Heroes of the Nations

EDITED BY

Evelyn Abbott, M.A.

FELLOW OF BALLIOL COLLEGE, OXFORD

FACTA DUCIS VIVENT, OPEROSAQUE
GLORIA RERUM.—OVID, IN LIVIAM, 265.

THE HERO'S DEEDS AND HARD-WON
FAME SHALL LIVE.

JULIAN

Coin of Rhodes.   Head of Helios.

AMS PRESS
NEW YORK

STATUE OF JULIAN.
FROM THE THERMES, PARIS.

JULIAN

PHILOSOPHER AND EMPEROR

AND THE

LAST STRUGGLE OF PAGANISM AGAINST CHRISTIANITY

BY

ALICE GARDNER

LECTURER AND ASSOCIATE OF NEWNHAM
COLLEGE, CAMBRIDGE
AUTHOR OF "SYNESIUS OF CYRENE"

G. P. PUTNAM'S SONS

NEW YORK
27 WEST TWENTY-THIRD STREET

LONDON
24 BEDFORD STREET, STRAND

The Knickerbocker Press

1895

Library of Congress Cataloging in Publication Data

Gardner, Alice, 1854–1927.
    Julian, philosopher and emperor, and the last struggle
of paganism against Christianity.

    Reprint of the 1895 ed. published by Putnam, New York,
which was issued in series: Heroes of the nations.
    Includes bibliographical references and index.
    1. Julianus, Apostata, Emperor of Rome, 331–363.
2. Roman emperors—Biography.   3. Philosophers—Rome—
Biography.   4. Rome—History—Empire, 284–476.
I. Title.   II. Series: Heroes of the nations.
DG317.G33   1978   937'.08'0924   [B]   73-14444
ISBN 0-404-58262-1

From the edition of 1895, New York.
First AMS edition published in 1978.

Manufactured in the United States of America.

AMS PRESS, INC.
NEW YORK, N.Y.

PREFACE

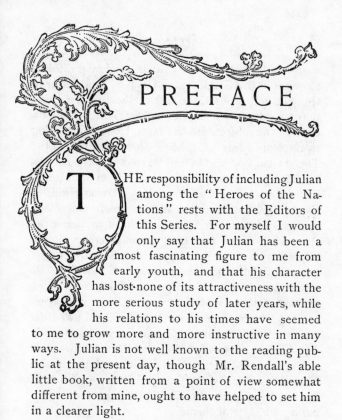

THE responsibility of including Julian among the "Heroes of the Nations" rests with the Editors of this Series. For myself I would only say that Julian has been a most fascinating figure to me from early youth, and that his character has lost none of its attractiveness with the more serious study of later years, while his relations to his times have seemed to me to grow more and more instructive in many ways. Julian is not well known to the reading public at the present day, though Mr. Rendall's able little book, written from a point of view somewhat different from mine, ought to have helped to set him in a clearer light.

It is always a pleasant task to acknowledge one's obligations to those who have helped one's work by counsel, criticism, or direction. I must be allowed in the first place to express my thanks to my brothers, Professor Percy Gardner of Oxford, and Mr. Ernest Gardner of the British Archæological School at Athens: the former for much general advice, and for assistance in selecting the illustrations; the latter for very useful criticisms while the work was in manuscript, and especially for help in rendering difficult passages in the Greek text. Dr. J. S. Reid, tutor of Gonville and Caius College, has directed my attention to many useful books, chiefly German, on portions of the subject, and has taken trouble in helping to elucidate some of Julian's laws preserved in the Theodosian Code. On this subject I have also received suggestions and information from Mr. Monro, likewise of Caius College. Mrs. Archer-Hind, of Cambridge, has kindly read my proofs and made some very helpful criticisms. I have to thank the Arundel Society for kind permission to obtain photographs of the fictile ivories at South Kensington. Mr. Collinson, who has travelled much in Asia Minor, has most kindly given me photographs taken by himself in or near Tarsus, with interesting comments. Messrs. Longmans have kindly allowed the reproduction of some curious Persian figures in *The Seventh Monarchy* of Canon Rawlinson. And the gentlemen in the Medal Room of the British Museum, especially Mr. George Hill, have been most kind in helping me to select my coins, and in procuring me casts of them.

I would here say a word as to my chief object in selecting my illustrations. Holding that their chief function was to *illustrate* the text rather than to adorn the book, I endeavoured to choose such as might make the story more vivid by enabling my readers to construct in imagination as much as possible of the environment in which Julian and his contemporaries lived, their personal appearance and dress, the most striking places where they dwelt, the scenes in which they habitually moved. I have not confined myself to contemporary art, which was during my period in a state of weakness and decline. One art, however, seems to have suffered less, and to have had a more continuous existence than the rest—that of carving in ivory. The ivory diptychs I have chosen, many of them from this period or a little later, give a clear notion of the dress and appearance of the men and women of the time. Some mythological subjects seemed a suitable addition, though belonging to an earlier period. Similarly, in addition to portraits and other coins of the period, I have selected some fine specimens of turreted and chariot-driven goddesses and radiant gods, struck in the great Asiatic cities, which help us in some measure to realise the Hellenic conceptions which Julian endeavoured to revive.

I have given, in suitable places, references to the chief authorities I have used. Of course the chief authority for the student of Julian must always be Julian himself.

ALICE GARDNER.

NEWNHAM COLLEGE, CAMBRIDGE,
    5th February, 1895.

CONTENTS.

CHAPTER X.

CHAPTER XI.

CHAPTER XII.

CHAPTER XV.

LIST OF ILLUSTRATIONS.

---

* I am bound to say that Bernouilli, in his *Iconographie Romaine*, throws doubt on the ascription of this statue to Julian. But the argument in favour of it seems pretty strong.

[1] Reproduced from Cohen's *Déscription historique des Monnaies frappées sous l'Empire Romain*.

[2] Reproduced by permission of the Arundel Society.

[3] Reproduced, by permission, from Rawlinson's *Seventh Monarchy*.

---

[1] Reproduced by permission of the Arundel Society.

[2] Reproduced from Boecking's *Notitia Dignitatum*.

[3] Reproduced from Cohen's *Déscription historique des Monnaies frappées sous l' Empire Romain*.

[1] Reproduced from Cohen's *Déscription historique des Monnaies frappées sous l'Empire Romain.*

[2] Reproduced by permission of the Arundel Society.

[3] Reproduced from Hopkins's *History of the Organ.*   Messrs. Robert Cocks & Co.

* From a photograph by Mr. Collinson.

[1] Reproduced, by permission, from Rawlinson's *Seventh Monarchy.*

[2] Reproduced from Cohen's *Déscription historique des Monnaies frappées sous l'Empire Romain.*

Coin of Constantinople: age of Constantine. Reverse, VICTORIA AVC:
Victory on the prow of a galley.

JULIAN,

PHILOSOPHER AND EMPEROR.

CHAPTER I.

THE ROMAN WORLD UNDER CONSTANTINE.
305–337.

" The time is out of joint, O cursed spite
   That ever I was born to set it right ! "—*Hamlet*, i., 5.
" ὀλίγου δεῖν ἅπαντα ἀπετράπη διὰ δὲ τὴν τῶν
   θεῶν εὐμένειαν σωζόμεθα πάντες."—JULIAN, Ep. 7.

URING the early years of the fourth century of our era, the fortunes of the Græco-Roman world were considerably modified by the frank and official recognition of three facts, which hitherto, though patent to thoughtful observers, had been more or less successfully hidden, under a mass of venerable fictions, from the eyes of the people at large.[1]

I

The first of these three facts was that the government of the Roman Empire had ceased to be a republic.

The second was that the Eternal City of Rome was no longer the one centre of the whole political system.

The third was that the worship of the ancient gods of Greece and Rome, neither in its earlier and simpler forms, nor in its later combinations with Oriental mythology and ritual and with theosophic accretions from the schools, could any longer be regarded as the religion of the people and their rulers.

The recognition of these three momentous facts was not simultaneous nor made by one person. It may be regarded as representing the chief lines of the policy followed by the Emperors Diocletian and Constantine. Yet Diocletian was so far from recognising the inevitable character of the religious revolution going on in the Empire, that his reign marks the last effort to check by stern persecution the rising tide of Christianity. In political and military affairs, on the other hand, some of the changes made by these great Emperors had been anticipated by others of earlier date. Thus the great soldier-Emperor, Aurelian, in his brief reign of less than five years (A. D. 270–275), had inaugurated several of the changes adopted during the succeeding period. But the reforms of the years with which we are now occupied are sufficiently homogeneous, and were carried out within a short enough period of time to enable us to draw here a line separating two historical epochs, which some German historians distinguish as that of the Princedom and that of the Absolute Monarchy.

It is, of course, far beyond our present purpose to examine and narrate, even in barest outline, the external fortunes and the internal developments of the Empire under the rule of Constantine and his immediate predecessors. Such a task would require powers equal to those of the great English historian who has written of this time, and whose work, in spite of its blemishes is not likely to be soon superseded. For although in many of our modern writers of history we may reasonably look for a more judicial impartiality, for a more scrupulous accuracy in detail, and for a greater breadth of sympathy, we should hardly dare to expect from the pen of any one of them as weighty, as impressive, and as inspiring a work as that of Edward Gibbon. Of late years, however, while some learned French and German writers have endeavoured to follow in Gibbon's footsteps, taking up his great subject as a whole, useful work has also been done by more special investigators of various nations who have restricted their labours to one or other of the sections into which that vast field may be divided. Those who would master the history of the Roman Empire, if not endowed with colossal powers, must adopt the maxim of the Romans themselves, and divide that they may conquer. But here the biographer finds his task simpler than that of the historian ; for him the division is ready-made, and his standpoint is definitely marked. He has to regard all the historical events of his period solely as constituting the environment in which his hero lived and laboured.   Thus for us, in our present study, no more of the Roman world and of contemporary history has to be considered than is absolutely essential for those who would understand the life and character of Julian.

Julian's career was greatly influenced by the recognition of the three great changes.   It exhibits in a striking manner the dominant tendencies of the age, tendencies against which, for the most part, Julian felt himself bound to maintain a vigorous resistance.   Not that he was unwilling to follow the policy of his predecessors in so far as it was conducive to the energetic defence and the efficient administration of the Empire.   But in his quick sympathy with the aspirations of past ages, and his entire devotion to ideas which had ceased to sway the minds of men, Julian felt himself out of harmony with the world in which he lived, and thus he came to throw all his powers and affections into the scale of reaction.   Perhaps some English and American readers, to whom the cause of progress and the cause of the right may seem to be identical, would regard the phrase " a reactionary hero," as a contradiction in terms.   Whether or no Julian deserves to be called a hero, we may be better able to judge at the close of our enquiry.   Here we would only say that the fact of his being a reactionary ought not unduly to prejudice us against him at the outset. For even if the upward progress of mankind were as sure and as steady as some optimistic philosophers

would have us believe, yet such philosophers cannot
deny that in the course of the march some good
things are often dropped by the way, in order, perhaps, that yet better things, incompatible with the
older, may be securely grasped. And if this is so,
the passing generation has no right to undervalue
the services of those who would call its attention,
sometimes, perhaps in overstrained and querulous
tones, to the glories of the treasures which are being
lost, but of which, perchance, some fragments may
yet be recovered.

Now each of the three changes, or acknowledgments
of change, which we have to consider, was abhorrent
to the mind and character of Julian. Hating pomp
and show, impatient of the petty, hampering rules of
Court etiquette, constantly dwelling in thought on
the ancient glories of democratic Athens and sena-
torial Rome, he could hardly view the orientalising
and inordinate exaltation of the Imperial dignity in
the light of a reform. Yet his almost single-handed
efforts to revive the great days of the Roman Senate
and of Greek municipal freedom were not productive
of very great results, either for good or for evil. Of
Rome herself, in spite of an antiquarian deference,
he was not as zealous a champion as he was of the
Græco-Roman culture which seemed to be bound up
in its fortunes with those of the great Empire,
threatened as both were in his day by adversaries on
the border and by discontented classes and nations
within. A prince whose two chief victories were
gained one on the Rhine and the other on the Tigris,
who devoted equal care to the military maintenance

of Roman defences and to the verbal championship
of Greek letters and ideas, may certainly be regarded
as having done his part in keeping up the integrity
of the Empire. As to the change in spiritual conditions, this was to him not merely an adverse element
of the environment in which he had to work; it was
the destruction of all that he held dear and believed
to be most necessary for the common good. He
felt bound to prevent such a destruction at any cost,
or to perish in the attempt.

To avoid vagueness, let us now consider very
briefly, and in relation to the main subject of our
narrative, how these great changes, political and religious, were being brought about, and what was the
exact significance of each one of the three.

I. Gibbon has defined the government of Augustus and his successors as " an absolute monarchy
disguised by the forms of a commonwealth." To
investigate the character of the monarchy and the
methods of its disguise does not belong to our present task. All who have even a slight acquaintance
with the history of the Roman Empire have read how
after the comparatively prosperous days of the Anto-
nines, the real power came into the hands of a violent and rapacious soldiery, destitute of national feeling, impatient of any attempts to enforce order and
discipline. Anarchy within and perpetual hostilities
on the frontier had brought the fortunes of the Empire to a low ebb, when there arose a succession of
strong rulers, beginning with Claudius II., an ancestor of Julian (268-270, A. D.), who were capable of
restoring discipline, of beating back insolent invaders,

and of taking steps towards the consolidation of the Empire. Still, the Imperial finances were on the verge of bankruptcy, and the Imperial defence in desperate need of a thorough reorganisation, when, in 285 A.D., Diocletian was called to the throne. This great Emperor, whose deep and powerful nature has been somewhat of an enigma to all historians, was not a Roman nor even an Italian by birth, but a Dalmatian of low descent, and was perhaps the better able to effect the necessary reforms in that he was but lightly bound by the traditions of the past. When he had overcome the rebellions that disturbed the earlier years of his reign, he devoted his energies to a series of administrative arrangements that should bring all parts of the Empire more directly under the control of the autocratic ruler, should increase the resources of the government, and diminish opportunities for usurpation and insurrection. He judged it expedient to surround the Imperial person with all the pomp and ceremony of Oriental monarchy, to insist that subjects admitted to his presence should kneel and kiss the border of his purple robe ; he assumed the title of *Dominus*, and accepted even that of *Deus*. The great functionaries of old time, the Consuls, had long ceased to have any but an ornamental existence. The Senate had lost all legislative power, and all freedom of speech. Imperial edicts and Imperial rescripts were the only forms of legislative action. The Emperor was supreme over the legislative, judicial, and administrative systems. His Court officials, especially the Master of the Offices, were among the greatest functionaries. His private fortune was hardly to be distinguished from the public treasure. His Council of State was presided over by an officer of his Court.   The pompous and ceremonious etiquette with which Diocletian and his successors surrounded themselves was extended to all who took part in the government.   The ranks in which men of high standing were placed—the Illustres, the Spectabiles, the Clarissimi, etc.—were clearly defined and minutely observed.   The nobility was for the most part of an official rather than of an hereditary character.   Even the title of *Patrician* became under Constantine a merely personal distinction.   In the lower grades of society trade and industry were fettered, and individual enterprise and liberty were reduced to a minimum by compulsory hereditary membership in the various corporations (of ship-owners down to those of bakers and chalk-burners) which enjoyed the privilege of carrying on their business in return for heavy dues rendered to the state. Under the all-powerful and ubiquitous authority of the Emperor, the administration was bureaucratic, and generally carried on by men who had begun their career with the study and practice of the law. The disorders of later times had often proceeded from the inordinate power of successful generals. A remedy to this danger was found in the diminution of the powers that could be held by any one man.   The Prætorian Præfects who had at one time been at the head of the army and also of the judicature were, under Constantine, deprived of all military command.   As an able modern historian has said,[2] " the separation of the civil from the military power becomes the foundation and corner-stone of the new administrative organisation."

This organisation was based on the division of the Empire into fairly large administrative areas, called *Dioceses.* Of these there were seven in the eastern and five in the western portion of the Empire, each under the rule of a *Vicar,* except such as came under the direct authority of the *Prætorian Præfects,* of whom we find two under Diocletian, four under Constantine. The *Provinces* which went to make up the Dioceses had their own governors, who generally bore the title of *Præsides,* and it seems to have been in the interest not only of the public peace but also of the comfort of the provincials, that a regulation was passed forbidding such office to be held by a native of the province over which the rule was to be exercised. The military governors who held command on the borders and elsewhere, and who generally bore the names *Duces* and *Comites,* had, as already stated, no connection with the civil administration. The army was not in any sense national in character. Some of the best regiments of the Guards were of barbarian race, and the defence of the borders was often entrusted to alien settlers, who held their land on a kind of military tenure.

II. The shifting, so to speak, of the centre of gravity of the Empire was a result gradually necessitated by a long course of events. The privileges of Roman citizenship, so ardently coveted and jealously guarded during the later days of the Republic, had been by degrees extended with ever increasing liberality, till by an edict passed some time in the reign of Caracalla (211–217, A.D.) they were granted to all free-born subjects of the Empire. Italy herself had been reluctantly subjected to the necessity of paying the land-tax formerly required from provincials only, and Rome, though retaining her municipal officers, saw, with the decline of the power of the Senate, the reduction of her prerogative to a level little above that claimed by some other leading cities of the Empire. Thus for instance Diocletian undertook measures for supplying to Alexandria the corn and other necessaries which the government had always secured to the capital. Diocletian himself had no capital, in the sense of a permanent royal residence, though Milan and Nicomedia were frequent resorts of himself and his colleagues, and as royal abodes enjoyed the munificence he loved to display in public buildings and shows. Even the founding of a new royal residence on the Bosphorus, one of the most notable acts of Constantine (about 330 A.D.), was probably not the result of a direct design against the dignity of Old Rome. The curious legend that Constantine abandoned the ancient city to the government of its bishops, is, of course, a fiction of much later times. Yet the facts remain that Constantinople did become politically a successful rival to Rome, and that the power of the Roman bishop was greatly increased by the unique position in which the act of Constantine had placed him.

Again, though the tendency to separation between East and West was furthered by the found-

ing of a new residence in eastern lands and also by
local separation in administration, yet it would b
a mistake to suppose that any so-called division,
effected by Diocletian or by any of his successors,
was intended to create two or more states out of
one.   When, in 286 A.D., Diocletian associated Maximian with him as Augustus; when, soon afterwards,
he adopted as his son, and forced Maximian also to
adopt, a young Cæsar who should be regarded as
the colleague and heir of each Augustus respectively,
there was still no notion that the Empire itself was
to be divided.   Laws still ran in the names of both
Emperors, and titles of honour were borne by both
alike.   Even in much later days, at the division
made on the death of Theodosius (in 395), there
was no project of establishing two entirely distinct
and separate governments, and one may almost say
that the final division into East and West became
permanent by accident.   Nevertheless, in any state,
and especially in an absolute monarchy, two sover-
eigns imply two Courts and two administrative
centres, and if there be already any tendency to
political separation (due to differences in religion,
in language, or in national character), such tendency
must needs be strengthened and hastened in its
operation by the sharing of the supreme authority
among two or more colleagues.

But Diocletian's plans even for a personal division
of Imperial authority and functions were doomed to
failure.   In 305 he and Maximian, his colleague
in the title of Augustus, abdicated, and their places
should, according to preconceived plans, have been

filled by the two Cæsars, who again should have been assisted and afterwards succeeded by two more regularly appointed Cæsars. The practical result, however, was a general scramble, a series of usurpations, and a destructive civil war. At one time six persons simultaneously asserted, and to some extent maintained, claims to the Imperial authority. But in the course of a few years, most of the pretenders had fallen in the field or otherwise disappeared from the scene. In 324 Constantine was sole master of the undivided Empire, and although he subsequently conferred the title of *Cæsar*, with some of the administrative functions pertaining thereto, on three of his sons and on some other relations, he maintained a position of supreme authority until his death in 337, when, as we shall see, a new division of territorial powers was accomplished. At that time Julian was about seven years old.

III. The relations of Diocletian and Constantine to the Christian Church, the semi-Christian sects, and the cults of Paganism, and the causes which determined those relations, form a large and attractive field of study. Here we can only notice a few points of immediate interest and importance.

Diocletian, though certainly not cruel by nature, nor unsusceptible to the softening and civilising influences of his time, was the last of the great persecutors of the Christians. The first objects of his rigorous measures were the Manichees, whose doctrine seems to have been a strange medley of Christian teaching with the tenets of the old Persian dualism as to the everlasting strife between the

A WARRIOR (THEODOSIUS?).
IVORY DIPTYCH.

powers of light and of darkness. It was not till comparatively late in his reign that the Christians, after a considerable time of security and of growing influence, felt his heavy hand. In 303 appeared the great persecuting edict, which ordered all churches and Christian books to be destroyed, and all Christians holding office at Court to take part in some heathen sacrifice, or else give up their civil and political rights. A second edict was specially directed against the Christian clergy. A third, in 304 affected Christians generally; all who refused to do sacrifice were made liable to imprisonment and torture.

The motives of Diocletian are, of course, not easy to discover. He may have thought that the celibacy, asceticism, and indifference to public affairs professed by some of the Christians were detrimental to the material and military interests of the state. This might at least easily account for his harshness to the Manichees. Or he may have considered the organisation of the Church, as it grew more powerful and spread more widely, likely to interfere with his administrative reforms. Or he may have been actuated, as was most probably his Cæsar, Galerius, by a genuine fear lest the decay of the old worships should alienate the favour of the heavenly powers. However this may have been, the persecution of Diocletian was short and sharp. Even before his abdication, in 305, it had considerably slackened, and the rivalry of the contending claimants to authority was favourable to Christian interests. Two of these claimants, Constantius Chlorus and his

son Constantine, have often been represented as
already attached to the Christian faith. With regard to Constantius (who died in 306) this seems by
no means probable, though the Christianity of his
wife Helen, the mother of Constantine, is beyond
doubt. With Constantine himself the case is somewhat different, yet we should greatly err if we attributed to him, now or at any time of his life, the
Christian zeal which was leading barbarian chiefs
to abandon and to cause their people to abandon
the superstition of their fathers. Constantius and
Constantine seem both to have been philosophical
monotheists, and their position in this respect was,
as we shall see later on, quite compatible with con-
formity, even with sincere and devout attention, to
ancient pagan rites and usages. The story of the vision of the Cross with the inscription, " By this sign
conquer," is not now generally accepted as historical,
and does not accord with what we know of the
character and position of Constantine. A few historians have regarded as due to Christian influence
the greater severity shown in the laws which bear
his name against crimes of impurity ; but some legislation on behalf of morality in this sense was begun
by Diocletian, and the dealings of Constantine,
especially with his ill-fated eldest son, are hardly
to be viewed as uniformly those of a strictly moral
and religious man. We may add that he postponed
his baptism till he was at the point of death. It is
also of great importance to observe that Christian
and pagan symbols occur together on his coins till
towards the close of his reign.[3]

A CONSUL, BETWEEN TWO COLUMNS.
IVORY DIPTYCH.

But whether a Christian or not, Constantine was a statesman, who hated all sources of division, and wished to unite all factions in loyal obedience to the Government. He was also by no means unsusceptible to religious impressions, or unaware of the importance of the spiritual factor in men's minds and lives. His edicts generally show a tolerant and liberal spirit, and his letters to contending ecclesiastics, if not always wise, are refreshingly redolent of a lay mind,—perhaps a rather blunt one. It seems most probable that, if circumstances had permitted, Constantine would have taken up and maintained an attitude of entire neutrality in all religious questions. The First Edict of Toleration, drawn up with the consent of the two colleagues (311 A. D.), which granted freedom of worship and commanded all men to pray for the Emperor, seems to show a dread lest pernicious results should follow the cessation of all worship on the part of those who were forbidden to exercise their proper cult. This view is yet more prominent in the Second Edict of Toleration, issued by Constantine and Licinius from Milan in 313, which granted complete freedom to the Christians, and promised the restoration of such churches as had been seized. The Emperors regard the granting of these privileges as a pious act, but they do not seem, if we judge from the words of the statute, to consider themselves as standing within the pale of the Christian Church.

Other laws of Constantine in favour of the Christians may be interpreted in accordance with the view that he desired to remain entirely neutral and

tolerant.   The grant made to the Christian clergy of
privileges similar to those enjoyed by the pagan
priests seems consistent with this policy, and even
the regulation for the observance of Sunday (*Dies
Solis*) may have a bearing on the worship of Mithras
as well as on the Christian holiday.   The prohibition
of sacrifices, however, though probably not strictly
enforced, as well as the decided position assumed by
the Emperor in ecclesiastical disputes, and also the
Christian education which his children seem to have
received, point to the fact that strict neutrality had
proved impossible, and that the Empire must henceforth reckon with the Church either as a close ally
or as a powerful and dangerous foe.

In two great controversies, we see the Imperial
power invoked and applied.   In 313, the secular
authority was appealed to by the faction of the
Donatists.   The real grounds of dispute in this case
and the nature of the principles involved are not
perfectly clear.   The immediate cause of disaffection
was a disputed election to the Bishopric of Carthage.
The question was complicated by a controversy as
to the rightful status in the Church of those who
had not held firm during the late persecutions.
Constantine evidently regarded the cause of Donatus
as that of insurrection and disorder, and therefore
gave all the weight of his personal and Imperial
authority to the suppression of the party that maintained it.   It is a notable fact that he committed the
enquiry to the Bishop of Rome.   The efforts made,
however, on behalf of peace and unity were not
effectual.   The Donatist sect continued for some

time an existence of violent and disorderly opposition to ecclesiastical authority.

The next occasion of Imperial intervention is of far greater interest, and had much more widely reaching results. The controversy between Athanasius and Arius presents great difficulties to the modern student; partly from the subtle discrimination required in those who have to discover the facts of the case from documents inspired by party hatred; partly from the extraordinary effort of historical imagination demanded of any person who would really put himself in the position of the metaphysical Alexandrians of the fourth century. We may, however, endeavour here to sketch in very brief outline the chief external events of the conflict, especially with reference to the indications they afford of the relations between the Church and the Empire.[4]

At the time when the great controversy first arose, the episcopal see of Alexandria was occupied by Bishop Alexander, a man apparently of no very extraordinary strength of character, but capable of taking up a very decided position through the influence of his secretary, the deacon Athanasius. Now Athanasius was a born ruler of men. He was also an Alexandrian of the Alexandrians, and as we shall see later on, the air of that city was, so to speak, impregnated with theological ideas of a highly metaphysical kind. His own belief was early formed and tenaciously held through life. His work on *The Incarnation of the Logos* seems to date from a time previous to the great dispute. Arius, an elder contemporary of Athanasius, was a presbyter in the

2

Alexandrian Church, but by birth a Libyan, and had
derived his education from Antioch, a city which
generally represents an essentially different school
of thought from that of Alexandria. The first controversy in which Arius was concerned arose as to
the relative positions which should be held by
bishops and presbyters. But the great Christological
dispute soon made the other sink into insignifi-
cance.

The doctrine of Arius brought upon him and his
followers the denunciations of Bishop Alexander,
and a sentence of excommunication against them
and of condemnation against their teachers which
was passed by a synod of about a hundred bishops;
yet it was not in form exactly like any modern
denial of the divinity of Christ. The distinctive
creed of Arianism may best be stated in the words:
"there was once a time when the Son of God was
not." After this doctrine and its upholders had
been condemned, Arius used such means to gain
partisans and to work towards his re-instatement as
brought down the wrath of his opponents. In particular he is said to have tried to gain over the
populace by embodying his doctrines in softly melodious verse, and he seems to have used in the interests of his party the jealous rivalry felt by various
cities against Alexandria. The dissensions soon
assumed dangerous proportions.

Now the Emperor Constantine was neither a theo-
logian nor a metaphysician, but from the standpoint
of a statesman, and of one duly appreciative of the
connection between unity in the Church and quiet in

A CONSUL, BETWEEN TWO COLUMNS.

IVORY DIPTYCH.

the State, he was bound to hate and suppress, if possible, everything that tended in either sphere to faction and disorder. On hearing of the dissensions,
he first endeavoured to pour oil on the troubled
waters by exhorting both parties to come to an
agreement. When his letters and commissions had
proved ineffectual, he took a step of momentous
import in its consequences and summoned the
Œcumenical Council which met at Nicæa in Bithynia in June, 325. At this council he was present,
and in spite of his professions of humility, there can
be no doubt that his influence was strongly felt. If
at first, as seems probable, he intended to hold the
balance between the contending parties, he was soon
led, by motives into which we cannot now enquire,
to support the policy of those who were most anxious to avoid all compromise and to find a symbol
the rejection of which might brand the holders of
the Arian doctrine as heretics. This symbol was the
term Homoousios (rendered in the English version:
" being of one substance with the Father,") and it
was accepted by all present except the African
bishops, though the Bishops of Nicomedia and Nicæa
refused to accept the accompanying *anathema* against
dissentients.

Athanasius and those who held with him seemed
to have triumphed; Arius and his adherents were
banished. Yet soon afterwards a reaction set in,
mainly owing to the efforts of Eusebius, Bishop first
of Nicomedia and afterwards of Constantinople, the
ablest and most statesmanlike leader of the party.
The Emperor returned to his previous attitude of

neutrality, and sent for Arius, who satisfied him by presenting a confession of faith from which the crucial word was omitted. Meanwhile, Athanasius had succeeded to Alexander, as Bishop (or Patriarch) of Alexandria, and he was now ordered by Constantine to reinstate the banished Arians. This, however, Athanasius persistently refused to do. And however much the modern reader may regret the want of forbearance and of kindliness on both sides during this unhappy struggle, it is refreshing to find that there lived at least one man who dared in the name of law and order to oppose the arbitrary command of the great autocrat. The spirit of liberty and independence had not entirely taken flight from among men.

We cannot enter into the charges brought against Athanasius by his enemies. They appear generally to have been of a malicious or of a trivial nature. Summoned to the Imperial Court, he maintained his ground, and was sent back to his diocese without dishonour.   Nevertheless, the behaviour of the Emperor changed once more, and Athanasius was forced to attend the Synod of Tyre, where his opponents had the upper hand. Having no hope of obtaining justice, he left the city, came to Constantinople, and boldly confronting the Emperor in the street, demanded an investigation of his cause. His request was partially granted, but the Emperor consented still, perhaps cherishing a hope of restoring peace and order, that Athanasius should be exiled to Treves. Arius was invited to Constantinople, and though he died suddenly just before the time appointed for his restoration to the Church, his faction, or rather a faction based chiefly on his teaching, prevailed generally through the rest of the reign of Constantine and during the period which followed. Athanasius recovered his see for a time on the death of Constantine, but had to go into exile once more from 341 to 346, and yet again from 356 to 361.

Some biographers of Julian would attribute considerable importance to the fact that during the years of his education and at the dawn of his intelligence, not the Catholic but the Arian party and doctrine were in the ascendant. We shall perhaps see cause to doubt this importance, but another fact should certainly be noted in this connection; that the activity of the Imperial authority in settling religious disputes afforded a precedent for decided intervention on the part of an Emperor of widely different views and character from those of Constantine. The earlier Emperors had exercised some sacerdotal functions and had held the office of *Pontifex Maximus*. In days when theological strife ran high, the religious professions of the monarch were by no means unimportant.

This brief survey may leave on our minds the impression that the age with which we have to deal is not strikingly heroic in character. In the state we have an absolute monarchy served by a sordid bureaucracy; in society, ranks and cliques, close corporations, and a grinding, benumbing system of supervision and taxation; in art and letters, little originality, a love of words, a paucity of ideas; in the Church, distractions and bitter divisions. Yet below the surface, forces were at work which bore in them the seed of better days. And those who could not reach forward into the future might escape from the ignoble present to rejoice in the greatness of the past, for they had within their grasp all the treasures of ancient civilisation, the literature and the monuments of older and grander times. What wonder if a sense of the worth of those treasures and of the poverty of contemporary life should force into the ranks of reaction one at least of the most eager and aspiring minds of the age?

Coin of Rome: age of Constantine. Reverse, Shepherd discovering Romulus, Remus, and the she-wolf.

NOTES ON CHAPTER I.

[1] It is, perhaps, unnecessary to specify, as it would be a lengthy business to discuss, the different sources which might be referred to as affording material for this sketch. The political and social state of the Empire at this time is set forth very clearly and thoroughly by Hermann Schiller in the third book of his *Geschichte der Römischen Kaiserzeit.* For ecclesiastical affairs, the general reader may be referred to Professor Gwatkin's little book on *The Arian Controversy* in the *Epochs of Church History* and to the translation of Gieseler's *Ecclesiastical History*, or to Cheetham's *Early Church History.* Also I would express my appreciation of Böhringer's *Athanasius and Arius.* Tillemont is, of course, a mine of wealth to students of this period. Gibbon is, or should be, the universal introducer to the subject.

[2] Schiller: *Gesch. der Röm. Kaiserzeit*, bk. iii., ch. 1, section 5.

[3] Schiller: *Gesch. der Röm. Kaiserzeit*, bk. iii., ch. 3.

[4] Perhaps, for the sake of any readers unacquainted with Church history, it may be permitted here to make two remarks: (1) That Arianism in its original form is as different as possible from modern Unitarianism. Channing or Martineau could no more easily have subscribed the creed which Arius professed than they could have accepted the Nicene. (2) The *Quicunque vult*, commonly called the "Creed of St. Athanasius," was not drawn up by him, but originated in the West, at a much later date. The real "Creed of St. Athanasius" is the original Nicene, (not precisely the one so-called by us), for which he contested manfully all his days.

Gold Medallion of Constans I. Reverse, SALUS ET SPES REIPUBLICAE;
Constantine, Constans, and Constantius standing.

CHAPTER II.

PARENTAGE OF JULIAN. HIS BIRTH AND CHILDHOOD.
CAREER AND END OF HIS BROTHER GALLUS.

331–354.

" Fair seed-time had my soul, and I grew up
Fostered alike by beauty and by fear."
WORDSWORTH.

"'Εντέτηκέ μοι δεινὸς ἐκ παίδων τῶν αὐγῶν τοῦ θεοῦ
['Ηλίου] πόθος." JULIAN, Or. iv., 130.

LAVIUS CLAUDIUS JULIANUS
was born, according to the generally
received account, in or near Constantinople [1] in the year 331 A. D. [2] As the
changes which made this city in a sense
the capital of the East were completed
about 330, his birth and that of New
Rome may be regarded as almost exactly coincident
in time.

24

The full name which Julian bore, but which is rarely mentioned, is a combination of several family names. The old Roman custom by which every man bore three names, that of the individual, of the gens, and of the family respectively, had long broken down, at least in the case of Imperial families. The *prænomen* (such as *Marcus*, *Gaius*, and the like) had dropped out of use, and though the *nomen* or name of the gens was retained, it was eclipsed by the names belonging to illustrious and distantly related gentes or families with which it was desirable to assert kinship. Thus, in Julian's case, the *Flavius* was a gentile name inherited from Constantius Chlorus, the *Claudius* was adopted by Constantine's family to bring them into connection with the Thracian Emperor, Claudius Gothicus (see Genealogical Table), and the *Julianus* was bestowed upon him by his maternal grandfather, who bore the same name himself.

A glance at the accompanying genealogical table will make Julian's relations to the other members of the Imperial family much clearer than a lengthy description could do. Of his father, Julius Constantius, son of Constantius Chlorus and of Theodora, step-daughter to the Emperor Maximian, we know very little. Libanius remarks that though (in consequence presumably of his legitimate birth and royal descent) he had a better right to the Empire than his brother who actually obtained it, he yet preferred to remain loyal to Constantine and to live on friendly terms with him. This observation shows either a confusion of mind or an affectation of ignorance on the part of the sophist of Antioch with regard to the elective character of the Empire, and it is not without interest as pointing to the growth of a dynastic idea and policy in the Imperial family. In a fragment of a letter[3] from Julian to the Corinthians, we find it stated that his father found repose in their city after a season of many wanderings. Julius Constantius was married twice, at least, and both his wives seem to have been ladies of good family and of considerable fortune. Basilina, the mother of Julian, was of the powerful and wealthy family of the Anicii. Her father, Anicius Julianus, was Prætorian Præfect at the time of the struggle between Maxentius and Constantine, and though he was on the losing side, he retained life and property under the conqueror.[4]

It seems probable that Julian owed more, both by inheritance and by influence, to his relations on the mother's side than to those on the father's. He bore, as we have seen, his grandfather's name, and this same grandfather provided for his early education. We have more than one reference in his letters to the property of his grandmother (almost certainly his maternal grandmother), and especially to a delightful little estate in Bithynia, in which he took pleasure from the days of his early boyhood.[5] The one kinsman to whom he writes as if expecting sympathy in his religious intentions (even before they were publicly declared) is his uncle Julian, in whom he also reposed political trust.[6] And beyond all this, we know that Basilina herself was educated in Greek literature, and thus it was probably to

GAMES IN CIRCUS.
IVORY DIPTYCH.

her that Julian owed his strong literary aspirations. Tastes like his are not prominent in his father's family, and are conspicuously absent from the disposition of his half-brother Gallus.

In affording to women opportunities of acquiring a good education, social influence, and scope for various kinds of activity, the fourth and fifth centuries of our era were more favourable than many other periods more brilliant and in some respects more morally sound.

Basilina's tutor was a certain eunuch, Mardonius, with whom she used to read Homer and Hesiod. Julian calls him a Scythian, but this title is used in the vaguest way by all writers of our period. A story is told of her,[7] that a little while before her son was born, she dreamed that she had given birth to Achilles. This is probably as mythical as most legends which gather round the birth and early days of great men, but if there is any truth in it, the dream probably followed a reading in the *Iliad* with Mardonius. But whatever Julian may have derived from his mother must have been physically inherited, not consciously imparted. Very soon after the birth of her only child, she was, in his words, "withdrawn in the bloom of youth from many sufferings by the Motherless Maiden-goddess."[8] Such a loss to a child of Julian's eager and susceptible temperament, and in his isolated position, was quite irreparable.

For while Julian was struggling through his motherless infancy, being probably brought up in his father's house in Constantinople, events were occurring which gave a peculiar colour to his whole life. In 337, Constantine the Great died at Nicomedia in Bithynia, after vainly trying a water cure at the neighbouring baths of Helenopolis. Now the policy of Constantine's later years was distinctly dynastic in character. Before his death, he arranged for a partition of the Imperial dominions among his surviving sons, and he included in this arrangement the two sons of his half-brother Dalmatius, Dalmatius the Younger and Annibalianus. Probably this partition was on the lines marked out by Diocletian,[9] and would not have involved such a complete separation of the different spheres of authority as a territorial distribution seems to imply. The project, however, was never carried out. Constantine had been essentially a soldier-Emperor, rejoicing in the good-will of the legions which he had often led to victory. His brothers and their sons seem never to have been conspicuous in military affairs. This contrast, being apprehended, was probably the chief cause of a movement among the troops (which was at least not checked by the sons of Constantine) against the sons of Dalmatius and all the other members of the Imperial family except the direct descendants of the late Emperor. The result was one of those horrible occurrences that so frequently darken the history of Oriental dynasties: Constantius, who seems to have been the favourite and the most able son of Constantine, after celebrating his father's obsequies, in very magnificent style, at Constantinople, either instigated or sanctioned after the event a general family massacre. In this way his two

cousins, who had received a claim to part of the
Imperial authority, two uncles (including Julian's
father), and some other kinsmen (including Julian's
eldest brother) fell victims to the rage of the soldiery and to the jealousy of the eldest branch of the
family. Julian himself only escaped in consequence
of his extreme youth, his brother Gallus through a
fortunate sickness which seemed likely to secure
his removal without involving anyone in blood-
guiltiness. According to Julian's statement, made
long afterwards, Constantius subsequently reproached himself for these murders, and regarded his
own childlessness as a divine judgment on his crime.
But for the time, the absence of rivals made the three
brothers secure in their possession of authority,
while their cousins, Gallus and Julian, having lost
their nearest and most natural protectors, led from
the first a precarious life, at the mercy of those who
had deeply injured them, and against whom they
needed to be ever on their guard.

A new division of the Empire followed. The precise nature of this division, the mutual relations of
the joint rulers, and the frontier lines of their spheres
of government are not easy to determine, though it
is clear that the East remained under the second
brother, Constantius, the northern and western
regions under the eldest, Constantine, and the
youngest, Constans. But the arrangement was
not lasting. Before very long, war broke out
between Constantine and Constans. Constantine
was entrapped into an ambush, near the city of
Aquileia, and put to death. Constans now added

his brother's dominions to his own. Meantime, Constantius was sufficiently occupied in distant parts. We shall have occasion later on to examine the relations between the Roman Empire and the only other far-reaching power of those days that had any claim to an inherited ancient civilisation,—the revived monarchy of Persia. This nation, or rather agglomeration of nations, which formed the last of the great kingdoms of the East, is sometimes called by the name of the *Parthian*, but those who ruled over it claimed to be successors of Cyrus and of Darius, and endeavoured to attach to their rule the prestige of ancient glories. The dynasty of the Sassanids (founded 219 A.D.) had frequently come into deadly conflict with the Roman power, which could only keep the enemy at bay by means of a chain of strong frontier fortresses, on the Euphrates and the Tigris. The Sassanid king contemporary with Constantius and Julian was Sapor, who began to reign at his birth (being a posthumous child) about the year 310. Very soon after the death of Constantine, Sapor took advantage of the change in government to invade the Roman province of Mesopotamia, and to lay siege to Nisibis and other important towns. Constantius, however, seems to have shown some ability in maintaining a vigorous resistance, and some of the sieges, especially that of Nisibis, were raised after an heroic opposition to all the resources which engineering science could then command. Several battles were fought, in one of which (that of Singara, in Mesopotamia, 348) the Romans, though victorious at first, suffered a severe defeat. The general

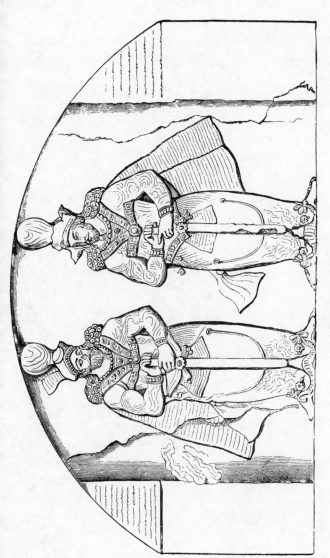

SAPOR II. AND SAPOR III.

RELIEF AT KERMANSHAH.

results of the campaigns of Constantius in the East
were not very favourable to the Roman arms.
Meantime, events had occurred in the West which
imperatively demanded his presence, and (possibly
after signing a truce with Sapor) he returned to
Europe.

These events were two insurrections, in Gaul and
in Illyricum, and the tragic death of the Emperor
Constans. The youngest of Constantine's sons was
energetic in his habits of life and orderly in his
government. The chief grievance raised against
him was that he promoted barbarians in the army,
to the disparagement of the old legionaries. The
disaffected faction found a champion in a certain
Magnentius, (who was, strange to say, himself of
barbarian extraction), and a serious rebellion broke
out in the Imperial Court at Augustodunum (Autun).
Magnentius assumed the purple. Constans fled
southwards but was captured and murdered in the
town of Helena, at the foot of the Pyrenees.
Meanwhile, a general of respectable reputation,
Vetranio, raised the standard of revolt on the
Danube, and in Rome itself young Nepotian, first
cousin to the Emperor [see genealogical table, p.
25] assumed the Imperial title, and maintained an
ephemeral state by the help of a band of gladiators.

Constantius was more successful against his rivals
in the West than he had been against his foes in the
East. In fact, the only insurgent who proved a
capable or dangerous opponent was Magnentius.
The speed with which Vetranio was induced, at a
peaceful colloquy with the Emperor, to return with

all his soldiers to his former loyalty, has led some
historians to think that in his case, at least, the
rebellion was not seriously meant.   This view seems
to be borne out by his coinage.[10]   Magnentius, however, had strengthened himself by assuming the
championship of various lost or distressed causes.
He posed as representing not only the cause of
Romans against barbarians in the army, but also
that of Bishop Athanasius and the Nicene Creed
against the Arians, who were generally favoured by
Constantius.   At the same time, with a curious inconsistency, he asserted some old claims of paganism
against Christianity.   But the forces of Constantius
were superior, especially in cavalry.   In a decisive
battle fought at Mursa on the Drav (September,
353) Magnentius was defeated with great loss, and
forced to fly.   Two years afterwards the remnant
of his adherents were overpowered at Lyons, and
he fell on his own sword.   Meantime the faction
of Nepotianus in Italy was speedily quelled.   Constantius stood alone at the head of the Roman
world.

But though no Augustus shared his honours,
necessity had already forced Constantius to appoint
a subordinate with the title of *Cæsar*.   Even the
lordship of the world cannot confer the gift of
ubiquity, and recent events had proved that a vigorous exercise of the sovereign power might be required in Gaul and in Mesopotomia at the same
time.   Constantius was still childless.   A temperament naturally jealous might, one would suppose,
have shrunk from reposing power in the hands of

almost the last scion of a deeply injured family. On the other hand, a genuine repentance for the ills inflicted might have suggested full and loyal compensation to the surviving sufferers. But Constantius seems to have been of that uncertain temperament which always prefers half measures. In want of a colleague he thought of his cousin Gallus. But subsequent events do not allow us to regard the authority with which Gallus was invested as having been bestowed in full and entire confidence.

Let us now go back to inquire how Gallus and Julian had fared during these stormy years. Although we have information from various sources, including some of first-rate authority, as to the character of Julian's education and the places where it was begun and continued, it is impossible to map out with chronological accuracy the vicissitudes of his childhood and youth. It seems on the whole most probable that his early boyhood was passed in Constantinople, though it is not unlikely that he may have resided for a time in the city in which he afterwards prosecuted his studies, Nicomedia in Bithynia. But however this may be, the chief part in his early education was taken by the eunuch Mardonius, who, as we have seen, had been tutor to his mother. At the age of seven, Julian was placed under the care of this man, who was to act as his *pædagogue*. This term indicates an office somewhat above that of an upper servant and below that of a private tutor. The pædagogue's duty was to escort his charges to school, to the games, and to the other resorts permitted to them, and perhaps also to see that they prepared their lessons at home. The character of Mardonius is one respecting which we have difficulty in forming a judgment. Libanius speaks of him in terms of high praise; Julian himself, on the other hand, has drawn a by no means pleasing picture of him and of his dealings with his pupil; but as this picture occurs in a writing, the chief object of which is to satirize Julian himself and to lay the blame of his idiosyncrasies on his educators, it is hard to see how much is meant to be taken in earnest. Two facts, however, are quite clear: that Mardonius was very strict in discipline, and that he both loved letters himself and strove to instil, on every occasion that arose, similar tastes and feelings into the mind of his pupil. On the walk to the school in which, without any special privileges or ceremonies, Julian shared the tasks of the other boys, he was always taken along the same streets. He was told that it was bad manners to stare about him as he walked along, and he was not allowed to go to the theatre or the games except on rare occasions. It is possible that Julian's grandfather was quite willing, with a view to the boy's security, to agree to such a mode of life for him as was prescribed by the suspicious jealousy of the Emperor. On the child himself the effect of so much loneliness and repression was to throw him upon his own resources, to stimulate an almost morbid delight in nature and in stories of the past. The fact that his childhood was passed under clear skies and by sunny seas was certainly of importance in the formation of his mind and character. He took an intense delight in observing the path of the sun and in contemplating the stars at night." Meantime his imagination was being nourished on the most wholesome food that it could have found in that or in any other age—the poems of Homer.

Homer was the standard text-book of Greek education. The first subject taught to boys was grammar, which included a good deal that we should put under the head of literature. The lessons learned at school were enforced by Mardonius at home, and he used to tell the boy, if he felt his life monotonous and wished for a change of scene, to take the book and read about the games of the Phæacians or the flowery gardens of Calypso; he would never find anything more beautiful in real life. Perhaps we might take a hint from Mardonius, and when we regret our inability to discover the details of Julian's early life, fall back upon the book on which he was brought up, and endeavour to realise the impression made on his susceptible mind by its pictures of heroic life and enterprise. Julian's intimate knowledge of Homer is shown by the frequent quotations he makes, even when writing hastily and at a distance from his books. This knowledge was accompanied by an enthusiasm almost religious in character. Homer has been called the Bible of the Greeks. This does not of course imply that Greek moralists never went beyond the primitive notions of the Homeric age, or that they did not freely interpret Homeric myths so as to adapt them to more recent modes of thought. Still Homer was always their starting-point, and their indispensable treasury of

illustrations and ideas. Dwelling comparatively near
to the very spot where the great deeds of Greeks and
Trojans were supposed to have been done, and
familiar with those deeds by daily readings, Julian
may well have seemed to himself at times to be
living rather in the world of Agamemnon and
Achilles than in that of Constantius and Athanasius.

It might have been supposed that the Christian
teachers and Christian influences by which Julian
was surrounded would exercise some force to counteract his passionate love of epic poetry. But of
such teaching and influence, we can find hardly any
trace. Whether Mardonius was a pagan or a Christian we do not know. If he was brought up in the
family of the Anicii, and was allowed by Constantius
to be always about his young cousin, Mardonius can
hardly have been an active opponent of the new
faith. Yet from what both Libanius and Julian say
of him, we can feel sure that he was penetrated with
the spirit of Hellenic paganism. According to Ammianus, [12] Julian's education was also in part conducted by Eusebius, Bishop of Nicomedia and
afterwards of Constantinople, the doughty champion
of the Arians, and distantly related (probably through
the Anicii) to Julian himself. Some historians have
found in the Arian belief of those who first undertook to impart to Julian the elements of Christianity,
the cause of his strong and bitter antipathy to
the Christian religion. Some form of that religion
which left more scope for mysticism might, they think,
have been both attractive and satisfying to him.
But when we come to examine the grounds of Julian's

anti-Christian feeling, we shall not see much to support this opinion. We may, however, observe that when party feeling runs high, the best of men are often apt to insist more on party principles than on deeper truths. Eusebius was a strong and skilful party leader, a faithful friend, and probably a sincerely convinced controversialist. If he did not make Julian a good Christian, it may be alleged in his excuse that at the time of his death Julian was only ten years old. In after days Julian looked back upon this time as one of spiritual darkness. His natural impulse would doubtless have been to yield to the religious ideas which dominated the literature in which he delighted. His teachers could to some extent restrain such an inclination, but they could not or certainly did not replace it by a counter-enthusiasm in favour of Christianity.

Yet these dark days were not without brighter moments. From Constantinople or from Nicomedia it would be but a short journey to the little Bithynian estate already mentioned, probably still in the hands of Julian's maternal relatives. Here he seems to have spent some pleasant visits. The letter in which he describes the place is interesting, as showing what we might consider a modern and refined taste for natural scenery, though of course in any man of the ancient world we must expect to find a preference for Nature in her tamer moods: " It is situated not more than twenty stadia (about two and a half miles) from the sea, so that no talkative merchant or quarrelsome sailor comes there to vex you, yet the gifts of Nereus are not wanting. There are fresh-caught fish to be had, and from a height near the house you can see the Propontid Sea, the islands, and the city which bears the name of the great Emperor [Constantinople.] And you can look out on all this, not standing on slimy sea-weed, offended by the sight and smell of the refuse thrown out on the sandy beach, but will find sand and thyme and sweet-smelling meadow grass beneath your feet. It is very restful to recline with a book, and to refresh the eyes from time to time with the pleasant view of the sea and the ships. When quite a young boy I delighted in the place, with its good springs, and pleasant bath, orchard, and shrubbery, and after I had become a man, I still felt drawn to the old way of life there, and I often visited the place again."

For a season, however, intercourse with schoolfellows and relatives, and free rovings in favourite spots, were to be forbidden to Julian and his brother. Whether any fresh suspicion actuated the mind of Constantius we do not know, nor is the exact time of the change certain. But we learn from Julian's testimony, as well as from that of others, that he and Gallus were taken away from their studies and condemned to a lonely sojourn of six years, without friends, companions, or exercises suitable to their age or station, in the remote castle of Macellum in Cappadocia. Where Gallus had passed his early youth is not quite certain. He is said to have studied for a time at Ephesus, and his sojourn there may have coincided with Julian's schooldays in Constantinople and Nicomedia. But wherever he may have been sent to school, he does not seem to have been carefully trained, and he certainly never acquired much intellectual culture.

The site of Macellum has been identified as that of a spot at the foot of the magnificent Arghi Dagh, in a wild and romantic region. But romantic scenery had little charms even to those among the ancients who felt most keenly the beauty of the sea, the heavens, and the exuberant life of nature. Had it been otherwise, the absence of teachers and friends would still have been an occasion of painful longing to Julian. His only companions were his brother Gallus and the attendant slaves. The way in which he mentions Gallus shows that he felt for him a strong brotherly affection, but he was fully aware of his glaring faults of character, and attributed them to his bad education. It must be borne in mind that the slaves with whom, in the want of other society and of congenial pursuits, Gallus was compelled to associate, would probably be people of low character and demoralising antecedents. Between the two brothers, whose dissimilarity reminded Ammianus (who knew them both) of Titus and Domitian, there cannot have been much real companionship. For himself, Julian says that the Gods preserved him from being corrupted by leading him to the study of philosophy. If, as seems probable, Mardonius accompanied him in his exile, the continuity of his studies was not entirely broken. Mardonius was not a mere grammarian, but an enthusiastic admirer of the works of Plato, Aristotle, and Theophrastus. Perhaps the deprivation of the best attainable teaching was not altogether an evil for Julian at that time, if he was already storing his mind with the works on which he should afterwards hear comments, and preparing himself, by solitary reading and thinking, to profit all the more hereafter by the academic training that was to fall to his share.

It seems probable that the retirement of the two youths at Macellum lasted till the year 350, when Gallus, then twenty-five years old, was summoned, as his brother says, from the field to the palace, to receive the dignity of *Cæsar*, and the hand of the Emperor's sister, Constantina, in marriage. Meantime, Julian was allowed to prosecute at Nicomedia those academic studies which we shall consider more fully hereafter.

There is no reason to suppose that Constantius intended from the first to place Gallus in such a position that his rude, untamable nature must needs bring him into difficulties and lead ultimately to his disastrous fall. A course of that kind would have been at least as dangerous to the interests of Constantius himself as to those of his cousin. Yet, if he had been acting with the most malicious designs, he could hardly have used more effectual means. In the first place, Constantina, was a woman of the kind certain to acquire a pernicious influence over a weak and passionate nature like that of Gallus. She must have been considerably older than he was, as she had previously been married to her cousin Annibalianus, who perished in the massacre of 337. The experiences of that time had not tended to sweeten her temper. According to one account,

she had a large share in the insurrection of Vetranio.[13]
Ammianus calls her a monster in human form, a living
megæra, and the stories which that usually calm and
impartial witness tells of her violence, cruelty, and
avarice, go far to justify the comparison. Nor was
Gallus much happier in the place of residence, than
in the wife appointed to him.

Antioch, the seat of his rule, was a gay, pleasure-
loving city, where he could indulge all the worst
proclivities of his nature, while the irascible, tumultuous character of the inhabitants afforded facilities both for the perpetration and for the punishment
of violent deeds. And even had his immediate sur-
roundings been less unfavourable, the task entrusted
to Gallus—the pacification and government of the
East—was one hardly suited to an ill-trained young
man, unused to the ways either of the camp or of
the council-chamber. The Persians were again invading Mesopotamia. The predatory inhabitants of
the Isaurian mountains were plundering and killing
their neighbours. The town of Antioch itself was
suffering from a famine, the blame of which was,
as usual, laid by the poor to the charge of the
wealthy.

Gallus can hardly be said to have made a vigorous effort to resist these calamities. He did not
take the field, though he despatched an expedition
against the Isaurians, which seems to have had some
success. His efforts against the famine consisted in
an arbitrary edict to fix the price of provisions, violent threats against all who remonstrated, and the
sacrifice to the rage of the people of certain officials

whom he chose to regard as responsible for the
deficient food supplies. Meantime he amused himself by holding boxing matches of the most violent
and brutal kind, deprived the law courts of all
respect by acquitting the guilty and condemning
the innocent for bribes, and encouraged espionage
of all kinds, even going about the streets *incognito*,
to listen for disaffected speeches against the government.

Constantius, now residing chiefly at Arelatum
(Arles), in Gaul, was informed of the turn things
were taking by the Prætorian Præfect Thalassius,
who seems to have been left as a spy upon Gallus.
Beginning as usual with tentative measures, Constantius sought a remedy by gradually diminishing the
number of troops under Gallus's command. A little
later, he sent a high official, Domitian, who had been
treasurer and was now præfect, to bring about the
Cæsar's recall and retreat from Antioch. Domitian
acted bluntly and without tact. Gallus, indignant
at his rudeness, seized his person, and when one of
the quæstors attempted to mediate between them,
Gallus appealed to the soldiery, and a disgraceful
tumult ensued, in which both Domitian and the
quæstor lost their lives. Gallus now declared that
a conspiracy had been set on foot against him, and
torture was employed to make suspected persons
reveal the names of accomplices. By such means,
many innocent persons were arrested, and several
were executed without any but a mock trial.
Among these were two who had been seized in mistake for others who happened to bear similar names.

A new person now appears upon the scenes, Ursicinus, Governor of Nisibis, whom the Emperor had ordered to go and investigate matters on the spot. He was accompanied by the historian Ammianus, from whom we have a graphic account of all the transactions at Antioch. Ursicinus was shocked at the violence and levity with which the trials for treason were being conducted, and wrote to inform Constantius of the state of affairs. But the suspicious ear of the Emperor had been gained by the rivals of Ursicinus at court, and the upright soldier was withdrawn from Antioch, on an artificial pretext, before Gallus was formally summoned thence. Meantime, Constantina was persuaded to leave her husband and pay a visit to her brother, probably in the hope of bringing about an understanding between them. But before she could cross from Asia into Europe, she fell ill of a fever and died. Perhaps the only good thing to be said of her is that her husband acted more foolishly (though certainly not more wickedly) after he had lost her. He seems now to have entertained designs of seizing the Imperial power. Nevertheless, he was persuaded by treacherous counsellors to leave Syria and come to the Emperor in Italy. He stayed in Constantinople on the way, behaved with foolish self-confidence, and held a chariot race, to the great indignation of Constantius. But so headstrong a man was sure to fall a prey to subtle courtiers covetous of his property rather than of his office, for Gallus, like Julian, had inherited considerable estates in Asia Minor. He proceeded on his journey, and only found that he had fallen into a trap when it was too late to retreat. When he had reached Petavio in Noricum, he was met by an officer who had formerly served under him, and who now came with a band of soldiers to arrest him. He was taken to the tower of Pola, in Istria, the scene, many years before, of the murder of Constantine's eldest son, Crispus. There he was subjected to an enquiry as to his violations of justice, and laid the blame of them on his wife. But his cowardice could not delay his punishment, and he was beheaded forthwith.

Gallus was at the time of his death twenty-nine years old, and had held the Cæsarship for four years. In external appearance he was handsome, tall, with well-proportioned limbs, soft yellow hair, and short beard. His vices seem to have been rather those of a weak and uncontrolled than of an actively evil character. Unlike his brother, he never rejected the religion in which he had been brought up, not, assuredly, that his moral proclivities were more naturally Christian than Julian's, but rather because he was totally without those intellectual aspirations which made Julian a votary of Hellenism.

It seemed desirable to narrate the history of Gallus in this place, partly because it illustrates the character of some of the persons and the complications of circumstances with which Julian himself had to deal, and partly because the wretched career and sudden fall of the elder brother made a deep and melancholy impression on the mind of the younger, whom it seemed likely to involve in a common ruin. But the Cæsarship of Gallus had not, while it lasted,

much immediate effect on Julian's life. The brothers corresponded occasionally and probably met
once. During those four years, however, Julian was
but little concerned with matters of court and of
state, being absorbed in those studies which seemed
to him of infinitely greater importance, living in an
intellectual world which he regarded as far more
real than any material environment.

Coin of Constantius Gallus. Reverse, GLORIA ROMANORVM:
Victory with wreath and palm.

FAMILY OF JULIAN'S MOTHER.

Claudius II. d. 270 — Quintillus — Crispus *a* (Claudia m. Eutropius)

Constantius Chlorus. d. 306
m. (1) Theodora, step-daughter of *Maximian*

Children of Constantius Chlorus:

- Dalmatius d. 337
  - Dalmatius d. 337
  - Annibalianus d. 337
- m. (2) Helen *b*
  - Constantine *c* d. 337
    - m. (1) Minervina
      - Crispus d. 326
    - m. (2) Fausta, daughter of *Maximian*
      - Constantine II. *d* d. 340
      - Constantius, d. 361 — m. (1) Galla "(2) Eusebia "(3) Faustina
      - Constans d. 350
      - Constantina d. 354 — m. (1) Annibalianus "(2) Gallus — A daughter
      - Helen d. 360 — m. *Julianus*
      - Constantia m. Gratian
- Julius Constantius m. (1) Galla
  - Galla m. *Constantius*
  - A son
  - Gallus d. 354 m. Constantina
  - m. (2) Basilina d. 363
    - *Julianus* m. Helen d. 360
- Constantia m. *Licinius*
  - Licinius
- Anastasia m. Bassianus
- Eutropia m. Nepotianus
  - Nepotianus d. 350

Julianus (*comes orientis*)
Julianus Anicius (Prætorian Præfect)
Basilina m. Julius Constantius
Flavius Claudius Julianus.

NOTES ON JULIAN'S PEDIGREE.—*a* Authority here: Trebellius Pollio, *Life of Claudius*, c. 13. *b* Helen was the second wife of Constantius, yet her son was older than those of Theodora. See Libanius, *Epitaph. Jul.*, etc. Some Historians would insert another son of Constantius to explain a reference to Julian's *Letter to the Athenians*, which may possibly apply to Constantine II. and his brother. *c* Zosimus says that Constantine were not the sons of Fausta, but of another early-divorced wife of Constantine. But the statements of Julian (especially in *Oration* i., 9) are to be preferred.

NOTES ON CHAPTER II.

The best authorities for the childhood of Julian are his *Letter to the Athenians* and the funeral oration of Libanius, with which may be compared *Misopogon*, and the *Hist. Eccles.* of Socrates, Bk. iii., c. 1. The history of Gallus is recorded at length in Bk. xiv. of Ammianus, who was eye-witness of some of the scenes which he describes, and in the concluding chapters of Zosimus, Bk. ii. Among modern authorities, see, besides those already mentioned, Mücke's *Julianus.*

[1] See especially Ep., 58.

[2] Socrates, the ecclesiastical historian, would place his birth two years earlier. This would make it possible for his exile to have followed speedily on the general massacre of 337 (as he seems to imply in his *Letter to the Athenians*), and yet for him to have passed part of his school time at Constantinople, as Libanius (*Epitaph :*) and others relate. (Though Libanius says that at the time of the massacres, Julian was only just weaned.)

[3] Fragment 5 in Hertlein.

[4] See Libanius, *Epit.*, and Reiske's note thereon. The Anicii were Christians, and Count Julian is said to have changed his religion in order to please his nephew. I do not think this probable, as such change must have occurred before Julian became Emperor.

[5] Ep., 46. Compare Fragment of *Letter to a Priest*, in which Julian mentions that he recovered his grandmother's estate after doing a kind turn to somebody.

[6] Ep., 13. Also one of the lately discovered letters of Julian published in the *Maurogordateion Bibliotheke. Cf.* Ammianus, Bk. xxiii., c. 1.

[7] By Zoraras.

[8] *Misopogon*, 352.

[9] The dominion of Annibalianus over Pontus and the neighbouring countries would seem to have been more independent, as he bore the title and insignia of *King*.

[10] On the coinage of Vetranio and Magnentius, and especially on the adoption by Magnentius of the symbolic letters A and Ω, see H. Schiller, *l. c.* iii., 3, sec. 21.

[11] See beginning of *Oration in Praise of King Helios.*

[12] Book xxii., c. 9.

[13] Philostorgius, iii., 22. See also Tillemont, *Hist. des Empereurs, Constance*, Art. 18.

| Coin of Nicomedia. | Coin of Nicomedia. | Coin of Nicæa. |
| Imperial Times. | Imperial Times. | A walled city. |

CHAPTER III.

JULIAN'S ACADEMIC EDUCATION.

350–354

"Εἴ τις ὑμᾶς πέπεικεν ὅτι τοῦ φιλοσφεῖν ἐπὶ σχολῆς
ἀπραγμόνως ἐστὶν ἥδιον ἢ λυσιτελέστερον τοῖς ἀνθρώποις,
ἠπατημένος ἐξαπατᾷ."

JULIAN, Ep. 55.

"What do you read, my lord?"
"Words, words, words!"

Hamlet, i., 2.

HE years during which Gallus held the
dignity of Cæsar, with the months that
immediately followed his fall, constitute a very important period in the
life of his brother. Julian henceforth
found himself partly, at least, liberated from the restraints under which
he had passed the preceding six years of his life,
and able to follow more freely his own intellect-

ual bent. Not that he was even now entirely his own master. We hear[1] of allegations made against him, that he quitted Macellum for purposes of study in the Asiatic towns, and that he had held intercourse with his disloyal brother. There can be little doubt, however, that Constantius, whether influenced by friendly feeling or by self-interest, was not sorry to see his young cousin's eager longing after a learned and intellectual life. The pursuits on which his heart was set would be less likely than any others to bring him into opposition and rivalry to the ruling powers. There was indeed the chance that he might fall in with some theosophic oracle-monger, who by playing upon his youthful enthusiasm might instil into his mind the belief that he had a special vocation to constitute himself the champion of the ancient gods and their votaries. The fear of such influences may have crossed the mind of the suspicious Emperor, but, if so, the result was to make him insist that Julian should openly profess adhesion to the Christian faith and should avoid teachers known to be zealous in the cause of reaction. It certainly did not prompt him to endeavour by enticements or threats to draw away his cousin from his academic studies.

Accordingly Julian, who seems, at least before his rise to power and supremacy, never to have been deficient in worldly prudence, early perceived the need of caution and dissimulation, if he were not to be debarred from following his ruling passion. As Libanius says (in one of the few bright remarks that occasionally enliven his wearisome and bombastic

4

pages), Julian reversed Æsop's fable, and became a
lion in an ass's hide. His mental disguise was so
successful that not only was Constantius disarmed,
but serious doubts have been caused among eminent
writers, down to our own days, as to what the
earliest religious beliefs of Julian really were, and
whether they were changed at the time when he
decidedly embraced Hellenism. Though the matter
cannot be regarded as settled beyond dispute, I think
that most students of Julian's life and works will see
little ground for the opinion [2] that his zeal in after
days was that of a pervert who had once been a
warm adherent of the opposite cause. The statement he makes in a letter to the Alexandrians [3] that
he " followed the way " of the Christians till he was
twenty years old does not imply any very sincere
adhesion to Christian beliefs and practices, nor do
we find traces of such early attachment in any of his
later works. He shows, it is true, considerable acquaintance with several books of the New Testament. This lends probability to the statement,
made by some Christian writers, that Julian at one
time held the ecclesiastical office of Reader. He
may also [4] have contributed, with his brother, to the
construction of the shrine of St. Mammas in Cappadocia. A silly story is told of supernatural forces
which caused the part undertaken by Julian to crum-
ble away and the part built by Gallus to stand
secure, a proceeding which showed little discernment
of character on the part of the saint, so far at least
as Gallus is concerned. All that Julian himself tells
us of his early habits and thoughts shows him to us

as a dreamy boy, devotedly fond of Greek poetry, and soon aspiring to the study of philosophy. His enthusiasm for Greek letters may naturally have developed into a zeal for Greek religion, or rather, may have itself become a religion to him, without any critical revulsion of feeling.

Still we have to face the knotty question, whether he had ever been baptised, since if it were so, it is the less easy to clear him in the eyes of the world from the opprobrious epithet that has clung to his name through all the ages. The statements of his fellow-student Gregory Nazianzen and those of Sozomen and the other ecclesiastical historians cannot count for much where their knowledge was imperfect and their hatred intense. Against their assertions, we may set the example of Constantine himself and of the members of his family, especially of Constantius, who only received baptism when at the point of death. The hard penances imposed for sins committed after baptism had led to this habit of delay, which we find very prevalent, especially in high quarters. But on the other hand we have it recorded of Julian, as already stated, that he was admitted to the ranks of those who received commission to read the Scriptures in church to the people. It was not customary to bestow this office on those who were as yet only in the grade of catechumens, though we are told that in at least one church[6] such cases were not unknown. Still, if Julian was formally admitted as a Reader, it seems probable that he had been baptised, even without the pressure of a dangerous illness; and once at least in his childhood he must have been in peril of death. Of course the matter would not afterwards appear to him as of great moment, though the story of his using occult means for counteracting the efficacy of the baptismal water is not at all inconsistent with his habit of mind and character.

The years of Julian's academic training (or, as we might say, of his university life) cannot be assigned with chronological precision to the various places at which we know him to have studied. He probably spent a considerable part of the time at Nicomedia, and also stayed in Constantinople. Towards the end of the period, he was a student at Athens, and he had probably made another sojourn there earlier. He also visited Ephesus, Pergamum, and other cities in Asia Minor, and it was the teaching acquired in these regions that seems to have influenced him the most profoundly. Some of the great Asiatic cities maintained at this time learned and eloquent men, who trained their youth at the public expense. Nor were endowments such as we know them entirely wanting. Marcus Aurelius had established four professional chairs of philosophy at Athens, to be held by the Platonists, Peripatetics, Stoics, and Epicureans respectively, and also chairs in politics and rhetoric. Athens retained her prestige for many generations, but the existence of the separate chairs for the four sects cannot be traced in the time of Julian. Meantime other endowments were founded in other cities, and students eager to sit at the feet of a noted professor would migrate from city to city like the wandering members of the mediæval universities, and many German students of our own day.

Our want of precise chronological data as to Julian's early days is partially compensated by the abundant information we can procure as to the manner of men by whom he was taught and the kind of life which he and his fellow-students had to live. Without attempting, then, a complete narrative of this period of his life, we may endeavour to picture to ourselves some of its episodes and to judge of its general results. We will therefore consider here very briefly the nature of the academic studies of the time, the character of some of Julian's principal teachers, and the habits of his friends and fellow-students.[6]

The system of education in vogue during the fourth century was, on its intellectual side, entirely based on literature. Grammar, logic, and rhetoric constituted both then and later on well into the Middle Ages, the basis of a liberal education. In grammar was included the elementary study of literature. Logic had already been developed into a very elaborate art, with its three branches of *apodeictic, biastic,* and *paralogistic.* Rhetoric had expanded in such fashion as to make all other arts and sciences subsidiary to herself. The physical and mathematical sciences were not a very important branch of ordinary education. Medicine was considered a necessary study for those whose health was not very robust. Arithmetic was in great part occupied with the mystical properties of numbers. History and politics, and even the lofty regions of metaphysics and theology were now dominated by the science and art of eloquence. The charge often brought against a purely literary education at the present day, that it tends to make men overvalue the power of expression, and undervalue the pursuit of hidden truths and lofty ideals, applies with ten-fold force to the system which prevailed before literary studies had been leavened with scientific method, while philology and historical criticism were yet unknown. To Greek school-boys it must have seemed as if the Athenians had conquered at Marathon, the properties of numbers had been investigated by the founders of mathematics, the immortality of the soul and its high destinies had been propounded by Plato, chiefly in order to furnish material for elegant and highly applauded themes. In the rhetorical exercises of which, we may well be thankful, not many have come down to our days, the youthful "heirs of all the ages," and the trainers of their minds eagerly sought to eulogise the great deeds of the past, or to show how those deeds might have been done better, to trace rambling analogies along conventional lines, and to prove the most vital of truths by the weakest of logical arguments. Illustrations of this perverse method of treatment are to be found in the works (still extant) of the Sophist Himerius, under whom Julian may possibly have studied at Athens. Among his elaborate discourses are some of a quasi-historical character which sufficiently display the tendency (ineradicable, perhaps, in the human mind) to regard all history not as a

A MUSE.
IVORY DIPTYCH.

field for patient labour and research, but rather as a happy hunting ground full of moral illustrations and fanciful analogies. Among them are orations supposed to have been delivered respectively by Hyperides for Demosthenes and by Demosthenes for Æschines, under circumstances that never arose nor were likely to arise, and one in the name of Themistocles, advising the Athenian people to reject certain Persian propositions of peace, of a kind that Xerxes most assuredly never could nor would have offered.

The more exact sciences suffered no less than the historical from the ubiquitous tyranny of rhetoric. Arithmetic furnished scope for fine-drawn disquisitions of fancied properties of numbers. We have an instance of this in a paper which appears among Julian's letters * and which may, perhaps, be a schoolboy exercise. It was to accompany a present of a hundred figs, and is devoted to a eulogy of the number ten, and of the figs of Damascus. Even medicine could not entirely hold her own. Considerations of practical expediency induced men of delicate health to make themselves acquainted with the ordinary methods of bodily regimen, as did Basil, the future Bishop of Cæsarea, while a student at Athens. But for such purposes a merely empirical knowledge sufficed, while among the masters of the art, some, at least, were enthralled by the all-powerful spirit of oratory. Thus we are told of a certain physician, Magnus of Antioch, that he excelled in rhetoric as well as in medicine, and rendered applicable to himself a story previously current concerning Pericles. As the rival

of Pericles complained that if he had thrown the
great orator, Pericles could persuade the people that
he had never been carried off his feet, so Magnus
could maintain an argument that those cured by
other physicians than himself were still sick.⁹ The
reporter of the saying does not go on to infer that
Magnus, by his powers of persuasion, could argue
his patients into the belief that they had recovered.

Still more curious and more dangerous was the
supreme influence of rhetoric in the law-courts. Two
anecdotes of Athenian university life in Julian's day
illustrate this fact. There had been in Athens one
of those not uncommon frays, of which we shall say
more presently, between the bands of pupils attached
to two rival professors. When the matter was
brought before a magistrate, both professors appeared to defend their quarrelsome disciples. They
were both armed with long speeches and with all the
paraphernalia for creating a sensation. The proconsul, however, cut short the scene by insisting that
the student who appeared as prosecutor should speak
for himself, and that the defence should be made by
a student from the opposite gang. The prosecutor,
being a youth readier with his fists than with his
tongue, failed miserably, and so brought down jeers
on the head of his professor, who, it was sarcastically
said, taught the Pythagorean virtue of silence. Then
came the turn of the defendant, Proæresius, afterwards an illustrious professor in the same university.
He rose to the occasion, implored the compassion of
the audience, praised the glories of his master, addressed a personal appeal to the proconsul, made a

telling allusion to the name of the prosecutor, (which
happened to be Themistocles), and threw all his
remaining energy into an eloquent peroration.   This
brought the proconsul bounding from his judgment
seat, shaking his purple robe in wild excitement.
Then, amid the applause of the audience and the
happy tears of the gratified professor, the accused
were honourably acquitted, and the accusers were
sentenced to the lashes which, in this case, they
probably deserved.

In later days, this same Proæresius, by an eloquent
speech in honour of the Emperor, obtained the
restoration of the tribute formerly due from certain
islands to the city of Athens.   But his oratorical
powers were put to a severer test on another occasion.   The machinations of a rival faction had caused
him to be sent into exile. On a change of proconsuls,
he was recalled, and the newly arrived magistrate
bade him display his oratory in rivalry with all his
foes.   Secure in his ability to defeat them, he asked
his enemies to choose themselves a subject for his
discourse.   When they had done so, he not only
spoke with most entrancing eloquence both for and
against the motion proposed, but on coming to an end,
repeated entirely both his speeches, so that the short-
hand reporters could not detect one verbal change.
The result was that he received almost divine honours, and was conducted home with military pomp.[10]

Furthermore, in the very highest regions of human
thought, the excessive power of words was largely,
though not universally, prevalent.   A few deeper
thinkers there were who realised that questions of

life, morals, and religion are not to be settled by
verbal jugglery or by pompously sounding phrases.
But among the sophists, especially at Athens, and
also to a great extent in Asia Minor, a discourse in
elegant form was regarded as sufficient refutation of
a whole reasoned system. Nothing, for example,
can conceivably be weaker than the arguments
directed by Himerius against the doctrines of Epicurus. Into the subject of the schools of philosophy
then prevalent we cannot now enter. We must
return to consider it in relation to the philosophic
views of Julian himself. Here, however, we may
mention two prominent characteristics of fourth-
century philosophy : its eclecticism, and its close
connection with religious belief and occult practice.
We look in vain for representatives of the great
philosophic sects. Everybody seems to hold more
or less the views of them all, except those of the
Epicureans, who never receive fair treatment at this
time, nor yet in some subsequent periods. The
sinking of formerly prominent distinctions may be
diversely explained. We may attribute it to a lofty
cosmopolitanism which recognises the unity of truth
under a multitude of interpretations. Or it may
seem more probable that a cloud of words has
enveloped and obscured distinctions that are nevertheless radical. As to the second characteristic
mentioned : the craving after some manifestation
of the supernatural is everywhere apparent, and may
be largely traced to that Oriental influence which,
ever since the conquests of Alexander, had been
continually streaming into western lands.

But Julian himself was, during his academic life, preserved by his earnestness of character from the worst tendencies to logomachy and sophistry prevalent all around him. This is shown in a very pleasing letter subsequently addressed (probably from Gaul) to two former fellow-students.[11] After some playful expressions of envy at their delightful occupation, and regret at his own danger of falling into utter barbarism, he gives them some sound advice as to their studies: "Do not despise light literature, nor neglect rhetoric and poetry. But pay more attention to mathematics, and give all diligence to learning the doctrine of Plato and Aristotle. Let this be your main work, your edifice from foundation to roof. Additional subjects may come in by the way, and should be prosecuted by you with more diligence than others show in the pursuit of what is really important."

Let us now briefly glance at the character and career of some of the men to whom at this time Julian seems to have owed most. We may thus perhaps grasp more vividly the characteristics which we have noticed in the general academic teaching of the time, as well as the particular influences that were most potent in the formation of Julian's mind and character. We will take representatives of three distinct and prominent classes: Maximus, the occult philosopher and pagan martyr; Libanius, the prolific orator and renowned trainer of youth; and Themistius, the sober-minded—perhaps rather coldhearted—upholder of eclecticism.

Maximus,[12] at the time when Julian first made his

acquaintance, belonged to the band of eager pupils that clustered round the famous sophist Ædesius at Pergamum. This city seems, from the days of the Attalids downwards, to have been a lively centre of Greek thought, art, and society, and it probably still contained a remnant of its once famous library. At this time, the tendency in Pergamene society seems to have been towards theosophy and occult mysticism. This disposition is especially manifest in some eminent ladies, a fact not surprising when we consider the liberty and consideration enjoyed by Ionian ladies in very early times, and also the freer life which Greek women generally began to enjoy under the successors of Alexander. The wife of Maximus seems to have been an ornament of this intellectual and spiritualist circle, but a yet more distinguished leader in it was a widowed lady, Sosipatra, of whose childhood strange tales were told. She had been given up, it was said, for five years to the charge of two ancient men who afterwards proved to be gods in human form. By them she was trained in the art of discerning things at a distance and of foretelling the future. Her receptions, or, as we might almost call them, *séances*, were as popular as the lectures of Ædesius himself, who lived on friendly terms with her, and educated her sons.

It was the fame of Ædesius that first attracted Julian to Pergamum, and this visit is regarded by some as marking the period in his life when he decisively made up his mind to renounce Christianity. It seems to coincide with the time when, as Julian declares, he "ceased to follow the former ways."

But if the story as told by Eunapius is in the main correct, Julian must have come with a clear notion of what he wanted, and quite emancipated from any shackles that his early education might have cast about his mind. Ædesius was at this time well stricken in years, and Maximus was at Ephesus, which seems to have been his native place.[13] Julian therefore consorted chiefly with two pupils of Ædesius, the genial high-flown Chrysanthius and the more rationalistic Eusebius. These told him tales of the wonderful doings of Maximus, especially how on one occasion he had caused a statue of Hecate to break into laughter, and the torches in her hands to kindle spontaneously. On hearing of these marvels, Julian cried, " He is the man for me," and started off to meet him. From that day to the hour when Maximus stood by Julian's death-bed, the relation between them was one of close and (on Julian's side, at least) of respectful friendship. It was to Maximus that Julian showed his works when he wanted a judgment on their merits, just as, he said, Celtic women tested their new-born babes in the waters of the Rhine. He slept with the letters of Maximus under his pillow, and found time, even when very busily occupied, to write to the philosopher a full account of all his doings.[14] One of the first results of his intercourse with Maximus seems to have been a desire for initiation into the Eleusinian mysteries, and this he was able to gratify. The solemn ceremonies, the mystic words, meaningless enough to the outsider, but fraught with power to the believer, the encouragement given (during this period, certainly, if not in the prosperous days of Greece) to the religious aspiration after purity and immortality, must have deeply impressed the mind of the young votary. He now felt that though he might still have to dissimulate for a time, yet for him the die was cast.

It is a curious fact that Maximus, with all his reverence for oracular and theurgic rites, when he sought responses from the Gods had no scruple in repeating his inquiries till the answer came in approximately the form he desired. We may also feel a little startled to learn that his chief literary work was a commentary on Aristotle's *Logic*.[15] The sanest and the insanest philosophic methods seem to have been blended in the mental operations of these eclectics of the fourth century. Maximus was a man of remarkable voice and appearance, with very piercing eyes and (in his old age, when Eunapius knew him) a venerable white beard. The favours which Julian subsequently conferred upon him will be recorded in a later chapter. His end was tragic. He continued the practice of occult arts after they had been authoritatively prohibited, and thereby brought down on his head the wrath of the Emperor Valens, and prepared for himself a martyr's death.

Libanius, the sophist of Antioch, was also a friend and correspondent of Julian in later days, though probably they did not meet often during this earlier period. Libanius expressly says that Julian had been forbidden by the Emperor to attend his lectures at Nicomedia.[16] He characteristically adds that Julian surreptitiously obtained copies of his works, and modelled his own style on them. To

this statement we may demur, yet the regard in
which Julian held the great sophist is amply attested
by the correspondence between them and also by
their public relations.

The voluminous works of Libanius which [17] are
still extant, including a minute autobiography, might
be expected to afford us a clear view of his life
and character, such as we cannot hope to obtain in
the case of Maximus. [17]   Unfortunately, however,
Libanius was not distinguished, even among his contemporaries, by an unbiassed pursuit of truth and
accuracy, and the chief impression we derive from
his works is of the profound respect he entertains for
rhetoric or "words," and of his yet deeper respect
for his own genius.   Left fatherless in his boyhood,
Libanius ran wild and unfettered by teachers till, in
his fifteenth year, his master-passion took possession
of him, and all things seemed worthless in comparison with the study of eloquence, and of literature as
an auxiliary branch of that study.   To the object of
this passion he remained faithful throughout his long
life; during his unhappy student days, at Athens
(where, by force of sheer bullying, he was obliged to
attach himself to another professor than the one he
had come to hear); during the four years in which
he held a subordinate position among the teachers
of the Athenian University; during a short period
of professional life at Constantinople, five happier
years at Nicomedia, and the forty years throughout
which he ruled supreme, as king of eloquence, in his
native city of Antioch.   He had many difficulties to
contend against : delicate health, the insubordination

of pupils, the treacherous machinations of rival teachers, the factions of a tumultuous populace. Yet he weathered all storms, and maintained his reputation and his own pleasure in it to the end of his prolonged career.

In religion, Libanius was an adherent of the old Gods, more perhaps from taste and temperament than from conviction. There was no trace in him of fanaticism, and the letters he wrote on behalf of oppressed Christians reflect great honour on his name. Human kindliness, and a certain degree of sound sense in matters where he was not personally concerned, redeem his character from the charge of triviality. One letter which he wrote on behalf of a poor man oppressed by a cruel governor is truly admirable. We must also respect his championship of the bakers of Antioch during a time of famine, when people were about to avenge the general sufferings on their powerless heads. His view as to the relative importance of religion and oratory is strangely shewn in a letter which he wrote to congratulate a friend on being made bishop, an office which afforded fine opportunities for applying the art of rhetoric. The blindness of such men as Libanius to the real import of the religious changes going on around them is curious and somewhat suggestive.

In estimating the deserts of Libanius and his school, we must not overlook their services to literature. It may be that ancient books appeared to them rather as a quarry furnishing raw material for manufacturers of discourses than as a mine containing treasures of the highest intrinsic value. But whatever their opinions and feelings might be, they helped to keep those treasures in existence for the men that were to come after them, and we are even now enjoying the fruits of their labours.

Themistius,[18] a Paphlagonian by descent, who lived and taught in Constantinople, Nicomedia, and elsewhere, differs from Maximus in being free from fanaticism, and, from Libanius in having a more just appreciation of the subordination in which words should stand to thoughts. The little treatise which Julian addressed to him, in answer to one which he had sent to Julian, on the Duties of Monarchy, would by itself suggest that Themistius was no commonplace man. Although in those days of oration-making he could hardly avoid being frequently called on for speeches, such as those which, revised by him, have come down to us, he set philosophy high above rhetoric. The work to which, by preference, he devoted himself, was the elucidation of Aristotle, though he did not neglect the study of Plato. The appointments which he received and retained under a variety of emperors, orthodox, heretical, and pagan, might suggest that he was of the fellowship of the Vicar of Bray. Such a judgment, however, would be very unfair, since Themistius probably never professed a religion that he did not hold, though his opinions were such as to make it difficult for some of his contemporaries to bring them within the range of any party or creed.[19] While believing in the truth and necessity of the fundamental principles underlying all religions, he held that different local and national rights ought to be maintained, as bearing

5

witness before the multitude to deep-seated verities. In subsequent days, when the Emperor Valens was persecuting those Christians that held to the Nicene symbol, Themistius opposed his attempts on philosophic grounds. "The Emperor," he said, "ought not to be surprised at the difference of judgment on religious questions existing among Christians, inasmuch as that discrepancy was trifling compared with the multitude of conflicting opinions among the heathen, which amounted to above three hundred. Dissension, indeed, might be an inevitable consequence of this disagreement; but God would be the more glorified by the diversity of sentiment, and the greatness of His majesty would be the more venerated from its being thus made manifest how difficult it is to know Him." [20] Themistius was on friendly terms with Gregory Nazianzen, and seems to have been tolerant in deed and not only in word.

We may thus note the fact which we shall have to consider more fully later on, that the relations between the professors of the old philosophies and the adherents of the new religion were not always or necessarily hostile. One, at least, of the philosophers at Athens in Julian's time was a professed Christian, though apparently not very ardent for the faith. Gregory Nazianzen and his friend Basil were both fellow-students of Julian in Greece. Christian and Pagan teachers had at least one large field to cultivate in common, the art of rhetoric, which demanded the labours alike of the candidate for the sophist's chair and of the aspirant to the bishop's throne. Whether the churchman desired to attain ecclesiastical preferment, or aimed primarily at the salvation of souls and the edification of the faithful, the rhetorical training of the Athenian school was for him equally necessary. Whether he could, with whole-hearted simplicity, receive at the same time all the best that the ancient culture had to offer him, is another question, the answer to which was made in the days that came after.

If we turn now from the teachers of the middle part of the fourth century to consider the life of the students, we may form a vivid picture of it, especially of life in the University of Athens, from the writings of Gregory Nazianzen [21] and of Eunapius. The chief feature which strikes us is the extraordinary want of discipline, which is all the more remarkable when we see the careful regulations to which the Attic Ephebi were subject in earlier times.[22] The professors were more like *condottieri* leaders than like the ruling authorities of a constituted educational body. Their pupils attached themselves to the person of their master rather than to the course of study he recommended, and were always ready to wage war on his behalf and to add to his band of scholars, by fair means or by foul. It has been supposed that non-paying pupils were turned to account by the professors (who were not always entirely dependent on their endowments) by being made recruiting sergeants to bring others. At Athens, as in the mediæval universities, the usual division was into nations, men from each particular province or region seeking out some eminent fellow-countryman under whom to study. But this rule was not universal. We have seen that Libanius was, on his arrival, forced by a tumultuous band to attach himself to a master of whom he had no desire to learn. The experiences of a "freshman" at our universities are mild indeed compared with those of the luckless, often sea-sick youth, on his arrival at the goal of his innocent hopes. His first journey to the baths seems to have been made the occasion of a rude initiation, trying to nerves and temper and probably sometimes dangerous to the bones. Two men are, by different authorities, recorded as having been exempted from this ordeal by special request. Basil, whose constitution was delicate, escaped by the influence of his friend Gregory. Eunapius, who was suffering from a dangerous illness, at the time of his arrival, was the object of a special appeal on the part of the gentle Proæresius to the good feeling of the ringleaders among the students.

Sometimes, as we have seen, free fights between bands of students furnished cases for the law-courts. Possibly better discipline might have been enforced if the professors had cared to use all their powers. Some, like Libanius, believed in the use of the rod. But such use, on the backs of young men at a distance from any parental control, would soon have led to empty lecture-rooms. What should we say to the appeal made by Himerius to the lazy students who failed to return on the right day after the vacations? [23]

" Presumptuous and overweening, heedless of my affection. Gladly would I have asked them: What for them is a sweeter hearing than my voice? What

sight more cheering than my radiant aspect? What
tuneful birds of spring utter such sweet and pleasant strains? What melodious, rhythmical chorus,
tuned to the flute or pipe, can touch their hearts as
the sound from this pulpit of mine? For indeed I
blame those shepherds who neglect to lead their
flocks with music and the pipe, but threaten with
chastisement and scourging. For my own flock
and my own nurslings—never may I see them with
sullen brows!—reason shall conduct them to the
meadows and groves of the Muses. Songs are for
them, not blows. Thus may our mutual love grow
and flourish, and my rule be ever guided by music
and by harmony."

A striking instance, surely, of faith in the supreme
power of persuasive words! Unfortunately we see
that in practice such power did not suffice to maintain order among a community of youths brought
together from all quarters and emancipated from
parental control.

Yet with all its drawbacks, university life had in
the fourth century both the present charm and the
germs of future profit which such a life must always
have while youth is youth and while the roads of
knowledge lie open. Those who had studied at
Athens felt for their *Alma Mater* in their after life
that loyal affection which we associate with the
widely different universities of modern times. The
excitement of a new and independent life, the first
realisation of the glorious inheritance bequeathed
by the past to the present age, the warm and stimulating influence of teacher on pupil, the influence

yet more rousing, to body and mind alike, of congenial fellow-students, the lively play of mind on
mind in places hallowed by centuries of noble
associations; such was the joy of university life at
Athens in those days as among us now. And if in
any way Julian had reason to complain that the
jealousy of his cousin excluded him from some
spheres of life suitable to his rank and station, he
might well thank the Gods that it was not in the
forced atmosphere of a court, but in the intellectual
freedom of great centres of culture, that he first
learned to test and use his mental powers, and
formed the most lasting friendships of his life.

Bundle of Manuscripts.   Rolled up.

Coin of Constantine II.
Plan of a camp on which stands
the Sun-god.

NOTES ON CHAPTER III.

[1] Ammianus, xv., 2.

[2] *Cf.* Mr. C. W. King and others.

[3] Ep. 51.

[4] According to Greg. Nazianzen, and Sozomen, v., 2.

[5] That of Alexandria, Socrates, *His. Eccles.*, v., 22.

[6] For much interesting information about the contemporaries and teachers of Julian at Athens, as well as about the whole system of University education at that time, I am indebted to M. Petit de Juleville, *L'École d'Athenes pendant le 4m siècle.*

[7] See Greg. Naz., *Oration in Praise of Basil.*

[8] Ep. 24. This letter is however, regarded by Cumont as the work of the same author who wrote those to Jamblichus. (*Sur l'Authenticité de Quelques Lettres*, etc. See *infra*). But in any case it may serve as a specimen of the models set before Julian for imitation.

[9] Eunapius, *Vitæ Sophistarum*, 180. The saying against Pericles is here given to Archidamus, not, as by Plutarch, to Thucydides son of Melesias in answer to a question of Archidamus.

[10] These stories are told by Eunapius (Vit. soph. : *Julianus and Proæresius*), and are also given in *Petit de Juleville*.

[11] Ep. 55.

[12] In his life by Eunapius. *Cf.* Zeller, *Philosophie der Griechen*, 2, 661.

[13] So says Ammianus. Eunapius does not mention his birthplace, but says that he was of good family.

[14] Epp. 15, 16, 37. The first two of these are disputed by Cumont.

[15] See Zeller, *loc. cit.* Also newly discovered series of letters by Julian (*Mavrogordateion*, etc.), No. 4.

[16] This statement might throw some doubt on the possibility of Julian's intercourse with Maximus. But we have already seen (*supra*, note 1), that one of his student journeys in Asia-Minor did bring Julian into trouble.

[17] Ed. Reiske. The autobiography is translated at the end of Petit de Juleville's charming essay, *Sur la Vie at la Correspondance de Libanius.*

[18] See Zeller, *Phil. der Griechen*, vol. iv., p. 739, and Brucker, *Hist. Phil.*, ii., p. 434, *et seq.*

[19] Thus he has been claimed as a Christian, and confused with the

leader of sect called *Agnoeti*, who professed ignorance as to whether Jesus Christ were or were not the Logos. The identification is tempting but will not stand. (See Brucker).

[20] Socrates, *Hist. Eccles.*, English translation, iv., 32.

[21] See especially his *Eulogy of Basil*. Petit de Juleville is excellent here, and he is followed by Mr. W. W. Capes in his bright little book on *University Life in Ancient Athens*.

[22] See Dumont, *L'Ephébie Attique*.

[23] *Oration*, xv., 1, 2.

Coin of Magnentius.
Reverse, SALUS DD NN AVC ET CAES. The Christian Monogram, between
A and W.

CHAPTER IV.

JULIAN'S ELEVATION TO THE CÆSARSHIP.

355.

"ἔστι δὲ . . . τὸ κεφάλαιον, ὅτι μήτε τὸν πόνον φεύγων
μήτε τὴν ἡδονὴν θηρεύων, μήτε ἀκραγμοσύνης καὶ ῥᾳστώνης
ἐρῶν, τὸν ἐν τῇ κολιτείᾳ δυσχεραίνω βίον ἀλλ᾿ . . . οὔτε
καιδείαν ἐμαυτῷ συνειδὼς τοσαύτην οὔτε φύσεως ὑπεροχήν,
καὶ προσέτι δεδιὼς, μὴ φιλοσοφίαν, ἧς ἐρῶν οὐκ ἐφικόμην,
ἐς τοὺς νῦν ἀνθρώπους οὐδὲ ἄλλως εὐδοκιμοῦσαν διαβάλλω."

JULIAN, *Ep. to Themistius*, 266, C.

" The forward youth that would appear
Must now forsake his Muses dear . . .
'T is time to leave the books in dust,
And oil the unused armour's rust."—A. MARVELL.

F his first intercourse with Maximus
and his initiation into the Eleusinian
Mysteries marked a mental crisis in
Julian's life, a similar crisis was
soon to follow in his outward circumstances. The one may be regarded as preparatory to the other,
since it is evident from Julian's writings, as well as

73

from the testimony of his friends, that his firm belief in his vocation to a divinely appointed task supported him as nothing else could have done in the difficulties and trials that he had to undergo.

The death of Gallus and the painful circumstances which attended it furnished a golden opportunity to the contemptible sycophants who abounded at the Imperial Court. Of the harassing persecutions and the judicial murders that disgrace this period, the chief responsibility must, of course, rest with the Emperor Constantius. Yet we should be wrong if we regarded Constantius as an exceptionally wicked man. Neither is he, in some ways, to be regarded as utterly weak. He had so far resisted the enervating influences of an Oriental court as to maintain an unblemished reputation for chastity and temperance. His habitual self-control was reflected in an imperturbable manner of look and behaviour which contrasted with the eager restlessness of his young cousin. He seems to have been guided by conscientious motives in the affairs of government, civil, military, and even ecclesiastical. But where his suspicions had once been aroused, he was as inaccessible to the dictates of pity as he habitually was to the sounds and sights around him. One person, indeed, could withstand the influences of the courtiers, not so much, apparently, by appealing to his better feelings as by cleverly flattering his self-interest. This was the brilliant and beautiful Empress Eusebia, Julian's good genius at the Court. Constantius having lost his first wife, Galla, had married Eusebia probably not long after the defeat

AN EMPRESS (PLACIDIA?) AND HER SON.
IVORY DIPTYCH.

of Magnentius.¹ She was a Macedonian by birth, of
a consular family, had been educated in Greek literature, and was singularly discreet in her behaviour.
She used her influence over her husband, an influence which she probably owed more to her mental than to her physical attractions, in favour of her
family, several members of which received promotion. This seems to have moved no great animad-
version against her, probably because in other ways
she advocated moderate courses, and was always in
favour of clemency and opposed to the corrupt influences of the eunuchs. If serious charges have
been brought against her by some historians, they
may be shown to rest on no very solid ground.²
Her habitual attitude in Court factions, as well as
her natural sympathy with a young Greek scholar,
constituted her the champion of Julian at Court,
and to her he owed his escape from peril, and his
rise to a position of power and importance.

Meantime, many suspected persons fell victims
to the vengeance which overtook the partisans of
Gallus. Ursicinus, the honourable soldier whose
mission in Syria has been already mentioned, and to
whose person the historian Ammianus was specially
attached, had a narrow escape from execution on a
charge which amounted to little more than a recognition of his capacity and popularity. The most
dangerous foe to all men of standing and ability was
Arbetio, consul in the year 355, whose serpent-like
wiles devised against his rivals were too often successful. Among the lesser functionaries who devoted themselves to the congenial task of tracking

out real or imaginary conspiracies, the most noto-
rious were a Persian of the name of Paul and a
Dacian called Mercurius. The former acquired the
nickname of "The Chain," because of his skill in
linking together every circumstance that could tell
against his victims. The latter was known as the
" Count of Dreams," owing to his habit of extract-
ing treasonable intentions from reports of nightly
fancies. At the same time Rufinus, who held the
office of Chief Apparitor of the Prætorian Præfecture,³ was eager to welcome any secret or treacherous information. One catastrophe caused by these
sycophants seemed likely to implicate Julian in its
issue. A dinner had been given at Sirmium, on the
Save, by the governor of one of the districts of
Pannonia. Talking freely over their wine, some of
the guests complained of the violent measures of
the Government, others spoke of a coming revolution, other lighter heads told stories of family fore-
casts which seemed applicable. But a Government
official was sitting among them. The hasty words
were speedily reported to Rufinus. The spy was
rewarded, the indiscreet talkers seized and brought
in chains to Milan, with the exception of one, who
contrived to commit suicide on the way. On this
occasion, however, they were so fortunate as to suffer only imprisonment and threats.⁴

Julian had meantime been summoned to Milan.
The weapons that his enemies sought to turn against
him were his alleged intercourse with his brother and
his journey in Asia of which we have already spoken.

Julian said afterwards that he had not seen Gallus at
all during the time in question, though he had occasionally corresponded with him. Ammianus says
that he was in Constantinople when Gallus passed
through the city. The statements are not contra-
dictory, and in any case Julian seems to have been
successful in clearing himself when he had an opportunity of so doing. But it was long before such an
opportunity was granted. For seven months he felt
himself a prisoner. Six months he spent in Milan,
without being once admitted to an interview with
his cousin, whom he had only once seen before,
namely, during his stay in Cappadocia. The Sirmium
troubles prolonged, most probably, his time of
duress. Libanius says that he behaved with much
discretion, not demeaning himself by denouncing
his dead brother, yet not bidding defiance to the
powerful Emperor. At length he was sent for a
time to Como, but he did not remain there long.
He soon found an opportunity of requesting the
Empress to use her influence so that he might be
permitted to return to his maternal estate in Asia
Minor, which he seems to have regarded as his home.
The permission was almost granted when events
occurred which made the Emperor anxious to loosen
the ties which bound his cousin to Asia Minor, and
perhaps also to keep him nearer to himself. Consequently, Julian was sent to study in Athens. The
months of seclusion and anxiety had occupied the
autumn and winter of 354 and the spring of 355.
They were probably of service to him in the oppor-

tunities they afforded of acquiring practical acquaintance with the Latin language, such as Libanius tells
us he afterwards possessed.

If in after days[5] Julian declared that he desired
nothing more than to live and die in the glorious
city of Pallas Athene, he need not be suspected of
affectation. Apart from the pleasantness of university life in the great centre of Hellenism to a young
man of studious habits, genial temperament, and
almost morbid sensitiveness to historical associations, the glimpses Julian had had of court life had
not been such as to make the other seem less desirable in comparison.

Constantius was the one successful man of his
family, yet his lot cannot have seemed a particularly
happy one, while he lived surrounded by rapacious
courtiers and hampered by perpetual cares. Of the
numerous male posterity of Constantius Chlorus, he
and Julian alone survived, the others having perished
by violent deaths. Meanwhile, sophists like Proæresius and Himerius lived to a green old age, and
the troubles which factious jealousy might arouse
against them were easily quelled. There was an
atmosphere of freedom in action and speculation
among the student bands of various nations and
creeds, which must have been most welcome to
Julian after his forced dissimulation and caution.
Nor were the leadings of ambition altogether in
favour of a more active life. We have seen the
extraordinarily high esteem in which the leading
sophists of the age were held, and Julian, himself, in
spite of his youth, was beginning to enjoy a high

degree of consideration and popularity among the students. Even if we discount the extravagant remarks of Libanius on the great sensation which his brilliant abilities and wide range of knowledge caused among his peers, we can easily believe that he had soon gathered around him a devoted circle of friends and admirers.

We cannot with certainty date any of Julian's writings as belonging to this period of his life, yet it was undoubtedly for him a time of great mental activity. The malicious pen of Gregory Nazianzen has drawn a portrait of Julian as he appeared at this time. It is a coarse caricature, yet if we compare it with the description given by Ammianus Marcellinus, and with what we might otherwise suppose, we may discern in it some foundation of fact. It was the eager, nervous restlessness of his gait, his unmethodical outpourings of excited speech, his sudden bursts of laughter, that seemed to the future bishop unworthy of a sober and dignified person. Ammianus,[6] who must have been very familiar with his appearance, describes it thus : " He was of middle height, with soft, fine hair, a bushy, pointed beard, beautifully bright and flashing eyes which bespoke the subtlety[7] of his mind ; fine eyebrows, a very straight nose, a rather large mouth with full lower lip, a thick arched neck, large broad shoulders, a frame compact from head to finger tips, whence his great physical strength and agility." To his physical culture, however, he would probably not have devoted much attention but for the sudden change in his prospects, the causes of which we have now to trace.

We have already seen that the eastern provinces of the Empire were by no means pacified, nor a permanent barrier set up against Persian encroachments at the time when Constantius had to turn and face his foes in the West. Musonianus, an Antiochene of eloquence and culture, had been appointed Præfect of the East. He had secured the favour of Constantius by the clearness with which he had explained to him the distinctive dogmas of the Manichees and of other sects.[8] In some respects he was worthy of his high post, but his besetting sin of avarice led him into courses detrimental to the eastern provinces and to the whole Empire. Meantime though the Persian king was, happily for the Romans, occupied in the far East, his lieutenants were making incursions into Armenia and Mesopotamia. It seemed probable that before long the presence of the Emperor would be required at the head of an army in Asia. Meantime, yet more pressing dangers threatened from the West.

The troubles from the German nations where perhaps in part an after-wave of the rebellion of Magnentius. Constantius has been accused[9] of cowardice and treachery in trying to stir up some barbarian tribes to invade the provinces at the crisis. If he did so, the act was not alien to Roman policy in dealing with barbarians and insurgents, and he did his best to repair the folly of it by taking the field in the spring of the year 354. The object of his attack was the tribe, or congeries of tribes, called the Allemanni, from whose ravages the Empire had suffered on many occasions since the reign of Caracalla, or possibly from an earlier period. The Emperor Aurelian, and in more recent times Constantius Chlorus, had dealt them severe blows, and they had been more or less held in check by the lines of fortresses along the Rhine frontier which had been raised and maintained by Diocletian and his colleagues. Now, however, they had broken through the barrier, and established themselves in the regions known in modern times as Alsace and Lorraine.

Constantius set out from Arelate (Arles) near the mouth of the Rhone, and marched north to Valentia at the junction of the Rhone and the Isere, expecting reinforcements from Aquitaine, the arrival of which was delayed by excessive rains. The troops which had been mustered about Cabillona (Châlons-sur-Saône) became impatient and even mutinous. The arrival at last of money and provisions was more effectual than the persuasions of the Prætorian Præfect, Rufinus, in inducing them to continue the march, and after many difficulties, owing to the early time of the year, they reached the Rhine not far from the site of Basel. An attempt to make a bridge of boats was frustrated by the enemy, who had been warned by some fellow-tribesmen holding office in the Imperial army. Owing however to reasons which cannot be with certainty assigned, the Allemanni were not eager to avail themselves of their own advantageous position or of the distance of the Romans, and envoys arrived in the Imperial camp from the brother-kings Gundobadus and Vadomarius desiring conditions of peace. Constantius set forth, in an address to the army, the grounds for deciding to accede to this request. A treaty was concluded with solemn rites, and Constantius returned to Milan, where, as we have seen, Julian also spent the following winter.

Next year, another tribe of the nation of the Allemanni made an incursion into Roman territory in the neighbourhood of Lake Constance (then called Brigantia), and Constantius again took the field. He did not, however, advance in person against the foe, but stayed in Rætia, while Arbetio, holding the title of Magister Equitum, penetrated with a large force into the mountain home of the barbarians. Here, in ignorance of the difficulties of the country, he was taken at unawares, and suffered a severe defeat. The credit, however, of the army was retrieved and the safety of the remnant secured by the gallant endeavours of three tribunes on the Roman side, who turned the fortune of the campaign. The uncouth barbaric names of these rescuers of Roman honour remind us how, for better or for worse, the mistress of the world had come to depend upon those she might affect to despise but could not afford to ignore. Such as this victory was, Constantius regarded it as entitling him to the honour of a triumph.

Arbetio seems thus to have been no general himself, and he pursued with revengeful envy those whose talents were conspicuous above his own. His machinations against the Frankish general Silvanus brought the western provinces into serious peril. This brave soldier, whose desertion of Magnentius at a critical moment had helped to secure the victory of Constantius at Mursa, had been sent in the capa-

city of Magister Peditum [10] to make head against the
invaders. An underling of his named Dynamius
entered into a conspiracy with Arbetio to compass
his destruction. Letters of recommendation were
obtained from him on plausible pretexts. The con-
tents of them were then erased and treasonable
matter substituted, and the transmuted epistles with
the signature of Silvanus, were brought before the
Emperor as evidence of his guilt. He was, however,
not without friends at Court, and it was decided to
send a commissioner who should induce him to return
to Milan, that he might, if possible, clear himself.
Unfortunately the mission was entrusted to a courtier
of the lowest type, who assumed the guilt of Silvanus
as certain, and made matters in Gaul much worse.
Silvanus regarded himself as a lost man. He would
have fled to his own people, the Franks, but feared
lest their desire to stand well with the Emperor
might lead to his betrayal. In desperation he threw
himself on the personal loyalty of his soldiers, and
in the city of Agrippina (Cologne), he assumed the
Imperial purple.

Meantime the astonishing trickery that had been
practised against him was brought to light. It is a
curious instance of the manner in which such affairs
were regarded at the court of Constantius, that one
of the prime intriguers shortly afterwards received
promotion. The practical problem now was to
secure the person of Silvanus. The mission was
entrusted to Ursicinus, whose ability and fidelity
made him so necessary at such a crisis as to silence
the tongues of the envious. With him were asso-

ciated ten tribunes, one of whom was the historian
Ammianus. They were to assure Silvanus as to the
security of his person and the continuance of his
dignities, provided that he returned to Court at once,
leaving Ursicinus to carry on his duties in Gaul. It
is with regret that we see honourable men like
Ursicinus and Ammianus condescending to the mean
deception of a culprit whom they regarded with pity
rather than with aversion. They were hospitably
received by the usurper, whose authority they judged
it prudent to acknowledge. Silvanus, with the levity
of a barbarian soldier, vented, in conversation with
Ursicinus, his indignation against the manner in
which both he and his principal guest had been
habitually treated by the Court. Ursicinus now felt
justified in meeting treachery with treachery. Some
of the soldiers of Silvanus were bribed to turn against
him. A tumult ensued, the usurper's guards were
put to the sword, and he was himself slain after he
had been dragged from a church into which he now
fled for refuge.

Proceedings such as these, though they might
temporarily avert an impending danger, did not tend
permanently to check the inroads of the Germans or
to encourage any generals who might be sent against
them. And while the horizon to East and West
was heavy with clouds, the sky was by no means
clear in the immediate neighbourhood of the Imperial
presence. In Rome, the Præfect Leontius, a man of
stern character, had with difficulty quelled a popular
commotion due to scarcity of wine. At the same
time, the Bishop Liberius had fallen into disgrace

through his championship of the Nicene party. Hampered by difficulties on all sides, Constantius, still childless, saw the need of taking a step that might secure the dynasty, and render the Imperial house more popular with the army and with the people.

This step was the elevation of Julian to a position similar in honour and title to that formerly held by Gallus, in order that his military abilities might be tested, and if found considerable, might be turned to the use of the Empire in its time of need. Darker motives have been attributed to Constantius in this course of action. He may have reflected that if Julian were not successful, many opportunities would arise for his convenient removal from the scenes. The conduct of Constantius on other occasions does not militate against such suspicions, and it must have seemed a most unlikely chance that a youth bred without any military training or acquaintance with the ways of the world, should prove capable of holding his own in a position which required a rare combination of practical talents. It is quite possible, however, to give Constantius the benefit of the doubt, especially since the course was urged by Julian's steady friend, Eusebia, and since the promotion was not intended in the first instance to carry with it very grave responsibilities.

When Julian was summoned from Greece to Milan he obeyed with great reluctance and gloomy forebodings. Not only was he obliged to leave, perhaps for ever, his favourite pursuits, his most esteemed friends, and all but a traveller's quantum of books;

the future was as dark to him as the immediate past had been bright. He felt, he afterwards said,[11] as if he were called to drive four spirited horses without having learned the art of the charioteer. He held up his hands towards the Acropolis, and besought Athena not to desert her votary. Then he travelled to Milan, and took up his abode in one of the suburbs. Julian afterwards described, with some humour, the process which he had to undergo in the transmutation from student to soldier and prince. Not only must his beard be shorn [12] and his sophist's gown exchanged for a soldier's cloak; he must also unlearn his student's irregular gait and affect the strut of the courtiers around him, on whom, all the while, he looked as the executioners of his family and as his own personal foes. The practice of military exercises, however necessary, was at first very irksome to him, and he was heard to mutter, "O Plato!" as he tried to catch the step of an elaborate military movement. Perseverance, however, made up for long neglect. A characteristic story was told of him afterwards, how, when he was engaged in a military exercise, his shield broke away in his hand. Without being disconcerted, he held up the handle before the by-standers, exclaiming: "I keep what I had hold of."

Meanwhile Eusebia reassured him both by messages and by kindly words spoken in a personal interview: "You have received somewhat from us already," she said, "you shall have more by-and-bye, with God's help, if only you are loyal and fair in your dealings with us." Her good-will was shown yet

RUINS OF IMPERIAL BUILDINGS, MILAN.

further in the highly-appreciated gift of a good library, to supplement the meagre stock of books that he had brought from Athens.

It was naturally to Eusebia that Julian felt disposed to apply in seeking some way of escape from the responsibilities and perils that awaited him in his new career. His actions, as well as the workings of his mind at this crisis, were afterwards described by him in his *Letter to the Athenians.* The passage may be quoted at length, as illustrating alike the painfulness of his position at the time, the means to which he commonly resorted in search of supernatural direction, and the Stoic sense of duty imbibed from the teachings of Socrates and of Julian's hero-model— Marcus Aurelius.

" Eusebia sent me friendly messages on several occasions and bade me write freely to her concerning my desires. Accordingly I wrote her a letter, or rather a petition, containing such vows as these; ' May you have children to succeed you, may you receive all good gifts from God, if only you will send me to my home as quickly as possible.' But I doubted whether it were safe to send to the palace a letter addressed to the Emperor's wife. I prayed, therefore, that the Gods would declare to me at night whether or no I should send my letter to the Empress. But they warned me that if I should send it, the most disgraceful of all deaths awaited me. I write the truth, and call the Gods to witness. Accordingly I refrained from sending the letter. And from that night a thought possessed me which is worth imparting to you. ' I have in my mind ven-

tured,' I said to myself, ' to resist the Gods, and have
thought to devise better schemes for my welfare than
those of the All-Knowing Powers. Yet human
reason, its eyes fixed on the immediate present, can
but attain passable fortune and avoid errors for a
short space. Wherefore no man takes thought for
the things which are to come thirty years hence, nor
yet for those which are already past. As to the future, deliberation is superfluous, for the past it is un-
availing. Man can only take counsel for what lies
near at hand, or on that which he can already see in
potentiality and in germ. But the Divine Reason
stretches far, nay, it comprehends all things, so as to
indicate rightly, and to accomplish what tends to good.
For the Gods, as they are the cause of all that is, are
likewise the origin of all that shall be. Thus must
they needs have understanding as to the things of the
present.' And as I thought thus, it seemed to me that
my second determination was better than my first.
And considering the justice of the matter, I reflected :
' Would you not be angry if one of your beasts were
to deprive you of its services, say a horse or a sheep or
a calf, and were to run away when you called it ? And
seeing that you wish to think yourself no beast but
a man, and not even a man of the common herd, but
one belonging to a superior and reasonable class,
would you deprive the Gods of their use of you, and
not be ready to accomplish whatever their will might
demand of you ? Beware lest you not only fall into
this great folly, but also neglect your rightful duties
towards the Gods. Where is your courage ? A
sorry thing it seems to be ; you are ready to cringe

and flatter from fear of death, when it is possible for
you to cast all anxiety aside, and to leave the Gods
to work their will, dividing with them the care of
yourself, as Socrates did ; thus in all things concerning yourself doing what you find possible ; leaving
the whole in their hands ; seeking not your own gain ;
seizing nothing for your own use, you might receive
in all security the gifts they bestow upon you.
This course seemed to me not only safe, but suitable,
to a man of reasonable mind, especially as it had
been pointed out by the Gods. For to rush head-
long into an unseemly course of present peril in
order to escape from dangers in the future seemed
to me unwise in the extreme. I yielded and obeyed.
Soon after, the title and the garb of *Cæsar* were
conferred upon me."

The ceremony of investing the new Cæsar with
the purple robe was performed in a great military
assembly at Milan, on the 6th of November, 355.
The soldiers applauded the Emperor's speech, and
were pleased at the modest bearing and animated
countenance of the young Cæsar. But while they
clashed their shields against their knees, he thought
less hopefully of the issue of the proceedings, and
repeated to himself a line of Homer :

" Him purple death obtained, remorseless fate." [14]

A few days afterwards, Julian married Helen, the
sister of Constantius. Of this lady we know almost
nothing, either for good or for evil. She was probably no longer very young, but if she was the child
of her father's old age, she may have been no older

than Julian himself, who is said to have attained his
twenty-fifth year on the day of his elevation to the
Cæsarship.[15] We have occasional mention of her in
some of Julian's letters, but not any that can enable
us to judge whether or no the marriage was a happy
one. Her influence over him was probably *nil*. In
any case, her death at the most critical period of his
life prevented her from acting much on his conduct,
either as a stimulus or as a restraint. They had one
child, who died at birth.[16]

On the 1st of December, Julian left Milan for
Gaul. The Emperor accompanied him as far as
Pavia, whence Julian struck west for Turin. He
had been obliged to remodel his household, and
only retained four of his former personal attendants,
of whom two were mere boys. Of the other two,
one, the only member of the party who shared
Julian's feelings as to religion, had charge of his
books. The other was the physician Oribazius,[17] a
pupil of the rhetorician-doctor Magnus, whom we
have already mentioned. How far the changes were
necessary, it is not easy for us to judge. The other
grievances which Julian felt, the restrictions placed
upon his own authority, are fully justified by the
total inexperience and the untried ability of the new
Cæsar.

At Turin bad news awaited the party. The great
colony of Agrippina (Cologne), in which Silvanus
had previously assumed the purple, had fallen into
the hands of the barbarians. No decisive action
could be taken before the beginning of spring, and
meantime Julian went into winter quarters at

Vienne. He received a warm welcome from the inhabitants of that city, and one blind old woman
declared that he was destined to restore the temples
of the Gods. It is not impossible that in some
minds the late misfortunes were associated with the
non-observance of the national cults.

Ammianus, in sketching the character of Julian
at this time, compares him to the Emperor Marcus,
whom he followed in his whole-hearted devotion to
the cause of duty and of right reason. Julian,
eagerly continuing his studies while preparing to
attack the Franks and Allemanni, may remind us
of his philosophic predecessor, noting down, in his
camp among the Quadi, his reflections on the government of the universe and on the laws of moral
life. If in some respects Julian may fall short of his
ideal, he was probably more successful than was
Marcus in arousing his energies from a life of contemplation to one of action. As a philosophic
idealist who was also a great military leader, there is
hardly a name, except perhaps that of Epaminondas,
that we can place beside his. His military achievements will occupy us in the following chapter.

Coin of Constantius II. Obverse, GAUDIUM ROMANORUM. Constantine receiving
a crown from heaven.

NOTES ON CHAPTER IV.

[1] For the probable date of the marriage of Constantius and Eusebia, see Tillemont, note xxi., on *Constantius. Cf.* also Art. xxvi. See Zosimus, bk. iii., ch. i., Julian's *Oration in Honour of Eusebia*, his references to her in his *Letter to the Athenians*, and several passages in Ammianus.

[2] See *infra*, note 16.

[3] *Adparitionis præfecturæ prætorianæ principem*, Am., xv., 3. He is elsewhere called Prætorian Præfect (or is it a different person ?).

[4] Am. Marc., *loc cit.*, *cf.* Julian's *Letter to the Athenians* 273, C. D. I cannot see that Mücke (*Julian's Leben und Schriften* p. 29) is to be followed when he infers that Julian was himself present at the Sirmium dinner.

[5] Libanius, *Epitaph. Cf. Letter to the Athenians*.

[6] Am. Marc., xxv., 4.

[7] (Or a look of perpetual inquiry.) Venustate oculorum micantium flagrans, qui mentis ejus argutias indicabant (some MSS., *angustias*).

[8] Am. Marc., xv., 13. He was *also* called Strategius.

[9] By Libanius and Zosimus.

[10] Or, perhaps, *Magister equitum et peditum*, Schiller, iii., 3, sec. 25. For the rebellion of Silvanus, see chiefly Am., xv., 5. *Cf.* Julian, Or. ii.

[11] Or. iii., 122.

[12] It must have grown again pretty rapidly, as it appears on his coins and medals.

[13] *Letter to the Athenians*. This would seem to show that Julian regarded the massacre of his relations as originating in the Court rather than in the Army. *Letter to the Athenians*, 275–7.

[14] Ἔλλαβε πορφύρεος θανατος καὶ μοῖρα κραταίη. See account of the proceedings in Am., xv., 8.

[15] This has been conjectured, perhaps on insufficient grounds ; see Tillemont, note i.

[16] We may here dispose of the unpleasant story, related by Ammianus, that Eusebia, by the use of pernicious drugs, caused the untimely death of Helen's children, and afterwards of Helen herself. The statement is entirely at variance with what we know, not only of the character, but of the lines of policy attributed to Eusebia. Of course, jealousy may incite to dark deeds women who are otherwise estimable. Yet in this case, we may be permitted to doubt the state-

ment of Ammianus. It is quite impossible that Julian should have written as he did concerning Eusebia, after both she and Helen were beyond reach of flattery or of vituperation, had he known of any such hateful machinations on her part. Nor could her practices have remained permanently unknown to him. At the same time, we are told that Eusebia suffered greatly, and shortened her own life, through the use of drugs taken to produce fecundity, a gift, as Chrysostom says, which she should have expected only from Heaven. What more probable than that being in the habit of using quack medicines herself, she should have recommended them to her sister-in-law, and that malicious tongues should have twisted an act of kindly-meant imprudence so as to give it a terribly criminal character ?

[17] *Cf.* with *Letter to the Athenians*, Eunap., *Oribazius.*

A Four-horse Chariot.

CHAPTER V.

JULIAN'S CÆSARSHIP IN GAUL.[1]

356–359.

'Αμφότερον, βασιλεύς τ' ἀγαθὸς κρατερος τ' αἰχμητης.
(*II., III.*, 179. *Chosen for inscription on Julian's Tomb.* Zosimus, iii., 34.)

> " Thine, Roman, is the pilum ;
>   Roman, the sword is thine,
> The even trench, the bristling mound,
>   The legion's ordered line ;
> And thine the wheels of triumph,
>   Which with their laurelled train
> Move slowly up the shouting streets,
>   To Jove's eternal fane."
>
> *Lays of Ancient Rome.*

THE new and arduous duties which began for Julian in the early months of 356 were not facilitated by any very clear and intelligible arrangements defining the character and extent of his authority. The system by which Diocletian had marked out the sphere of activity belonging to the Augusti, the Cæsars,

94

and the civil and military authorities that acted under them, had, as we have already seen, scarcely survived his abdication. The partial division of Imperial authority among the sons of Constantine, and the delegation made in the more recent and equally unlucky case of Constantius and Gallus, can hardly have been looked on as furnishing convenient or safe precedents. The authority of the Cæsar was not regarded as entirely superseding either the civil powers of the Prætorian Præfect, or the military command of the *Magister Equitum et Peditum.* The Prætorian Præfect of the Gauls was the same Rufinus who has been already mentioned.[2] He was brother to the first wife of Julian's father, and therefore uncle to his brother Gallus, and probably well inclined to the new-made Cæsar. But we shall see that Julian had serious difficulties to encounter from the Præfect appointed in 357. In military matters he was supposed to act conjointly with the *Magister Equitum* Marcellus, and with Sallust, the holder of some military office which is not specified.[3] Of these Sallust was an able and loyal man, Marcellus was either incapable or perfidious—probably both. No reasonable person can blame Constantius for not at once entrusting full powers to an entirely untrained and untested man. But he seems, in accordance with his character, to have subjected Julian to a system of espionage irksome to his feelings and detrimental to his efficiency. As Julian afterwards said, Constantius sent him not to rule, but to bear about the image of the Imperial ruler—to represent, we may say, in his person the majesty of the Em-

pire. Yet, if the speech before the soldiers, which
Ammianus, in Thucydidean fashion, puts into the
mouth of Constantius, may be taken as indicating
the nature of the charge given, Julian was not to
serve as a mere figure-head : " Come and share my
labours and my perils, and take upon yourself the
care of the Gauls, that you may by beneficent action
alleviate the pains with which they are stricken. If
you are called to go against the enemy, your place
is close to the standard-bearers. Be wise in inciting
to opportune action, lead with caution while you
arouse the courage of the soldiers, be at hand to support the wavering, moderate in reprimand, a faithful
witness alike of good deeds and of short-comings."

"The Gauls," of which the charge was thus entrusted to Julian, did not constitute one very definite
territorial area. The Præfecture of the Gauls, which
coincided almost, if not entirely, with the regions
over which Constantius Chlorus, Julian's grandfather, had ruled as Cæsar, comprised not only
modern France and Belgium, but the British Isles,
Spain,* and parts of Germany and Holland. On the
other hand, the Diocese of the Gauls did not include
Aquitaine nor yet the old province of Narbonne.
Julian's power was certainly exercised in these latter
parts, but he seems to have had no concern with
Spain, nor yet with Britain, except in so far as
Britain constituted the granary of Gaul in the nar-
rower sense. The Gauls, in ordinary speech, comprised all the country between the Pyrenees, the
Alps, the Rhine, and the Ocean, and included many
provinces in very various stages of civilisation.

In the south-east was the earliest Roman province in Gaul — Gallia Narbonensis, sometimes called Viennensis. These regions were as thoroughly Romanised as was any part of Italy, and contained the flourishing cities of Arelate (Arles), Valentia (Valence), and Vienna (Vienne). Aquitania was, roughly speaking, in the form of a square, of which the sides were respectively formed by the Pyrenees, the Ocean, the Loire, and the Rhone. To the north was Lugdunensis, an irregular triangle, having its apex near the great city of Lugdunum (Lyons), and its base in a line running from the mouth of the Seine to that of the Loire. Further north was Belgica, and still further north the two Germaniæ, the home of independent warriors who still, especially in the further parts, disdained any kind of subjection to Rome, though they often served for Roman gold in the Imperial armies, and held lands on the border on condition of military service.

At this moment, however, the system of border defence had utterly broken down. Devastating hosts of free Germans had destroyed the fortifications on the frontier from Cologne to Strasburg, overthrown forty-five walled cities, and established themselves considerably to the south of their former boundaries. The losses and the misery caused to the peaceable provincials were very great. Men of gentle birth and official rank, with their wives and children, were often led away in captive trains. Perhaps the most hopeful feature of the situation lay in the hatred felt by the Germanic tribes for life in walled towns, which prevented them from repairing and oc-

7

cupying the fortifications they were able to seize, and
so rendered the recovery of the strong positions a
less desperate task.

The three provincial tribes, or unions of tribes,
whose ravages had worked the greatest confusion in
Gaul, bore names which in the course of history
have been at times associated with the three great
nations of modern Europe: the Allemanni, the
Franks, and the Saxons. Of the Allemanni and
their encroachments from their early abodes on the
Upper Rhine and the Danube we have already
spoken. The Franks, who were likewise a nation,
or incipient nationality, had in early times inhab-
ited the country to the north of the Allemanni, on
the right bank of the Rhine, from the Maine almost
to the vicinity of the North Sea. The expeditions
they sent out, however, traversed very great extents
of territory. In the middle of the third century, we
find that a band of them have passed through Gaul,
seized Tarragona in Spain, and even sailed across to
Carthage. The victories obtained over them by
energetic Emperors, such as Claudius, Aurelian, Probus, and Constantius Chlorus, might for a time check
their advance or compel them to retreat, but did not
avail to break their power. Meantime their valour
was used and their fidelity tested in the Roman
armies. The case of Silvanus, which we have just
considered, is an instance of this policy and of its
consequences.

With the third great Teutonic foe of Rome, the
Saxons, Julian was not much concerned, except in
so far as their invasions had caused other tribes to

adopt a migratory life. They dwelt between the mouths of the Rhine and the Elbe, and were the terror of the opposite coast of Britain, where a special officer (the Count of the Saxon Shore) had been appointed to withstand their ravages, which often rendered it difficult for the Gallic provinces to obtain the supplies of British corn and other produce on which they depended.

Julian arrived at Vienne, as we have seen, about midwinter, 355–6. Next spring, while he was engrossed with harassing business and distracted with conflicting rumours, tidings came that the city of Augustodunum (Autun) had been attacked by a host of barbarians, probably Allemanni, and had only been saved from capture by the prompt aid of a band of Roman veterans. This news determined Julian to take active measures as soon as possible, and having made the necessary arrangements for the campaign, he set out from Vienne, and arrived at Autun (for familiarity's sake we will give the modern names), on the 24th of June. He had decided to carry the war into the enemy's country, and a rendezvous had been arranged for his forces and those of Marcellus at Reims. At Autun he held a council of war, in order to select the safest route. On hearing that the road leading through Auxerre and Troyes was the shortest, he resolved to follow it, and though much harassed by flying bands of the enemy, against which he had to be continually on his guard, he reached Reims in safety, and was met there by Marcellus and also by Ursicinus, who was to remain with him for that one expedition. After a good deal of deliberation, the army pursued its way to the Rhine. While on the march, it encountered imminent danger from an attack of the Allemanni on its rear. From this time forward, Ammianus tells us that Julian became more cautious, a statement which, with the record of previous dangers and escapes, has led later historians to read between his lines the story of sundry small disasters, at the cost of which the general's experience was purchased.

Now began the main work of the campaign, the recovery of the towns and fortunes on the Rhine recently lost, or, where that was impossible, at least of their sites. Brumath (Brucomagus) was the first to come into Julian's power, after a conflict with the Allemanni, in which he obtained the advantage by arranging his forces in crescent form and enclosing the enemy between the two horns. But his greatest success was the recovery of Cologne from the Frankish kings or chiefs, who were forced to sign a treaty favourable to Rome. This town seems to have suffered less than others from the barbarian conquest and occupation, probably on account of the superior strength of its fortifications. No other of the Rhine fortresses was left standing, except Remagen, and perhaps a part of Coblentz.[5]

The Roman army now retired through the territory of Treves to take up its winter quarters at Sens ("apud Senonas"). It soon became evident how slight and superficial any conquest or recovery must be unless confirmed by the settling of garrisons in strong posts. The need was also seen of a large

army that should not be materially weakened by
the loss of such forces as Julian was obliged to leave
in places like Cologne, Brumath, and Remagen, or
in the more flourishing towns in which, for economy's sake, they were quartered. A host of barbarians speedily overran the country that Julian had
just traversed, and even ventured to besiege him in
Sens. They retreated after thirty days, but Julian's
deliverance was due rather to the unskilfulness of
the Germans in siege warfare than to any measures
which, in his newly-acquired virtue of military prudence, he was able to take, or to any succour from
outside. Marcellus, who was quartered in the neighbourhood, never attempted a diversion. He seems
to have let Julian have his way in the summer campaign, but to have been by no means eager in saving
him from personal inconvenience and danger. In
fairness to Constantius it must be said that as soon
as he heard of the misconduct of Marcellus, he recalled him, and sent out in his place one Severus, a
man of capacity and merit. It was probably at the
same time that Julian received, through the inter-
cession of Eusebia, a considerable extension of his
powers, and was permitted to summon volunteers to
his standard. His guard of three hundred and sixty
he regarded, according to Zosimus, as good for little
else but praying; a strange criticism, if it is really
Julian's own, seeing that he more often reproaches
the Christians with lack than with excess of devotion. On the departure of Marcellus for the Imperial Court, Julian sent thither a faithful eunuch,
named Eutherius, an Armenian by birth, and singu-

larly free from the faults supposed to be generally engrained in men of his class. Eutherius was successful in averting any blame that might have been thrown on his master, and Marcellus was ordered not to remove from his native town of Sardica.

Between the campaigns, in the winter months, Julian had sufficient occupation in making preparations for the next expedition, and in examining into the affairs of the provinces, while he strengthened body and mind with military exercises and literary studies. He earned the affection of the soldiers by his thoughtfulness in providing for their welfare. Giving a military turn to his Stoic principles, after the example of his hero-model, Marcus Aurelius, he reduced the list of luxurious dishes to be provided for his table by striking out pheasants and other delicacies, and himself partook of the fare of the common soldiers. It may be mentioned that strict temperance, or rather ascetic abstinence, marked his behaviour now and throughout his life.[6] Although, as we have seen, his authority did not supersede that of the ordinary civil governors, he was often besieged by petitioners for redress of private grievances. In judicial matters he seems to have erred rather on the side of clemency than on that of sternness, but before taking action in answer to petitions, he ordered full inquiry to be made by the provincial governors. He devoted considerable attention to financial affairs, and determined to effect an alleviation of the heavy taxes, by steadily declining to grant such exemptions as might benefit the rich at the expense of the poor.

For his studies he had little time except what he stole from the night by his habit of rising before the dawn. He generally slept on a kind of rug, and after a very brief time of rest, arose and invoked the aid of Hermes before he passed to his tasks of business or of literature. It is at about this time that we must date three long orations of his that have come down to us, written in honour of Constantius and of Eusebia.[7] We have already had occasion to refer to these, especially to the panegyric of Eusebia, as furnishing material for the personal history of Julian and for that of his family. In his laudations of the Empress there is nothing that clashes with the views expressed in those letters of his which seem to convey his undisguised feelings. With regard to the two orations in honour of Constantius, the case is otherwise, and those who feel respect for the high moral qualities of Julian's character must regret that he was capable of writing them. At the same time, we must remember that complimentary orations were at that time so much in vogue, and the composition of them was regarded as so essential a part of the work expected from a young rhetorician, that no one would be likely to take the adulatory expressions as seriously meant, or to interpret the high-sounding comparisons as representing the genuine feelings and sober thoughts of the orator. Still, there is a demoralising tendency in the art by which a rhetorician describes as superior to all the Homeric heroes, and as uniting in his own person all virtues and all talents, a character which, when writing freely, the same orator reproaches as arrogant, cruel, and unjust. The orations are, of course, overloaded with literary and historical illustrations. They are, however, marked by considerable vigour of style, and they afford scope for bringing in a good many of the author's own sentiments. Thus he sketches the character of an ideal monarch, to which sketch the features of Constantius have to be accommodated. We observe the importance Julian attaches both to the dignity and to the responsibilities of the Imperial position, and the stress he lays on the gentler and more private virtues, such as clemency and chastity. In the oration in praise of Eusebia, the permission he had obtained by her means to study at Athens affords an excellent opportunity for eulogising the city which stores up and distributes fertilising knowledge for all the world, as the Nile fructifies the thirsty land of Egypt. Her gift of books suggests a similar digression on the value of literature generally. More interesting however, in this oration, is the evidence it affords of the high esteem in which Julian held the character and dignity of women, and his especial admiration for the more domestic types of female virtue. This respect for women also appears in those letters of his still extant which were written to various ladies. We may add that since all rhetorical compositions of this kind were cast in old Hellenic forms, Julian was free to express his own views as to the duty of piety towards the Gods, and as to the relations of man to Gods and dæmons, without borrowing at all from Christian phraseology or conceptions. Thus if perhaps an excessive dissimulation is to be found in these orations, they are at least free from any taint of religious hypocrisy.

Although Julian was a great gainer by the substitution of Severus for Marcellus, a new difficulty presented itself in the campaign of 357. He had to co-operate with another colleague whose sphere of authority lay to the east of his, and who was therefore independent of his command and unwilling to contribute to his success. According to some historians, Constantius himself took the field against the Allemanni in 356, starting from Rhaetia and advancing along the Upper Rhine.[8] If so, he did not accomplish much, but soon returned to Milan, and thence to Rome, where he and the Empress were received in great splendour. Alarming movements of the Quadi and other tribes in the Danubian countries required his presence in Illyria. Meantime he despatched Barbatio, the *Magister Peditum*, from Italy to Basel, with an army of 25,000 men. Barbatio was a much-older man than Julian, he had contributed as much as anyone to the fall of Gallus, and being in direct communication with the Emperor, he had no intention of taking commands, or even advice, from the young Cæsar. The design was to restrict the field in which the Allemanni roved and devastated at will, by means of a preconcerted march of two Roman armies from opposite sides. However, the tribe of the Laeti were too swift to be taken in this way. They advanced between the armies and came as far as the neighbourhood of Lyons, which town, however, was able to make a defence. Julian at once took steps to secure

the three passes by which the barbarians could effect
a retreat. This plan was on the whole successful.
In one pass the Laeti suffered a defeat, and had to
relinquish some of the booty. But the pass nearest
to the army of Barbatio was purposely left unde-
fended, and two military tribunes, Valentinian (afterwards Emperor) and Bainobaudes, whom Julian had
sent to secure its occupation, were falsely accused
to the Emperor, and removed from their posts.

In other ways Barbatio continued to thwart
Julian's plans. Rather than let the Cæsar have
certain boats required for a bridge over the Rhine,
he preferred to set them on fire. When a convoy
was on its way to Julian, he intercepted it, and
burned all that he could not use. Julian made
up for the want of boats by ordering an attack on
one of the islands in the Rhine, where the stream
was fordable. Rafts and booty were obtained, and
a terrible slaughter followed, which caused the Germans to decamp with their families and property
from the neighbouring islands. The missing convoy
had to be supplied by the gathering in, on the part
of Julian's soldiers, of the corn which the Germans
had sown for themselves. Meanwhile the restoration of the fortifications on or near the Rhine,
especially those of Zabern, was actively carried forward. But the Allemanni had taken alarm and
determined on an invasion *en masse*. Barbatio was
severely defeated and forced to fall back on Basel,
with the loss of great part of his supplies. Unable
to attempt anything in reparation or in revenge,
the inefficient general sent his men into winter

quarters, and himself repaired to the Imperial Court.[9]

The barbarian host which was advancing towards Julian's position consisted of thirty-five thousand men under the command of King Chnodomar and his nephew Agenaric or Serapio, who had received the latter, rather incongruous name in token that his father had been initiated into certain Greek mysteries. Five lesser kings followed with their contingents, and there were other tribal leaders of high rank. Before attacking the Romans, Chnodomar, who had been informed by a deserter of their comparatively small number, sent an offensive message to Julian, bidding him restore to the Germans the territory that properly belonged to them.[10] Julian kept the envoys by him until he had finished the fortifications of Zabern, then marched in careful order, the infantry protected by the cavalry and light-armed troops, in the direction of Strasburg (Argentoratum). They arrived in sight of the enemy after a march of twenty-one Roman or about nineteen and one-third English miles, and Julian wonld have preferred to stay for the night, to give his men rest and refreshment. But the feeling of the army and the advice of the Prætorian Præfect Florentius were for instant action, and with vigorous exhortations to the soldiers Julian agreed to give battle. The day was hotly contested, and the result seemed for a long time doubtful. Julian's cavalry on the right wing began to give way, and needed all his efforts to keep it from wild flight. He afterwards punished the cowardly band by making them show themselves in

the camp in women's dress. Their panic seems to
have been caused partly by the Germans' device of
mixing a few foot-soldiers among the horsemen, who
inserted themselves between the enemy's lines, and
wounded the horses from beneath. The Roman infantry, especially the Prætorian band, stationed in
the middle of the host, stood firm, and finally the
better discipline and arms of the Romans, aided by
the ubiquitous activity of Julian, the military skill
and energy of Severus, and the fidelity and courage
of the Gallic allies, prevailed over the superior numbers and great physical strength of the barbarians.
Six thousand Germans fell, and only 247 of the
Romans. Many of the fugitives dashed into the
waters of the Rhine, and Julian had to issue strict
orders that they were not to be pursued further.
King Chnodomar was taken prisoner in a wood near
by. His courage had deserted him, and he disgusted Julian by pleading for his life. He was sent
captive to the Imperial Court, as a tangible proof to
Constantius of the result of the conflict.

This great victory," won in trying circumstances,
and against great odds, was momentous in its effects,
principally, perhaps, from the terror it struck into
the German tribes all around. Julian sternly re-
pressed the acclamations of the soldiers which would
have conferred then and there upon him the title of
Augustus. It was more prudent for him to allow
the Emperor to assume to himself the honour of the
victory. This was not contrary to Roman Imperial
usage, yet in the credit he took for a battle fought
hundreds of miles from the place where he then was,

Constantius reminds us of the belief into which (as report says) George IV. persuaded himself, that he had been personally present at Waterloo.

After the victory, Julian returned to Zabern. He left his prisoners and his booty in the neighbourhood of Metz, and begun an advance into the enemy's country, crossing the Rhine near Mentz. Like all expeditions of the kind, this march was of a destructive and devastating character. The houses of the natives were burned down and all their property wasted. The Romans marched on till they came to a thick wood, probably in the neighbourhood of Aschaffenburg on the Main. But the autumnal equinox was past, snow was beginning to fall, and the attempt to make further progress in a difficult and hostile country would have been decidedly rash. The Allemanni were at last willing to retreat. Julian granted them a ten months' truce, and received humble submission from three kings who had fought at Strasburg. He now prepared to go into winter quarters, but he had first to dislodge a company of six hundred Franks, whom Severus had come upon in his march towards Reims, and who had occupied two fortresses on the Meuse. It was not till after a long siege, in frosty weather, that they were obliged to yield themselves prisoners of war.

The place in which Julian passed the winter of 357–8 is one that had been of some slight importance from much earlier times. Yet he must be credited with having perceived the peculiar advantages of its position, and contributed not a little to its future greatness. " Beloved Lutetia, as the Gauls

call the little city of the Parisii," comprised as yet
little more than the island in the Seine, now covered
by Notre Dame and the adjacent buildings, and the
palace to the south of the river where Julian took
up his abode, and which is still associated with his
name.[12]   It was near the junction of several military
roads, and as a French historian has said, "the town
was becoming what Paris is to-day, the centre of
resistance to Germany."   In later times, writing in
the far-off East, Julian remembered its good situation, the purity of its water, the even flow of the
river, and the temperate climate, which allowed of
the culture of the vine and the fig, if their roots
were covered with straw in winter.   He told a story
against himself how, confiding in that agreeable
climate, he had, in Stoic fashion, refused to have
his rooms warmed with a furnace, till, when the cold
became intense, he sent for braziers, and narrowly
escaped asphyxiation from the steam which exuded
from the damp walls.[13]

While in Paris, Julian threw himself with energy
into the work of financial reform.   Here he was
hindered by the Prætorian Præfect Florentius.   We
have already seen this man in the camp before the
battle of Strasburg, giving advice which, though
justified by the event, was contrary to the judgment
of Julian and to the ordinary calculations of prudence.   Florentius declared that some additional
imposts were imperatively required.   Julian denied
the necessity, and refused to entertain the suggestions.   Florentius appealed to Constantius, who
wrote to Julian, bidding him place confidence in

THE THERMES, PARIS.

the experience of the Præfect. Thereupon Julian replied that, wasted as the province had been, it could not possibly afford to raise more than the ordinary revenue. His firmness had the desired result, and at the same time he asked and obtained power to rearrange the method of collecting taxes in the second province of Belgica, greatly to the alleviation of the distress from which the provincials were suffering.

In the spring of 358, Barbatio, assisted by a competent cavalry officer, was sent into Rætia to chastise the Juthungi, a tribe of Allemanni who had apparently not been comprised in the truce. Meantime Julian had gathered from Aquitaine supplies (including biscuit, which seems to have been a novelty), sufficient for a long expedition, and now led his army towards the mouths of the Rhine. On the way he met a deputation of Salian Franks, which tribe had lately settled in Zealand, or perhaps in the country more to the south. These had come to demand terms of peace. Julian dismissed them with presents, then fell suddenly on the main army, and reduced them to sue for peace on more humiliating conditions.[14] The Chamavi, another tribe of Franks, next felt his strong hand, and that of Severus. Having granted them peace on condition of retreat, he proceeded to fortify the line of the Meuse. At the same time he re-established the water communication between Britain and the Rhine country, which had for a time been interrupted. For this purpose he had to cause the building of a new fleet, in spite of difficulties which Florentius regarded as insuperable. It was apparently through the machinations of this disappointed financier that some of the soldiers, being defrauded of their pay and worked upon by agitators, showed dangerous signs of insubordination. Even Severus seemed to be wavering in his loyalty and courage. Julian's intimate friend, Sallust, was recalled on suspicions received against him, a blow bitterly felt by Julian, as he showed in an apparently sincere though elaborate farewell address. Nevertheless, the result of the campaign was favourable to the Roman arms, both on the Upper and the Lower Rhine. The stream was crossed, and a king of the Allemanni, named Suomar, who seems to have ruled between the Maine and the Rhine, was obliged to sue for peace. A barbarian free-lance, Charietto, was induced to enter the Roman alliance, and afterwards proved very useful. Another barbarian king, Hortar, was forced to deliver the Romans whom he had captured in his devastating raids, including some that he tried to keep back, till Julian suspected his attempted fraud and speedily defeated it.

The winter months were again given to inquiries into civil affairs, and to judicial proceedings which Julian regulated with great attention, insisting on publicity, and on acquittal in absence of adequate proof of guilt. The next year (359) was marked by the establishment of corn magazines, the erection of fortresses on the Rhine (at Bonn, Andernach, Bingen, and other places), and by another expedition across that river, in which Julian penetrated further than he had done before, and reached the confines of the Burgundii and the Allemanni.

It is noticeable that in marching through the territories of those kings who had made peace the year
before, Julian studiously avoided all kinds of plunder
or vexation. The submission of the several chiefs
of the more distant tribes was now secured.

The story of wars of civilised against semi-bar-
barous peoples is generally distinguished by deeds of
cruelty and of perfidy. The Gallic wars of Julian are
not an exception to this rule. But they had the
merit of success. At the end of his fourth campaign,
Julian may be regarded as having accomplished the
task he had been sent to perform. The Gallic provinces were not likely to be soon again disturbed by
the barbarians who had received so hard a lesson.
The frontiers were again protected by fortresses;
food was secured to the provincials who dwelt inland. The oppressive taxation could now be light-
ened. Peace and security reigned in Gaul, and the
distant Germans again reverenced the majesty of the
Roman name. If Julian received no gratitude from
his cousin, he probably expected none. Yet his
achievements were none the less profitable to the
Empire, and may strike us now with admiration, and
seem, considering the character and education of the
man who did them, almost unique in character.
History knows of young military geniuses, like Alexander the Great, or Charles XII. of Sweden, who obtained wonderful victories without previous experience. Yet the bent of Julian ·had been distinctly
non-military, and he had been summoned from the
lecture-room to the camp. History knows also of
men of riper years, such as Epaminondas, Timoleon,

8

and Oliver Cromwell, who only began a military career after their minds had been formed in other pursuits. But Julian became a great general while still full of youthful ardour for the studies which he was compelled to lay aside. There is in his character and powers a wonderful diversity, which seems, as it were, to blend several lives in one. He had become a general, a statesman, and a man of the world, without ceasing to be a student, an ascetic, and a religious idealist. If, in his letters to his friends, he lamented the literary leisure of by-gone days, if he constantly asserted that the contemplative life was worthier than the active, and the merit of Socrates infinitely above that of Alexander, he let no such preferences appear openly, and shunned no irksome tasks in the camp or in the council chamber. If he stole hours from sleep to spend them in devout meditation, aspiring speculation, and elaborate composition, his daily life showed, at this stage of his career, no trace of pedantry or of indecision. His success on new and strange ground may be accounted for partly by the versatility of his mind. The man who could write the *Oration on the Mother of the Gods* in one night must have been able to move swiftly with brain and pen. But the main cause of that success lies deeper. The secret of it is to be found in the possession of an iron will, controlled by a stern sense of duty, and in an unswerving faith in the final triumph of good over evil.

(*For designs of coins selected as illustrations for this chapter, see page* 262.)

NOTES ON CHAPTER V.

[1] For this narrative, we have Ammianus, books xvi., xvii., and xviii., Zosimus, book iii. (apparently a far less trustworthy account), Julian's *Letters to the Athenians*, Libanius' *Funeral Oration*, etc. Of recent accounts, I have made most use of Mücke's *Julians Kriegsthaten* (Gotha, 1867), a careful and valuable study, though, perhaps, not quite fair towards Constantius, and H. Schiller's *Römische Kaiserzeit*, iii., 3. A considerable difference of view prevails as to the extent to which the story of Julian's achievements is based on his own narrations. Mr. Hecker regards Julian's lost *Commentaries* as the source whence Ammianus, Zosimus, and Libanius alike drew their statements. It does not seem probable, however, that the sober and impartial Ammianus blindly followed such records, even if they existed in as complete a form as Mr. Hecker supposes.

[2] Tillemont, *Constance*, xxxv., xxxix., etc.

[3] Afterwards Præfect of the Gauls, *not* the Sallust that accompanied Julian in his last campaign.

[4] Jul., Or. ii., 51, D. *Cf.* Tillemont, *Notes sur Diocletian*, xii.

[5] Ammianus seems to confound Remagen and Coblentz. His language is here not quite clear. Mücke regards the important fortifications of *Tres Tabernæ*, mentioned by Ammianus on several occasions, as the lines connecting Zabern in Alsace, Bergzabern, and Rheinzabern.

[6] Of Julian's earlier life we have hardly sufficient knowledge to assert this positively, though the very slightest tendency to licentiousness would undoubtedly have been made matter of accusation in the invectives of Gregory Nazianzen and others.

[7] Mücke (*Julian's Leben und Schriften*) considers that the first oration in honour of Constantius was delivered in Milan, near the end of the year 355 ; that the second was worked up from the first while Julian was in Gaul ; and that the one in honour of Eusebia was composed just after her arrival in Rome, in the spring of 357. (Possibly Eusebia visited Rome in 356).

[8] See Tillemont, notes xxxviii., xxxix., etc. It is difficult to account for all the movements of Constantius at this time.

[9] I follow the account of Ammianus, who, however, was not present at these events, as Ursicinus, to whose service he was attached, had been sent to the East.

[10] Not only Libanius (*Epit. Jul.*) but also the church historian Socrates (iii., 1) represent the barbarians as producing letters on this occasion by which Constantius had authorised this march. What the letters really amounted to is uncertain. But Chnodomar probably interpreted them in very liberal fashion.

[11] The circumstances and topography of the battle of Strasburg have recently been the object of a thorough study by M. Wiegand, in *Beiträge zur Landes und Volkeskunde von Elsass-Lothringen.* He considers that the accounts of Libanius and of Ammianus are probably from Julian, and he finds them remarkably exact, and easily fitting in with indications of topography. He would place the battle-field more to the south-west than the generally accepted site.

[12] The " Thermes de Julien," near the Luxembourg and Palais de Clugny.

[13] *Misopogon*, 340, 341.

[14] Mücke's version of this affair would acquit Julian of bad faith towards ambassadors, but I cannot reconcile it with Ammianus.

Roman Ensigns.

That to the left that of the Celtæ ; that to the right that of the Petulantes.

CHAPTER VI.

MILITARY MOVEMENTS IN EAST AND WEST.   JULIAN BECOMES EMPEROR.[1]

359–360.

"Καίτοι χρῆν δήπουθεν πιστεύοντα τῷ φήναντι θεῷ τὸ τέρας θαρρεῖν. ἀλλ, ἠσχυνόμην δεινῶς καὶ κατεδυόμην, εἰ δόξαιμι μὴ πιστῶς ἄχρι τέλους ὑπακοῦσαι Κωνσταντίῳ."

JULIAN, *Letter to the Athenians*, 285.

"Perfidus ille [Julianus] Deo, quamvis non perfidus urbi."

PRUDENTIUS.*

HILE we are tracing the fortunes of Roman arms and the efforts towards civil reform of upright Roman governors in one corner of the vast Empire, we are apt to forget that, thousands of miles away, events may be happening pregnant with results to the Imperial house and to the whole Imperial system.   In fact it may seem that at no time

---

* A Spanish Christian poet, contemporary with Julian.

between those days and our own has there been such a close sympathetic connection between the frontier fortresses in the heart of Asia and the political capitals of Western Europe. Now, as then, no place in the civilised world can be regarded as entirely shut out from the influence of political disturbances or military movements that may occur in distant regions. All countries are again bound together, for good and evil, though not with the ancient cords.

Thus, to understand the crisis which arrived in Julian's life while he was still occupied with the reconquest and the administration of Gaul, we must turn our attention to the course of affairs on the Danube and on the Tigris. Indeed the causes of the breach between Julian and his cousin seem to have been determined too superficially by those who have not grasped some important factors in the problem. By some, Constantius has been accused of a superfluous assertion of authority in making unreasonable demands. To others, Julian appears as an ungrateful subordinate, preferring his own ambitious plans to the welfare of his patron and to the interests of the whole Empire. A careful examination of the general conditions of the case may lead us to the conclusion that the demands of Constantius, though not made with a prudent regard to time and circumstances, were not determined upon without pressing need, while Julian's opposition had also its grounds of justification, apart from its unforeseen and far-reaching results.

It has been already remarked that it is not easy

to account for all the movements of Constantius
during the years of Julian's campaigns in Gaul.
His principal residence was at Milan, whence several
of his laws are dated.   Whether or no he made an
expedition against the Allemanni in 356 is a question we must leave on one side.[2]   The matters
which chiefly occupied him were a ceremonious
visit to Rome, sundry expeditions against the tribes
to the north of the Danube, and some ineffectual
attempts at negotiation with the Persian king, followed by preparations for active hostilities.

The object of the Emperor's visit to Rome was,
according to his detractors, a childish desire to
make a notable display of pomp and power in
celebrating, some time after the event, his triumph
over Magnentius.   And there seems some reason in
the complaint that a moment at which war was
either imminent or actually being waged, in several
provinces, was hardly the one to choose for extravagant expenditure on meaningless ceremonies.
Yet it is quite possible that Constantius may have
acted with some statesmanlike purpose when he
determined on making this progress.   Even if it
were not so, it was surely a laudable curiosity that
made him desirous of a personal inspection of the
great sights of the Eternal City.   Political prudence
would suggest the expediency of showing himself,
with all the paraphernalia of Oriental majesty, to the
sight-loving populace that still considered themselves as *par excellence* the Sovereign People of
Rome, and to the wealthy dilettante officials who
seemed to themselves to perpetuate the glories of

the Roman Senate. The enthusiasm with which
he was received might be considered to justify
some munificent expenditure, for though it may not
have been a matter of great moment what the actual
denizens of Rome thought of their ruler, yet the
dignified associations which clung to the ancient
names might still be, as they again became centuries
afterwards, a source of strength to the Imperial
power. The attitude which Constantius took up
towards the pretensions of his ancient capital is
shown by two laws which date from about this
time: by one, he withdrew from the Præfect of
Rome the cognisance of cases of appeal from Italian
and Sicilian courts; by another, all senators were
bidden to reside in or near the city.[3] Thus Rome
was not to hold a position of political headship in
Italy, but at the same time Roman municipal dignities were to involve definite civil and financial
duties, and not to be regarded as a mere ornament.

Constantius was accompanied on this occasion by
his wife Eusebia and his sister Helen, who seems to
have come on a visit from her husband in Gaul, as
we find her there before and afterwards. The entry
into the city was very imposing. The Emperor was
seated alone in a golden chariot, preceded by legionaries with their standards held aloft and surrounded
by guards in brilliant plate-armour. He preserved
his usual imperturbable demeanour in countenance
and manners, though startled once or twice at the
loud roar of the cheering multitude and at the novelty of the spectacle before him. He condescended,
however, to allow some indulgence to the fancies of

CHARIOT-RACE BEFORE A CONSUL.
IVORY DIPTYCH.

the Roman people in the manner of holding the
equestrian games, and he made a public speech from
his seat in the Forum as well as one to the nobles in
the Senate-house.   He devoted some time to visiting all the principal buildings, baths, theatres, and
temples.   Though desirous of purging the city from
pagan rites, to which end he had lately caused the
removal from the Senate-house of the altar to Victory, on which incense used to be offered, neither he
nor those with him seem to have felt any scruple in
admiring the temples which, even if according to
law no longer used for religious purposes, must still
have been full of religious symbols and works of art.
In fact, the monument with which Constantius determined to enrich the city, in memory of his visit,
was one of a distinctly pagan character.   Constantine had issued orders for the removal to Rome of
an obelisk which had adorned the city of Thebes in
Upper Egypt, and which was connected with the
worship of the sun, and bore inscriptions in honour
of a solar deity and of one of the Egyptian kings.
Augustus had once thought of bringing it away, but
had refrained in order to spare the religious feelings
of the people.   Constantine, however, had no such
scruples, for he considered, as Ammianus says, "that
it was no injury to religion to remove a religious
object from one temple to dedicate it in Rome, the
temple of the whole world."   The attempts of Constantine to remove it were cut short by his death,
but Constantius carried out the project.   With vast
labour it was brought to Rome and set up.   In later
times it was thrown down, but was re-erected by

Pope Sixtus V., and stands to this day before the church of San Giovanni Laterano.

The original idea of Constantius had been to give an equestrian statue to the city, like that in the Forum of Trajan, with which he had been much impressed. But a Persian fugitive who accompanied him suggested that such a steed would require a stable to correspond, and Constantius did not intend to construct another Forum. If Hormisdas had suggested that the rider also should be of Trajanic mould, the remark would have been equally to the point. This same Persian, on being asked what he thought of Rome, replied that he was glad to learn that men died there as elsewhere. Whether the remark was dictated by a spirit of Oriental fatalism or by dislike of an overpopulated city, we are not told.

Constantius was obliged to abridge his agreeable visit to Rome and hasten northwards, because of alarming news received from the regions of the Danube.

The vast plains of the southern and western parts of the country known to us as Russia-in-Europe, with some regions more to the south, including the district between the Danube and the Theiss, were at this time the abode of wandering hosts of fierce and predatory horsemen, belonging to the race known as Sarmatians. These had given a good deal of trouble to preceding emperors. Diocletian and afterwards Constantine seem to have flattered themselves that they had reduced them to subjection, but people of their character and habits of life are not easily subdued, as King Darius had experienced long before. According to the ordinary lines of Roman policy, the people of the Thracian Chersonesus had been engaged to make war on the Sarmatians, and had been rewarded for their successful intervention, and subsequently, when the Gothic power in those countries became more formidable, Roman aid was given to the Sarmatian tribes, into which a Vandal element seems to have been received, against the yet more dangerous foe. When, however, the Sarmatians found that the Romans were either unwilling or unable to give them much help, they adopted the imprudent course of placing arms in the hands of a subject race, or of subject races, known as the Limigantes. These were successful not only in defeating the Goths, but in establishing their own independence against their former masters, and obtaining fixed territories for themselves. When thus weakened, the Sarmatians received more encouragement from the Romans, and were permitted to settle in Pannonia and other border provinces. Some of them, however, preferred the alliance of other barbarian hosts, especially the Quadi, who seem to have been of Germanic race, and while Constantius was in Rome, he heard that the Quadi and the Sarmatians, as well as the Suevi, were ravaging the Danubian lands. He does not seem to have accomplished much against them that year, but he wintered at Sirmium, a town on the Save near the Sarmatian frontier, so as to be ready for military operations in the spring.

Early the next year (358) news came that the

Quadi and Sarmatians had joined their forces and
were doing great mischief in the provinces immediately to the west of the Danube, below the point
of its great bend southwards and to the south of its
lower course (the Pannonias and Upper Mæsia). At
the same time the not far distant province of Raetia
was being invaded by German forces, with which, as
we have seen, Barbatio had to contend. The Emperor himself, at about the end of March, crossed
the Danube and marched into the enemies' country.
The barbarians fled to the mountains. But the sight
or the tidings of their burning homesteads (as they
had something to burn they cannot have been entirely nomadic) induced both Quadi and Sarmatians
to sue for peace. Constantius prudently contrived
to keep the two sets of negotiations distinct. After
some difficulties, terms were arranged. Hostages
were to be given, captives restored, and the hosts to
retreat. A fine young barbarian named Zizais, who
had taken an active part in bringing about the agreement, was acknowledged by the Emperor as King of
the Sarmatians, and that formidable race was thus
made to own the authority of Rome. This authority
involved the duty of protecting the client people
against their foes and former slaves. The Limigantes
had not been behind their quondam superiors in
taking advantage of the opportunity given of invading the Roman provinces. Nor were they behind
the others in making professions of submission and
requests for terms of peace. The Emperor had determined to insist on a wholesale migration of the tribe.
But he consented to a parley first, and even invited

them to cross the Theiss and come to his camp for
that purpose.   They arrived *en masse* in warlike
array, and their formidable mien, together with a
real or assumed attempt to attack the sacred person
of the Emperor, seemed to the Roman generals to
justify an onslaught which degenerated into a massacre in which neither age nor sex was spared. The
remnant of the Limigantes retired humiliated to the
distant lands assigned to them, while the Romans
advanced up the rivers into the territory of those
Sarmatian and allied tribes that yet held out, and
reduced them to some kind of subjection. Constantius again wintered at Sirmium. He had taken the
title of *Sarmaticus,* but his task was by no means
complete.   Next year news came that the Limigantes were wandering away from their new quarters.   The Emperor advanced into north-eastern
Pannonia. Here another conference with the host
was projected, and this time the treachery seems to
have been on the side of the barbarians. When they
perceived that the Romans were unprepared for an
attack, they raised their war-cry and advanced towards the Imperial throne. Constantius only escaped
by riding off at full speed. Subsequently, the barbarians were very severely defeated in the encounter,
but there was also some loss on the Roman side.
The success of the Roman arms seemed, however, to
have rendered the frontier in these regions fairly
secure. The Emperor returned to Sirmium, and
thence proceeded to Constantinople, to devise means
for meeting the yet more serious dangers that threatened the Empire from the East.

Meantime, Paul, "the Chain," was doing more damage probably than any barbarian chief to the reputation and authority of his master, by instituting a series of prosecutions based on reports of dreams and oracular responses. Constantius has the credit of certain measures for putting a stop to soothsaying and other pagan superstitions. It would not be easy, however, to determine how far his zeal against such practices was aroused by a jealousy on behalf of Christianity, and how far by the more personal jealousy of his restlessly suspicious temperament.

At the same time, negotiations had been going on between Constantius and the great ruler of the East, in which probably both parties desired rather to gain time than to establish a permanent understanding. These negotiations were begun, apparently, without direct Imperial authorisation, by the Præfect of the East, Musonianus, and the *Dux* of Mesopotamia, Cassianus. Sapor, as already stated, had gone to repel an invasion on his eastern frontier, and it was long before he could receive the letter from his general, Tamsapor, respecting the Roman overtures. In 358, however, he made peace with the chiefs of the warlike tribes, against which he had been contending, and some of which—especially the Chionites, acted as very valuable allies in the war which ensued. Feeling now at liberty to turn his attention to his western provinces, he sent a certain Narses with presents and a letter for Constantius. The embassy arrived at Sirmium in March, 358. The letter (given by Ammianus) is thoroughly Oriental, both in style and in significance. It begins: "Sapor,

King of Kings, Sharer in the Stars, Brother of
the Sun and the Moon, to my brother, Constantius Cæsar." The King goes on to congratulate
Constantius on his having renounced the desire to
acquire the goods of others, and after making the
questionable statement that it is the great privilege
of those in high rank always to speak their own
minds, he roundly requests him to give up Armenia
and Mesopotamia, as rightfully belonging to Persia,
the ancient boundary of which had been the river
Strymon. He dwells with complacency on his
own virtues, declaring that he never from early
youth has done any act of which he has had to repent, advises the Emperor to consult for the well-
being of the whole by cutting off the superfluous
parts, and finally declares that if his ambassador
does not bring back a favourable answer, he will pre-
pare to take the field, with all his forces, next spring.
Constantius, in reply, could not but repel the insinua-
tion that Mesopotamia was a " diseased limb to be
cut off." He rejected the humiliating terms offered,
and expressed his confidence in the ultimate success
of the Roman arms. Nevertheless he sent complimentary presents to Sapor, and an embassy of three,
one of whom, Eustathius, belonged to the rhetorical philosophers of Asia Minor, whose influence in
education and in the ornamental part of public
affairs we have already noticed. But in this case,
in spite of the pleasure which the eloquence of
Eustathius is said to have given to the Great King,
the breach was too wide to be filled by a load of
rhetoric. The proposal that the *status quo* should

be maintained was rejected. The embassy returned disappointed from Ctesiphon in Babylonia where Sapor had given them audience. One more mission was sent, with no better success. It was evident that a serious war was at hand.

It was fortunate for the Romans that the Sarmatians had been subdued and that Gaul was well-nigh pacified. It was probably at this time that Julian sent to the Emperor a considerable force, both of infantry and cavalry, that had acquired experience and glory on the Rhine. But two serious disadvantages made the Roman cause less hopeful. One was the desertion of a certain Antoninus, who had been an official in the finance department of the eastern provinces, and whose fortunes had been broken by ruinous law-suits and unfair decisions. Having vainly attempted to recover them at the expense of the State, he fled with his family, his possessions, and what was far more important, his knowledge of government secrets, to the army of the Persians, where he was received with open arms. The other misfortune which befell the Romans at the outset was the withdrawal of power from the one man likely to be able to meet the storm. Ursicinus had been holding command in Commagene, the most north-easterly province of Syria. Meantime, his foes at Court were plotting against him, the suspicions of the Emperor were aroused, and he received a sudden summons to return to Europe. When hostilities broke out, however, he was quite indispensable. He was accordingly sent back to Mesopotamia with the office of Commander of the

Infantry lately held by Barbatio. That General, with his wife, had, in consequence of foolish tamperings with diviners, met with the same fate which during this reign overtook many much worthier people. But though entrusted with some military authority, Ursicinus was placed in subordination to a wealthy and inert old man named Sabinianus, who, though totally incapable of conducting a campaign himself, was able to thwart the measures of his abler colleague.

In all his military expeditions, Ursicinus had a devoted supporter, and, except when the fortunes of war parted them, a constant companion, in the historian Ammianus Marcellinus. Thanks to his literary labours, we are able to realise the character of a war which, in its romantic incidents and circumstances of pomp and show, suggests to us other wars carried on in much the same regions many centuries later. The hostilities between Sapor and the generals of Constantius can hardly be considered as a crusade, though they were waged between Christians and fire-worshippers. But though the religious element was not prominent in the conflict, it forms part of the unending struggle between East and West. The romantic character is partly due to Sapor himself, who shows touches of chivalrous feeling in his courtesy towards ladies, both in the case of dedicated virgins, and of the beautiful wife of a Roman official who fell into his hands. Ursicinus also has interesting traits of character. We are told of his efforts to save a stray child, and of a dramatic interview between him and the traitor

9

Antoninus. The story is full of hair-breadth escapes
and of deeds of daring, especially on the part of the
Gauls, who abhorred the slow work of defending
besieged towns, and could only be kept in subordination by being allowed to indulge their appetite for
warlike exploits. On the other side are splendid
Asiatic barbarian leaders, like old Grunbates, King
of the Chionites. The details need not be given
here. Ursicinus and Ammianus left their superior
to his inert leisure and hurried into Mesopotamia,
where they put the city of Nisibis in a state of defence. The town of Carrhæ was abandoned and the
surrounding country wasted by fire, to check the
progress of the Persian and allied hosts arriving up
the Tigris from Nineveh. Amida, a very important
town on the Tigris, near the borders of Armenia,
Cappadocia, and Mesopotamia, was taken after a
siege of seventy-three days, during which great
valour and great engineering skill were shown on
both sides, and the efforts of Ursicinus to relieve the
city were foiled by the excessive caution of Sabinianus. Further insult and injury were heaped upon
Ursicinus, in that the loss of Amida was punished
by his degradation from his military rank. He in-
dignantly protested against the false view which
Constantius derived from his courtiers of the state
of affairs, and exhorted him to take the field himself. Constantius had probably made up his mind
to do so soon after the Sarmatian war was over.
Meantime Sapor retreated with the booty of Amida
and went into winter quarters.

From this brief narrative some points are manifest

which we must bear in mind in forming our judgment as to succeeding events. More troops were certainly wanted in the East, and also a capable commander. And far the best troops were those that came from Gaul. One detachment from Illyria had been ignominiously cut to pieces early in the campaign. In Gaul at this time was a numerous and well-seasoned army. And if "that goat," as Constantius called his bearded cousin, had achieved all the victories, of which the court was tired of hearing, he could surely spare some soldiers to his hard-pressed superior and imperial colleague. The præfect Florentius, who, as we have seen, had reasons of his own for not loving Julian, offered advice which Constantius was only too ready to follow. Possibly, as Julian afterward asserted, their ultimate project was to divest the Cæsar of all his military authority. The immediate demand was that four of the best companies of auxiliary troops, the Heruli, Batavi, Petulantes, and Celtæ, together with a detachment of picked men from the other forces, should be at once despatched under the command of Lupicinus, for the Persian War.

Libanius, who does poor service to Julian by persistently blackening the deeds of Constantius, asserts what is simply absurd when he would make us believe that there was no special need for soldiers in the East, and that Constantius had no serious intention of making an oriental campaign. The Emperor probably wished to test Julian's fidelity to the utmost, and it is not probable that he thoroughly realised the difficulty of obeying his commands. The orders were not likely to be the more agreeable from being entrusted to commissioners whom Julian believed to be personally hostile to his interests, especially to the tribune Decentius. Had Constantius merely signified, in a confidential manner, his needs and desires, without specifying the regiments or the commander, it would have been only right and reasonable for Julian, his colleague and possible successor, to show himself forward in considering the needs of the East as of the West. But in the way of executing these specific commands there lay difficulties familiar enough to Julian, with which Constantius was but imperfectly acquainted. In the first place, the pacification of Gaul was not so completely effected that so large a contingent of troops could be safely withdrawn. Had that pacification been complete, the commissioners would not have found Julian without crossing the British Channel. A devastating raid of the Picts and Scots across the border of the British provinces demanded the prompt intervention of Roman troops under a Roman general. Had Julian considered it prudent to leave Gaul at this juncture, it is not impossible that London, instead of Paris, might have witnessed his elevation to the Empire. Under the circumstances, however, he thought it wiser to send over an efficient force under the Magister Armorum Lupicinus, a man of ability and experience. This created a further difficulty in the way of executing the Emperor's orders, since Lupicinus had been nominated to the command of the soldiers who were to go to Asia, and among those under his command

in Britain were some of the bands expressly
demanded, especially the brave Batavians, whose
ancestors had given great trouble to the Roman
authorities, and who are commonly regarded as the
progenitors of the doggedly heroic Dutch nation.
Some of the Germanic auxiliaries had only joined
the Roman armies on the special condition that they
should not be sent South of the Alps, and Julian
might well complain that it would be impossible
ever to obtain recruits if Rome refused to keep her
plighted word to her barbarian allies. Many of the
men, too, had wives and children, whom, if they left
them now, they had faint hopes of ever seeing
again.

In fact it would seem that Constantius, though
head of a military monarchy, failed to realise the
conditions on which supremacy can be exercised
over the whole extent of a vast empire. Soldiers
who were well aware that on their shoulders rested
the whole effective power of the reigning house, were
not likely to consent to be moved like pawns across
the Imperial chess-board to subserve the interests of
nobler pieces, or of the immoveable director of the
game. Of the three motive powers by which masses
of armed men can be readily swayed, patriotism, the
hope of glory and gain, and loyalty to a personal
leader, all were in this case either absent or operative in the opposite direction from that indicated in
the Imperial commands. What patriotism existed
in Julian's army was Gallic, not Roman. His men
knew and cared nothing about Mesopotamia, but
they felt the importance of not suffering Gaul to

become the prey of barbarous northern hosts. The advantages they might gain for themselves in the East were very shadowy. Roman arms had not of late been very successful there, the country was unknown to them, and the risk great, while Constantius had no military prestige to attract them. They were ready enough, most of them, to follow Julian, because he had shared in their hardships, and led them to glorious victories. They, or their officers, saw in the projected movement the beginning of a process by which their beloved leader was to be deprived of all credit and authority, and possibly brought before long to share the fate of his luckless brother Gallus.

Julian was placed in an exceedingly difficult position. Though not prepared for opposition, he consented under protest, at least so far as the auxiliaries from beyond the Rhine were concerned. He requested the commissioners to wait till Florentius, who was at Vienne in South Gaul, and Lupicinus could be summoned to Paris to give their advice. But Florentius preferred to leave his superior alone in this extremity. The fidelity of Lupicinus, too, was doubtful, and he had work to do beyond the sea. The commissioners meantime urged haste, and the tribune, Sintula, began to raise levies, paying no heed to warnings or remonstrances. Julian, in despair, offered to throw up his authority altogether, and retire into private life, but the suggestion seems not to have been taken seriously.

The act which brought about the crisis is (according to Zosimus) to be attributed to some of the officers in the army. Inflammatory notices were anonymously drawn up and circulated in one of the chief bands commanded to march, the Petulantes. They ran somewhat in this fashion : " We are banished, like condemned criminals, to the ends of the earth. Our dear ones, whom our swords have rescued from captivity, will fall again into the hands of the Allemanni." A disturbance was naturally aroused, and tidings of it were brought to Julian, who had not left his winter quarters in Paris. He hastened to avoid dangerous consequences, as well as to satisfy the justice of the complaints, by making arrangements for the wives and children of the soldiers to accompany them on the march. At the same time, he advised Decentius not to arrange the route so that the forces should pass through Paris. This advice, like the rest which Julian had offered, was disregarded.

When the troops arrived before Paris, Julian went out to meet them, and endeavouring to make the best of a bad business, spoke cheerfully to the soldiers of the great rewards for which they might hope in the East, and invited the officers to a farewell dinner, at which he encouraged them to make any parting requests of him that they desired. Of course it might easily be alleged afterwards by Julian's enemies that he was secretly at the bottom of the resistance of the soldiery, that the anonymous papers were drawn up at his instigation, and that the farewell dinner gave an excellent opportunity for an outbreak of insubordination. On the other side we can place Julian's most solemn assertions, to friends such as Maximus, as well as to public bodies, that what was done occurred without his connivance, and even against his will. And, considering all the circumstances, this seems the most probable view of the case, though we may never be able to decide, and perhaps Julian himself scarcely knew, exactly to what extent personal ambition, the belief in his special vocation, and a profound distrust of the Emperor, may have influenced him in permitting what he was after all powerless to prevent.

During the night, the excitement in the camp waxed high. Julian retired to the apartments in the palace which he occupied with his wife, but was soon aroused by the din of arms and of many voices uttering the momentous cry " Julian Augustus." He endeavoured at first to pacify the men by assuring them that he would secure the withdrawal of the Imperial order for their removal. As he prevailed nothing, he kept the bolts of his room fastened, and, looking through an opening in his chamber to the starry skies, he besought Heaven for a token. Some sign, probably a meteor, at once appeared, yet with the inconsistency of most people who consult oracles and observe stars, he did not at once resign himself to the decision. After a while, however, the door was broken open, the soldiers forced their way in, and hoisted him on a shield. A cry was raised for a diadem with which to crown him. No such thing, of course, was at hand, and it was proposed to take a necklace or coronet from among his wife's jewelry. But Julian rejected what would have seemed to prognosticate an effeminate character for his reign. Finally a standard-bearer belonging to the Petulantes unbuckled his military collar and placed it on Julian's head. This rough act of coronation accomplished, Julian, in fear for his life, as some said, or wishing to prevent the Imperial honour from being accepted by another, as he afterwards said to Constantius, yielded to the storm. The die was cast and he was Emperor.

Yet the partisans of Constantius made at least an effort, by bribing the ringleaders, to create dissensions among them or to reverse their act. An officer of Helen's household discovered their machinations. There was a fresh rush of soldiers to the palace, and the cry resounded: "Soldiers, both strangers and citizens, never give up the Emperor!" When they found him alive and safe in the council-chamber, their joy knew no bounds. They next prepared to wreak their ill-will on the leaders of the opposite party, but Julian succeeded in saving their lives. Decentius was permitted to escape, and he returned at once to the Imperial court. Florentius, when he heard at Vienne what had been done, departed, as might have been expected, in the same direction. His family and his property were scrupulously respected by Julian. Lupicinus, on his return from Britain, was placed under temporary arrest.

The first tasks which lay before Julian under these changed circumstances were to make sure of the disposition of the whole Gallic army, and to attempt to come to some sort of understanding with Constantius. Of these, the first undertaking was far easier than the second. The smaller band which, under the command of Sintula, had already begun its march, returned to the main body, and the new-made Emperor, who had, on accepting the diadem, already promised the usual donative to the soldiery, made a harangue to the army, expressive of his gratitude to them and of the community of fortunes which bound them together, and announcing his intention of making all military appointments with regard solely to the merits of the candidates, without giving ear to personal recommendations. He immediately put this rule in practice by refusing promotion to some members of the commissariat-staff of the Petulantes and Celtæ whom their comrades wished to see in higher offices. He seems, however, to have given no umbrage by this refusal.

He next drew up a careful letter to Constantius, who, he doubted not, had already heard from Decentius and others of the unexpected turn which affairs had taken in Gaul. He protested his own loyalty, to which his labours and conflicts since his elevation to the Cæsarship had abundantly testified. He showed the great provocation under which the army had acted, and his own unwillingness to accept the dignity violently forced upon him. He urged the necessity, in the present circumstances, of avoiding a breach between the rulers, and the expediency as well as the wisdom on the Emperor's part of pardoning what had been done and accepting the conditions offered. These were that Julian should furnish him with Spanish horses and with certain contingents of barbarian forces that could be spared;

that the Emperor should appoint men of worth to the post of Prætorian Præfect, and leave other appointments, civil and military, in the hands of Julian himself, who also claimed the selection of his own guards.   He again warned Constantius against the scheme of removing the flower of the Gallic Army into Asia.   Finally he expressed his desire not to insist on his new dignity, as he preferred to appeal to past experience and future prospects in urging a course which might make for peace.

This letter as Ammianus gives it (though he does not profess to make a perfectly literal translation) agrees in the main with what is told us by Julian himself.   But now comes in a rather puzzling difficulty.   Ammianus says that with this reasonable and modest letter was sent another, drawn up in very different terms, and full of biting reproaches. This document he declines to publish, as he would not consider such publication to be seemly.*   Now Ammianus generally aims at giving an honest and impartial account of the events he is narrating, he is not slow to reproach Constantius on his own account, nor does he try to hide Julian's faults when he considers him unfair or undignified.   What could have prevented him from telling us more about so important a document?   Again, we can hardly believe that Julian was likely to spoil the effect of a carefully written letter by sending with it a childish ebullition of petty spite.   His great desire, according to his own writings and to the probabilities of the case, was to avoid a rupture as long as possible.

* Or because he had not been allowed to see it.

Why should he have gone out of his way to give perfectly gratuitous provocation to the Emperor? That some private letter was written seems indubitable, if our text of Ammianus is correct. Three hypotheses may be suggested : (1) That we have a confusion here between the communications made by the embassy and those which came later, after Julian's offers had been rejected. (2) That the second and secret letter was sent with the other, but not to be delivered if the first were favourably accepted : or (3) That the secret letter was a part of Julian's original communication but that it contained matter on which Ammianus preferred to be reticent. Here I would hazard a conjecture : May it not have related to religious affairs, and have insisted, as an additional demand, on freedom of ritual and profession to Julian himself and to those who with him adhered or wished to adhere to pagan ways ? Ammianus always seems to have been a sober-minded neutral in religious matters ; he had no sympathy with Julian's ruling passion, and would probably have regarded his demands as very unreasonable ; he was desirous, moreover, that his work should be read by men of all parties, and should steer clear of burning controversies ; thus he might have regretted that such a letter was ever written, and seeing that it had been written, might wish to say as little about it as was consistent with his love of truth and fairness. But however this may be, there can be little doubt that the primary object of Julian in sending the embassy was to make a satisfactory accommodation.

To our notions of military subordination and administrative authority, it may seem that Constantius could not, consistently with the dignity of his position, acknowledge the result of a mutiny as if it were a lawful act. But the experience of centuries had forced the rulers of the Empire to regard the preference of the soldiery as a factor seldom omitted in the elevation or destruction of potentates and dynasties. There were examples, too, like that of the rise of his own father, Constantine, in which the forcibly expressed choice of the soldiery had subsequently received the sanction that could not safely be withheld. But either Constantius, or those whose influence prevailed with him, felt too bitterly against Julian to receive his advances in a pacific spirit.

His friend and well-wisher, the Empress Eusebia, was already dead, and he had now probably no friends at court. Constantius, in his progress, had reached Cæsarea in Cappadocia when the ambassadors arrived. Having received their despatches, he exhibited such wrath as to strike terror into them, and refused to give them audience. They were, however, permitted to return in safety. At the same time the quæstor Leonas was sent with a letter to Julian, bidding him confine himself to the authority he had previously held, and making sundry appointments in the government of Gaul. In particular Nebridius was to succeed Florentius as Prætorian Præfect.

When Leonas arrived at Paris, Julian received him with personal friendliness, but as the letter from Constantius was received and read aloud in the presence of the whole army, there was not much likelihood that the conditions, especially as to the proposed abdication, would be accepted. Leonas was sent back with a description of the opposition made by the army to the Emperor's suggestions. Of the new appointments, that of Nebridius alone was recognised.

Other negotiations, the details of which are unknown, were carried on, both parties being unwilling to begin a civil war. A certain bishop Epictetus was commissioned to assure Julian, from Constantius, that at least his life would be secure if he complied with his cousin's requirements. But, ambitious motives apart, Julian had to consider his duty to the soldiers and the provincials who had entrusted themselves to his care. He declared at once his political intentions and his religious belief in proclaiming openly that he preferred to trust himself and his life to the Gods rather than to the words of Constantius.

Different stories are given as the ground of Julian's confident assurance that the events which had raised him to the Empire were a call to a divinely appointed task. According to his own narrative, he saw, at the critical moment, the sign he had prayed for in the heavens. Others tell of his dreams, or of his enquiries, made by means of the occult sciences. Modern readers can hardly justify a usurpation for which no higher sanction can be brought. Nor can they easily discern a *vox dei* in the shouts of an insurgent army. But if we must acknowledge Julian's accession to be, in a sense, a departure from the legitimate order, we must also remember how little legitimate principle was to be found in the common practice of succession to the Imperial throne, and how hopeless it was to find any orderly means of discovering and enthroning the man whom the crisis of events demanded. The Petulantes and the Celtæ boldly cut the knot, and decided that he alone who had driven away the devastating hosts of the enemy deserved to hold supreme power over the lands he had saved.

Coin of Julian.
Reverse, Securitas Reipvblicæ. The Bull Apis ; above, stars.

NOTES ON CHAPTER VI.

[1] The chief authorities for the circumstances of Julian's elevation to the empire are his letter to the Athenians, and Ammianus, Book xx. The accounts given in Libanius, *Epitaph*, and Zosimus, iii., 9, are apparently based on Julian's own accounts. We have no detailed narrative written from the opposite standpoint. Ammianus is excellent for the Persian War. I have followed him closely also for that with the Sarmatians.

[2] See Tillemont, *Constance*, Note xxxviii.

[3] Cod. Theod. xi., 30, 27 ; vi., 4, 11.

Coin of King Sapor II.
A.D. 340–370. Reverse, Fire-altar.

CHAPTER VII.

WARS IN EAST AND WEST CONTINUED. DEATH OF CONSTANTIUS AND BEGINNING OF JULIAN'S REIGN AS SOLE AUGUSTUS. [1]

360–361.

Οὐ πώποτε ηὐξάμην ἀποκτεῖναι Κωνστάντιον, μᾶλλον δὲ ἀπηυξάμην. Τί οὖν ἦλθον; ἐπειδή μοι οἱ θεοὶ διαρρήδην ἐκέλευσαν σωτηρίαν μὲν ἐπαγγελλόμενοι πειθομένῳ μένοντι δὲ ὃ μηδεὶς θεῶν ποιήσειεν.

JULIAN's *Letter XIII.* (to his uncle, Julianus).

"By my prescience,
I find my zenith doth depend upon
A most auspicious star, whose influence
If now I court not, but omit, my fortunes
Will ever after droop."—*Tempest*, I., 2.

HEN we read the narrative of the exciting events in Paris described in the last chapter, the elevation of a successful general to the supreme Imperial authority by the unconstitutional and unauthorized conduct of a scarcely national army, and the acceptance of that authority by the man of the

soldiers' choice, as of a vocation direct from heaven, we are prepared to pass at once to the story of a disastrous civil war. And, in fact, if Julian had marched eastward or Constantius westward in the spring of 360 A.D., backed as each was by an experienced, brave, and devoted army, hostilities must have ensued of a most destructive and demoralising character to the whole Empire. It is, perhaps, to the credit of both rivals, though partly owing also to propitious circumstances, that this was not the case. Neither was animated by a feeling of goodwill or a conciliatory disposition towards the other. Neither can have hoped for a successful issue to the negotiations that had been set on foot. But both had enough of the spirit of military rulers to prefer not to leave undone the tasks still in hand, nor to risk, in a struggle of personal rivalry, the safety and resources of the great empire which was the stake for which both were contending. Both wanted to gain time. Julian had his work to finish in the West. Constantius desired to make a serious beginning of what he had undertaken in the East. Thus, between the elevation of the rival Augustus at Paris and the beginning of the internecine war which seemed its necessary consequence, we have two campaigns, or parts of two campaigns, both in Gaul and in Asia, in which the Roman armies contended against barbarians, not against one another.

Early in the year 360, before Constantius arrived on the scene of war, Sapor crossed the Tigris and laid siege to the already memorable town of Singara. Like the other sieges of the war, this one

was conducted with much engineering skill and formidable artillery, and sustained with great determination. The town was taken by storm, there was
a general massacre, and the survivors of the garrison, consisting of two legions and a company of
cavalry, were captured, led forth with hands bound,
and sent off to a distant part of the Persian empire.
The chief part of the Roman forces, however, were
stationed at a little distance from Nisibis, which
town Sapor made no attempt to take. Pressing on
northwards, he laid siege to another important
frontier port, Bezabda or Phœnice, situated on the
Tigris near the border of Mesopotamia and Armenia.
The garrison consisted of three legions, which
received the assailants with storms of arrows. In
self-defence, the Persians placed in the front the
prisoners taken at Singara. After a good deal of
fighting and an ineffectual attempt at accommodation made by the Bishop, the fate of the town was
decided by the fall of a much battered tower. The
massacre and pillage which ensued seems to have
been more extensive than at Singara. The town
was refortified and strongly garrisoned against any
Roman attempt at reconquest. Another strong
place, Virta, an old fortress of Alexander, was
the next object of attack, but the King's army
had probably been considerably weakened in the
course of the other sieges, and he thought best
to retire.

Constantius, meanwhile, was trying to obtain
allies in his projected campaign for the next year.
He advanced into Cappadocia and secured the

friendship of Arsaces, King of Armenia, by giving him the hand of a noble lady formerly betrothed to the Emperor Constans.   He then set out in the late summer or early autumn, crossed the frontier into Armenia, and then struck south to Edessa.   In September he advanced northwards to Amida, now a heap of ruins, and determined to attempt the recapture of Bezabda.   This important post proved, however, no more easy of attack by Romans than by Persians.   In spite of the use they made of an enormous battering-ram, which had previously belonged to the Persians, and had been left behind at Carrhæ, all attempts to storm the walls were frustrated by the courage and energy of the defenders, who made vigorous sorties and set fire to the Roman machines.   Constantius determined to turn the machine into a blockade, but when the rainy season came on, the discomfort felt by the besiegers, combined perhaps with a superstitious dread of the frequently appearing rainbows, led him to abandon the attempt for the present, and retreat to Antioch for the winter.   There he married his third wife, Faustina.   Before the next campaign he sent rich presents to the kings of Armenia and Iberia, whose alliance he felt to be of great importance.   Another measure imperatively required was the despatch of some trusty person to take precautions against any attempt that Julian might make on the coast of Africa.   The man chosen for this task was Gaudentius, who had formerly been an Imperial agent attached to Julian's establishment in Gaul, and who bore him no good-will.   Gaudentius accom-

plished what was required of him promptly and
efficiently.   He speedily raised a force of Mauri-
tanian cavalry, with which he watched the coast, and
prevented any invasion which might have been
made from East Gaul or from Sicily.   Early in May,
Constantius left Antioch and marched to Edessa, as
he had heard that Sapor was again about to cross
the Tigris.   He was, however, in a doubtful state of
mind.   Julian, he heard, had left Gaul and marched
through Illyria, on his way to Constantinople.   It
would not be safe to weaken the army in the East
by a very adventurous campaign.   Fate seemed generally to declare for Constantius when he contended
with internal foes, against him when he strove
against foreign potentates.   Yet he could hardly
have left affairs in Asia to go and meet his enemies
in Europe, if Sapor had taken advantage of his em-
barrassed position.   Why he failed to do so, we cannot tell.   The hostilities in Mesopotamia lasted but
a short time, and the Roman officers had special
directions to run no unnecessary risks.   Sapor
seems to have found the auspices unfavourable, and
probably also his presence was required elsewhere.
He retreated, and Constantius feeling able to do the
like, moved back to Hierapolis, about midway between Edessa and Antioch, and there, in a great
military meeting, he set forth his own deserts, the
ingratitude and enormity of Julian's conduct, and
his hope of speedily crushing the insurrection.   The
army expressed its readiness to march against Julian,
and light troops were sent on ahead to prevent, if
not too late, the occupation of the pass of Succi

which the usurper must cross in his march on Constantinople.

Julian meantime had been actively occupied in the West. As has been already said, he felt the necessity of completing the pacification of Gaul before marching against the Emperor. The summer campaign of 360 was chiefly occupied with the punishment of the Attuarian Franks, who occupied the territory about Cleve, and had made incursions over the Gallic border. This involved another expedition across the Rhine which was entirely successful. Having taken many captives, and imposed conditions of peace, Julian marched along the frontier to make sure of all the important posts, and passed by Besantio (Besançon, a place vividly described in one of his letters and to judge from its remains, an important town under the Roman Empire), to Vienne, where he stayed for the winter. During the winter months, it was necessary for him to mature his plans for the future. He soon resolved to postpone no longer the assumption of the Imperial pomp and dignity, the symbols, in the eyes of the soldiers, of the authority which they had conferred upon him, and which the Emperor did not seem inclined to recognise. Thus he celebrated the completion of the fifth year of his Cæsarship in solemn fashion, wearing a magnificent diadem. In religious matters he seems to have advanced tentatively. In a letter written in the course of the next year,[2] he expresses his delight that public sacrifices are being offered, and that the army is devoted to the ancient cults. Yet we are positively told by Ammianus that while at Vienne he went publicly to church and took part in the celebration of the Feast of the Epiphany. It is not impossible that he may have been thinking of carrying out an idea of Constantine, and of joining together men of various religions in a common ceremonial. The Feast of the Epiphany was one of the very earliest ever observed in the Church, and the precise nature of its significance only came to be defined much later. In Julian's day it was not specially commemorative of the Adoration of the Magi. It was generally associated with the baptism of Christ, although in some churches it was not distinguished from Christmas, and regarded as part, if not the whole, of the Festival of the Nativity. This confusion is not found in the Gallic churches, but probably existed in those with which Julian was acquainted in the East. Now we shall see later on that there was another festival occurring just at Christmas time which Julian most strongly desired to have celebrated with due honours, the "Birthday of the Unconquered Sun." He probably thought that to the day set apart "in honor of the manifestation on earth of creative and life-giving power" he might hereafter give a Mithraic character without destroying all the associations that it had for the Christians.

It must have been about this time that Julian lost his wife. She probably died in her confinement, but, as we have already shown, nothing definite can be stated as to the manner of her end. Neither politically nor personally had her influence been of importance, and her removal seems to have made no change in the plans and prospects of her husband.   Her body was sent to Rome, to be laid beside that of her sister Constantina.

In his anxiety to ascertain the course he should pursue, Julian had recourse to the various arts of divination.   The results seem to have been favourable, and the historians have preserved some rude hexameter lines,[3] communicated to Julian in the visions of that night, in which a sudden and speedy end to Constantius was attached to certain planetary conjunctions.

Meantime, the world must be prepared for the coming changes, and partisans must be secured. There was hardly anything like a public opinion to which Julian could appeal to judge between himself and his cousin.   If there had been such an opinion, he would probably not have treated it with deference. But he strongly desired to have on his side the sympathy and the counsel of those who represented, in his eyes, the collective wisdom of the world.   It is very characteristic of his mental attitude that he issued manifestatoes not only to the Senate of Rome (to which some kind of address might seem necessary), but to the " Senate and People " of the Athenians, the Spartans, and the Corinthians.   These letters were not issued till the next summer, but it seems probable that they were prepared during the winter. The appeal to the Roman Senate was, as we shall see, a lamentable failure.   Julian's intercourse with Greek and oriental philosophers and with Gaelic soldiers had not fitted him to deal with Romans who thought themselves statesmen.   The very fact

that he thought it worth while to appeal to the
venerable cities of Greece shows how far his mind
always was from comprehending the distance between the present and the past.   It can surely not
have mattered greatly to Julian what the fourth-
century Spartans thought of his proceedings, and
the opinion of the commercial city of Corinth, if it
had any opinion, was not representative of any influ-
ential society.   These two addresses have perished,
except, perhaps, a fragment of that to Corinth,⁴ and
we can only guess at their substance and character
by that which survives, the letter to the Athenians.
We have already seen Julian's extravagant regard
for that unique city, the brightness of whose ancient
glories has often blinded the eyes of enthusiastic
admirers to her later decrepitude.   And to Julian
Athens was not only the great city of the past, she
was the headquarters of sophists and scholars.   It
was not unnatural that his long pent-up feeling
should find an outlet in the little autobiographical
treatise which he wrote to justify himself in the eyes
of the fellow-citizens of Aristides the Just, and in
which the rhetorical form does not entirely hide the
burning passion beneath.   We have already had
several occasions to cite this letter, which is one of
the most important sources of information about
Julian's early life and his Gallic campaigns.   Not
that he writes with the idea of drawing up a complete autobiography.   He only dwells upon those
points which are likely to secure for him the sympathy of those to whom he is writing, and the style
is that of a rhetorical manifesto, not of a sober his-

tory.   In apology for his usurpation of the Imperial
authority, he urges the shameful treatment he had
received from Constantius, the compulsion used by
the soldiers, and the manifest will of the Gods.   He
expresses his willingness even yet to come to terms
with Constantius, but he has evidently given up
hope of a peaceable settlement, and therefore sees
no reason to be reticent on the expression of his
feelings both towards his so-called benefactor and
towards the Gods of Hellas.

One of the charges brought by Julian against
Constantius is that of stirring up barbarians to invade a Roman province.   The last enemy with
whom he had to cope in Gaul was a chief of the
Allemanni, who was either in communication with
Constantius, or seeking to secure his own ends by
trimming between the rivals.   We have already seen
that in the year 354, Constantius forced terms of
peace on two brother-chiefs, Vadomar and Gundo-
mad, who dwelt on the borders of Rætia.   Gun-
domad was now dead, and Vadomar, who bore a
great reputation for cunning, wrote very subservient
letters to Julian, addressing him not only as Emperor, but as a god.   A messenger of his was, however, seized, and a despatch to Constantius was taken
from him, in which the warning was given: "Your
Cæsar is becoming insubordinate."   This must have
been before the great event at Paris.   But early in
361, Julian, at Vienne, received tidings that the
Allemanni were pillaging the province of Rætia.
Accordingly he sent the brave Petulantes and Celtæ,
under a certain Libinio, to chastise the barbarians

and restore order. The Roman commander, however, was taken at unawares, and in an engagement fought near Sanctio (probably Seckingen, in the Aargau), Libinio was killed and his troops put to flight. Julian determined to secure the person of the slippery chieftain. For this purpose, he sent his trusted and able secretary, Philagrius, on an embassy to Vadomar, furnishing him with secret instructions which he was not to look at until Vadomar had crossed the Rhine. On finding that this was already the case, Philagrius consulted his directions, and found that he was ordered to make Vadomar his captive. This was accomplished without difficulty at the conclusion of a social meal. Vadomar was conveyed into the presence of Julian, who treated him with more clemency and forbearance than he seems to have expected, and merely ordered his withdrawal to Spain.[6] We afterwards find him acting as *Dux* in Phœnicia. This step was followed on Julian's part by another crossing of the Rhine (the fifth he had made during his government of Gaul), and by a brief campaign which led the barbarians to sue for peace.

Julian now had leisure to turn his attention eastwards. Before he began his march, he made a spirited harangue to the soldiers, in which, after recapitulating the work of conquest and of settlement which they had accomplished together, he showed them how desirable it was to take possession of Illyria, while it was so scantily supplied with troops, to advance to the frontier of Dacia, and there to await the course of events. Throwing

himself on their loyalty and sympathy, he besought
them to identify their cause with his by taking an
oath of fidelity. He further requested them to
respect the property and all the rights of private
citizens and the safety of the provinces. The speech
was received with loud applause, and the desired
oath taken with great fervour. One man, Nebridius,
the Prætorian Præfect lately appointed by Constantius, and approved by Julian, had the courage
and the loyalty to his old master to refuse it at the
peril of his life. Julian interposed between him and
the infuriated soldiers, and while refusing him any
demonstration of confidence, permitted him to retire
into Tuscany.

It would thus seem that many of the very soldiers
who had remonstrated so loudly against being withdrawn from Gaul to serve under Constantius in the
East, were ready to follow Julian to the ends of the
world. Yet he must have found it necessary to
leave a considerable force behind him, and his continued care for the Gallic provinces was shown by
the appointment of his friend Sallust [6] as Præfect
over them. Other promotions were made, both in
the army and in the civil government, to fill the
places of those whose fidelity was doubtful. Nevitta,
a Frank, was set over the cavalry, and a certain
Dagalaif over the guards. It is evident that in spite
of the reproaches that Julian directed against the
promotion by Constantius of barbarians to offices of
trust, he could not escape from the necessity of
following the same policy himself.

His forces amounted altogether to about twenty-

TRIUMPHAL ARCHWAY, RHEIMS.

three thousand men. Feeling anxious lest this
small number might appear contemptible, and lest
they might be surprised on their way, he divided
them into several detachments, and impressed on
the leaders of each the necessity of taking abundant
precautions.   Jovius and Jovinus were to lead one
division through North Italy.   Nevitta was to conduct another portion of the army through the Swiss
passes and the land known as Rhætia.   He seems
himself,[7] with a band of picked troops, to have
penetrated northwards through the Black Forest
to the sources of the Danube, on which he embarked
as soon as he came to a navigable part of the river.
The divided forces were to be concentrated near
Sirmium, which lay, as we have seen, on the Save,
near its junction with the Danube.   This important
post had been left in the care of Lucillianus, while
the governments of North Italy and that of Illyria
were in the hands of Taurus and of Florentius
respectively, both of whom were consuls for this year
361.   Both these officials fled as Julian's army approached.   Lucillianus, in Sirmium, was surprised by
Dagalaif with a chosen band, seized in his bed, and
brought into Julian's presence.   He seemed scared
out of his wits, but on being allowed to kiss the
Imperial purple he recovered sufficient voice and
confidence to volunteer some good advice to the
adventurous leader who was pressing on so rapidly
among unknown dangers.   Julian replied with a
smile: "Keep your wise counsels for Constantius;
I did not reach the purple to you because I wanted
your opinion, but to remove your fright."   Lucil-

lianus was withdrawn and Julian proceeded to the
city, where he was received with much enthusiasm.
The next day he rewarded the good-will of the
people by delighting their eyes with a chariot race.
Immediately afterwards, he proceeded to occupy
the important pass of Succi, between the mountain
chains of Rhodope and Hæmus. Leaving it under
the care of Nevitta, he retreated for a time to Naissus, in Upper Dardania.

Hitherto, his progress had been continuous and
easy. But now unexpected dangers arose in two
different quarters. We have already mentioned the
letter which he addressed to the Senate of Rome.
Though it has not been preserved, it seems to have
contained a justification of Julian and an arraign-
ment of Constantius of much the same kind as are
found in the *Letter to the Athenians*. We can
imagine that it was couched in flattering terms and
was bristling with rhetorical illusions, and that the
old Roman hatred of tyrants was appealed to as in
the other document the Athenian love of fairness.
But there yet remained more ballast in the Roman
Senate than in the so-called "Boulé and Demos"
of the Athenians. The recent visit of the Emperor
had probably increased his popularity, and the expenditure which Ammianus blamed as lavish had
thus, after all, achieved some result. The Præfect,
Tertullus, read the letter to the senators, who indig-
nantly uttered in one breath the laconic reply : "We
require you to respect your superior." Two senators,
Symmachus and Maximus, were deputed to go to
the Court of Constantius. At Naissus they were

intercepted [8] and well received by Julian, who made Maximus Præfect of Rome in the place of Tertullus. We may regret that he did not see his way to continue in office so bold an opponent as Tertullus, but the appointment of Maximus, said to have been dictated by private motives, is partly justified by results, seeing that he was able successfully to cope with a serious famine that threatened Rome.

Far more dangerous, however, was the action of two legions of soldiers who had been quartered in Sirmium, when he acquired that city. Strangely unmindful of his late experience with the Gallic army, or perhaps acting on an exaggerated impression of his own powers over soldiers that had not, like the Gallic legions, shared his fortunes for better and worse, he ordered the troops from Sirmium to march westward into Gaul. But the terror of the German enemy and of the chilly and unknown western lands was as formidable to these eastern troops as was the dread of the dry desert and of Asiatic siege-warfare to the Petulantes and the Celtæ. To complete the turning of the tables, the ringleader in the military agitation, Nigrinus, was a native of Mesopotamia. The determination to resist was, however, kept secret till the legions reached Aquileia, at the head of the Adriatic Gulf. They then swooped upon the city, the inhabitants of which were favourable to Constantius, and summoned all the disaffected in Italy to join them. Julian felt his position to be critical, especially as he had heard that forces were being raised against him in Thrace. Jovinus, with the portion of the army that had taken the most southerly route, was ordered to go to Aquileia, and if possible to bring the rebels to reason without resorting to force. His efforts at negotiation, however, proved futile, and the siege began in earnest. The assailants, finding a difficulty in bringing their machines against the walls, stationed in the river and bound firmly together three vessels on which towers could be raised, so as to give a vantage ground for the hurling of missiles. The defenders, however, succeeded in firing the towers, and in other ways inflicted great loss on the besiegers. How the affair would have ended, apart from startling news that arrived from the East, it is useless to conjecture.

This news was of no less an event than the sudden death of the Emperor Constantius. He had already, as we have seen, determined to march against Julian, and in the autumn of 361 he left Antioch and travelled through Cilicia. But his health seems to have been weakened by the anxiety and fatigue he had lately undergone, and at Tarsus he was attacked by a fever, such as, in the very same spot, had well-nigh cut short the career of Alexander the Great. At first he hoped to drive away the malady by exercise, or perhaps rather by removal from an unhealthy region, and proceeded on his way, but when he arrived at Mopsucrene, not far to the north of Tarsus, he was forced to make a final halt. Feeling the approach of death to be near, he had recourse, as his father had before him, to a death-bed baptism. The rite was performed by Euzoius, the Arian bishop of Antioch. According to one report he left directions that Julian should be appointed his successor. His young wife gave birth, shortly after his death, to a little girl, who was in course of time married to the Emperor Gratian.

Though the death of Constantius occurred at a most opportune moment for his far more interesting kinsman, and perhaps also for his own reputation, it is natural to feel a passing regret at the sad and distressing circumstances in which the last male descendant of the great Constantine ended his days. Constantius was not by any means a great man, nor yet a man whom we greatly esteem, yet he seems to have acted under a sense of duty in his military and civil government, and even in his unfortunate ecclesiastical policy. Cool and self-controlled in his demeanour and chary with his favours, he could not stir much enthusiasm, though it is evident that there was a strong feeling in his favour both in Italy and in the army of the East. His good intentions were foiled by the want of an independent mind resolved to see things for itself and not only through the eyes of overbearing and interested persons, while his natural inclination to justice and forbearance was entirely counteracted by the vice, so constantly besetting the despotic ruler, of jealousy and suspicion. And his whole reign, with its record of foreign wars and civil rebellions, of failure and exhaustion, forms a dark setting to a somewhat pitiable personality. His efforts to alleviate the financial distress of the Empire riveted yet more closely the bands which attached the mechanic to his art and the peasant to the soil. His attempt to restore unity in the Church had borne, as we shall see, no better fruit than had his military expeditions against the Persians. "Such as he was, he was," wrote Julian, "may the earth lie lightly on him."

Some of the courtiers who had devoured the Imperial resources under Constantius, especially the infamous chamberlain Eusebius, saw their only hope of safety in the project of setting up another rival candidate to Julian. But no such scheme could be set on foot, and two military legates, who bore the barbarous names of Theolaif and Aligild, were sent to inform Julian of what had happened and to recognise him as Emperor. Meantime, the corpse was conveyed to Constantinople in a funeral car, on which was seated the "Protector Domesticus," Jovianus, who from his somewhat ghastly elevation celebrated games and received gifts in the towns through which he passed. In later times, this circumstance was regarded as a prognostic of the high dignity to which Jovian was destined to rise, and the brief period during which he was to hold it.

Julian was still in Dacia when the messengers came. We have already seen that certain omens had made him inclined to hope for a speedy issue to the conflict. Another which is recorded at this time is like many which illustrate the skill of a ready-minded leader in giving an encouraging interpretation to little accidents. When he had one day mounted on horseback, the soldier who had assisted him fell to the ground. "He who helped me up is fallen himself," said Julian. Whether expected or not, the news was accepted thankfully, as delivering him from the necessity of further bloodshed, yet without

A CONSUL, BETWEEN TWO DIGNITARIES. BELOW, CAPTIVES.
IVORY DIPTYCH.

any unseemly exultation. He speedily marched
through the pass of Succi to Philippopolis and
thence to Constantinople. His easy and triumphant
march made his pagan friends think of the progress
of Triptolemus. He entered Constantinople on the
11th of December, and was received by senators
and people with great demonstrations of delight.
When the corpse of the Emperor arrived, he received
it with all honour and acted as chief mourner in the
funeral ceremonies. It seems probable that he was
then present at Christian rites for the last time.

The peaceable acquisition of Constantinople led,
as might have been expected, to the surrender of
Aquileia. The besieged legions were not easily
convinced of the genuineness of the message sent to
them, but as soon as they were satisfied on that
point, they gave themselves up. The ringleaders
were punished with that refinement of cruelty which
marks the executions of this period. The bulk of
the men were allowed to depart unhurt.

Julian had now three great tasks to accomplish
before he could think of an eastern campaign or of
any but the most pressing affairs of the Empire.
The first was to visit with condign punishment the
detested ministers of the late Emperor. The second
was to purge the palace and the whole city of the
miserable hangers-on that sucked the blood of the
provinces and infested the palace and the government
offices. The third was to establish on a sure basis
those religious changes which he had long contemplated. We must postpone these latter changes till we
can interpret them in the light of Julian's religious

system and ideals. The first measure that he undertook seems to have been executed more summarily
than was desirable or necessary. A special commission of six, at the head of which was the new and
worthy Præfect of the East, Secundus Sallustius (not
to be confounded with the other Sallust, Julian's
friend in Gaul,⁹) held sessions at Chalcedon, on the
Asiatic side of the Bosphorus, to hear charges and
pass sentence against several notable officials of
Constantius. Some were undoubtedly deserving
of the hard fate that was measured out to them.
Paul " the Chain " and Apodemus the Sycophant
perished by the hideous death, which seems to have
been a not uncommon sentence, of burning alive. The
chamberlain Eusebius also suffered death, and there
were numerous sentences of banishment. The dignity of ancient Rome was offended by the banishment of the fugitive Taurus in the very year of his
consulship. The other consul, Florentius, had hidden
himself, and did not reappear during Julian's reign.
The hardest sentence was that pronounced against
the finance minister Ursulus, who, it was said, ought
to have been an object of Julian's gratitude, since he
had secured supplies to him in Gaul. But Ursulus
had incurred the anger of the soldiery by some
scathing remarks about the loss of Amida, and
several officers of the army took part in the proceedings at Chalcedon. When Julian heard that he
had been put to death, he declared that the sentence
had been carried out in consequence of military
demands and without his own knowledge. The
strangest part of the affair is that the moving spirit

of the commission was the miserable Arbetio, who had been mixed up with many of the least creditable proceedings of the late reign. The most plausible hypothesis is that Julian allowed Arbetio to sit on the tribunal for the sake of fair play, and as representing different factions and interests from those of the other judges, and that he trusted to the respected Sallustius to maintain order and justice, but that Sallustius, being a very old man, was not equal to coping with Arbetio. In a letter written at this time,[9] Julian vehemently denies (what some one must have asserted) his intention of visiting the crimes of these men too harshly. The many-headed hydra, he says, must be dealt with, and where there are charges, judges must be appointed to hear them. The difference between his spirit in administering justice and that of Constantius was shown in his indignant refusal of an offer made to reveal the lurking-place of Florentius. After all, the cases of capital punishment inflicted were few, and probably almost all were very richly deserved.[10]

A like indifference to vested interests and public opinion was shown in Julian's palace reforms. A sudden reduction of the numbers of those directly and indirectly nourished at the public expense, must, however just and expedient, inflict some losses on innocent people and lead to charges of oppression and favouritism. Doubtless the fact that many of these schemers and idlers bore the reputation of having waxed wealthy on the spoils of temples combined with Julian's hatred of government by espionage in leading him ruthlessly to thin their ranks.

Long accustomed to plain living, and combining a philosophic with a military aversion to luxury, he had little tolerance for the costly paraphernalia of Court life.   When he sent one day for a barber, and a pompous individual in costly clothing entered his apartment, he exclaimed in feigned surprise : " I sent for a barber not for a finance minister." Nor did the " artist " rise in his esteem by admitting that he expected as remuneration twenty rations of food per day with the like for his horses, an annual salary, and various extras.   Julian's disgust at all which savoured of pomp and effeminacy dictated a policy not unlike that which a cold-blooded economy would have recommended.

But if Julian wished to economise in the salaries of personal servants and of useless dependents, he was only too demonstrative and lavish in favours he conferred on his philosophic friends.   He eagerly invited several of his former teachers or fellow-students to come to him, and allowed them free passage by the public conveyances.   One of them was his revered master, Maximus of Ephesus." He arrived while Julian was presiding at a meeting of the Senate, and the Emperor seemed to some critics oblivious of his Imperial dignity, as he rushed out to meet the old man and bring him into the illustrious assembly. The sophist Chrysanthius had been summoned at the same time, but he, finding omens adverse, had declined the invitation.   No omens were sufficient to deter Maximus, who persisted in his enquiries till the gods gave the desired answer.   Priscus likewise came from Greece, and Himerius followed in about

A CONSUL, BETWEEN TWO DIGNITARIES. BELOW, CAPTIVES.
IVORY DIPTYCH.

a year's time. Among those promoted to high
offices, we find several whose literary tastes and profession had recommended them to the Emperor.
Thus the rhetorician Mamertinus was one of the
consuls for the year 362.

During his stay in Constantinople, Julian did much
to increase the dignity and beauty of the city, which
he regarded with much affection as his native place.
He increased the powers of the Senate, enlarged the
port, and built and furnished a library. The defence
of the Thracian provinces and the reorganisation of
the army also occupied his attention. He celebrated
the inauguration of the consuls with due solemnity,
and having performed an act of manumission which
properly belonged to the new consuls, acknowledged
his error by paying the judicial fine. He received
embassies from many remote peoples, from Armenia,
Mauritania, and far-off India. But no part of his
work was in his own eyes and that of his sophist
friends so important as the restoration of the ancient
worships, and the remodelling of the religious system in accordance with the ideas of which we have
now to take a brief survey.

(For designs of coins selected as illustrations for this chapter, see page 262.)

NOTES ON CHAPTER VII.

[1] The chief authority for this chapter is Ammianus, books xxi., xxii. Zosimus gives a few additional particulars (bk. iii.), but is slight and brief ; Libanius (*Epitaph.*) agrees in the main, but is, as usual, rhetorical and indefinite.

[2] Letter 38.

[3] Ammianus gives them as follows, and there is hardly any difference in the version of Zosimus :

Ζεὺς ὗταν εἰς πλατὺ τέρμα μόλῃ κλυτοῦ ὑδροχόοιο,
Παρθενικῆς δὲ Κρόνος μοίρῃ βαίνῃ ἐπὶ πέμπτῃ
Εἰκοστῇ, βασιλεὺς Κωνστάντιος Ἀσίδος αἴης
Τέρμα φίλου βιοτοῦ στυγερὸν καὶ ἐπώδυνον ἕξει.

[4] Given in Hertlein, *Fragment*.

[5] There is perhaps here a discrepancy between Ammianus and Libanius.

[6] For the two Sallustii, see Tillemont, *Notes sur Julien*, v.

[7] This seems to be the usual interpretation given to the statements of Ammianus, which are not perfectly clear.

[8] Or possibly they passed through Illyria on their return journey.

[9] Letter 23. Hermogenes is not mentioned by Ammianus as a member of the commission, and I see no ground in the Letter for regarding him as such.

[10] For stringent measures to secure the wealth of the proscribed, see *Cod. Theod.*, ix., tit. 42.

[11] According to Eunapius, Maximus had already visited him in Gaul, and Julian seems to have hoped to meet him there. See Letter 38.

Coin of Julian and Helena: Heads of Serapis and
Isis. Reverse, VOTA PUBLICA : Isis and
Nepthys, face to face.

Coin of Rhodes.
Head of Helios.

CHAPTER VIII.

JULIAN'S RELIGION AND PHILOSOPHY.[1]

Εἰμὶ τοῦ Βασιλέως ὀπαδὸς Ἡλίου.

JULIAN, Or. iv., 130.

Ὥσπερ γὰρ ἀλήθεια μία, οὕτω δὲ καὶ φιλοσοφία μία,
θαυμαστὸν δὲ οὐδὲν, εἰ κατ' ἄλλας καὶ ἄλλας ὁδοὺς ἐπ'
αὐτὴν πορευόμεθα.

Orat. vi., 184.

"We needs must love the highest when we see it."

TENNYSON.

IN a letter which Julian wrote to the
philosopher Maximus,[2] most likely
during the latter part of the year
361, from which we have already
had occasion to quote, he expressed
his gratitude to the Gods that his
success in the office which he had
unwillingly accepted had hitherto been free from
bloodshed or spoliation, and that he was now able

169

to sacrifice publicly hecatombs of oxen, his army entering sympathetically into his religious changes. He also stated his purpose of resolutely carrying out the work from which he had reason to expect good results. The attitude of mind shown in this letter, and very frequently throughout his writings, is one which cannot be apprehended without difficulty, yet it is that which chiefly attracts the student of human nature to the career of the reactionary theosophic emperor. There is sufficient paradox about that mental attitude and that career to have tempted historians of all ages to try to solve the problems they offer. How was it, it has been asked, that a man whose moral standard was, to say the least, higher than that of his contemporaries, had no respect for the morals of the Sermon on the Mount? How could the follower of a highly spiritualised theology and cosmology prefer in religious worship the sacrifice of hecatombs of oxen, which some of the Neo-Pythagoreans already felt to be brutal and disgusting,[2] to the prayers and praises offered in the Christian assemblies? How could a reformer, painfully aware of the religious and moral degradation of his own times, be so blind as he was to the real character of the only forces by which a healthier society could be erected? We may set aside the justification he has received at the hands of some strongly anti-Christian writers, especially of some "philosophers" of the last century, whose patronage has probably been worse for his reputation than the invectives of his foes. To those in any degree familiar with the high-flown and

imaginative strain of his religious musings and with
the violence of all his attractions and repulsions in
regard to persons and things of religious character,
the idea that even the force of a common hatred
could induce the rationalist opponents of superstition to claim him as an adherent is almost ludicrous.
Modern friends of Julian's fame are perhaps likely
to err in another direction and to minimise that abhorrence of Christianity which, it cannot be denied,
was one of the ruling passions of his life. It has
been suggested that his earliest ideas of Christianity
were of a religion in the name and the strength of
which his Imperial relatives had persecuted his nearest and dearest, and had murdered the chief members of his house. Again, it is said that Christianity
was always presented to him in an uninteresting and
unattractive manner, and some, as we have seen,
have laid on the Arian bishops of the Court the burden of his apostasy. None of these reasons is without some weight, yet none of them goes to the root of
the matter. We have seen that the poems of Homer,
in which Julian from childhood took such keen
delight, were presented to him by Mardonius in as
unattractive a guise as were ever the narratives of
Bible story to children of strict Puritans. He showed
himself quick enough, when dealing with the apathy
or with the crimes of those who shared his views, to
distinguish between the logical and the practical
results of religious beliefs and between the offices and
the persons of religious authorities. Again, in his
polemics against Christianity, he boldly attacked the
Christian Scriptures, not any imperfect or mislead-

ing interpretation of them. With those Scriptures he was well acquainted, and he had at least as good facilities as most men of his generation for separating the grain from the chaff, a process he was well able to perform with regard to all systems save the Christian. If he had been a mere visionary, without any practical acquaintance with men and with life, his enthusiasm for an effete system might have been less surprising. But, as we have seen, the perils, vicissitudes, and responsibilities of his early life had developed in him a high degree of mental energy and promptness in thought and action. Then again his views of life and duty seem in some respects much more like those which have grown up under Christian teaching than like those of the joyous, life-loving paganism of the best days of Greece. Yet nowhere is he more bitter in his denunciations of Christian depravity than where he is exhorting to what we are accustomed to regard as peculiarly Christian virtues.

In fact we can only approach the question with any hope of success if, without any thought of accusation or of apology, we study his beliefs, first on their positive and afterwards on their negative side. The great problem is not so much why he was not a Christian as what made him such an ardent Hellene. For it was the ideas of Hellenic mythology and philosophy which so entirely possessed his mind as to make the reception, or even any faint comprehension of the Christian ideal a total impossibility to him. While he was yet in his student days, his young and enthusiastic mind, saturated with Greek culture, mov-

ing in a world peopled with the imaginations of Greek
poets and illumined by the splendid speculations of
Greek philosophers, felt a bitter scorn and indignation in seeing this culture and this world receding
before the inflowing tide of new principles totally
foreign to his whole view of life. For whatever may
have been the case with less ardent souls or with
more quiet minds, with him, at least, no compromise
between Christianity and Hellenic culture was in
any degree possible. It is interesting to observe
the inconsistency in the feelings expressed at different times by the more cultivated of the Fathers
of the Church as to the value of the old records of
pagan wisdom and the character of the philosophers
and poets of ancient Greece. Gregory Nazianzen, Julian's fellow-student at Athens, denounces
the greatest names of antiquity with the scurril-
ity of a fish-wife, yet he is driven to quote the
writings of those very men in illustration of his meaning, and had thought it worth while to undergo a
costly training in order to familiarise himself with
their methods of thought and speech. Nobler and
gentler spirits like Origen showed some respect for
the philosophers, and would derive part of their
wisdom from Palestine, yet even they scorned the
tragic writers and regarded the Olympic deities as
actually existing malicious demons. Augustine, with
all his contempt for secular learning, expressed a
hope that the great men of old might have been the
" spirits in prison " to whom the Gospel was preached.
One is almost driven to relinquish any attempt to
discover the mind of the early Church on the subject,

and to fall back on the hypothesis that in so rhetorical an age, the alternate invectives and laudations represent not so much the conflicting views of a divided society or the varying moods and phases of individual minds, as different fashions of speech, corresponding to the various methods according to which subjects of this kind had to be handled. Now Julian was himself something of a rhetorician, else he could not have been a fourth-century Hellene. But at the same time he was imbued with a whole-hearted loyalty to the great men of the past and to the teachings and the mode of life that had come down from them. The heathen writings which his Christian contemporaries regarded as a dangerous though necessary article of diet, only to be taken with copious antidotes, were to him the staff of life and the medicine of the soul. He could not divide his allegiance. With all his short-sightedness, he perceived some things that were hidden from most men of his time. In the triumph of Christianity he foresaw the Dark Ages. We cannot wonder that he did not see the Renaissance on the other side.

But apart from his attitude toward Christianity, there is yet another paradox in the position taken up by Julian as to the beliefs of his day. His religion was Hellenism ; he aspired to be a Greek of the Greeks. Yet both in his religious philosophy and in the religious cults which he chiefly preferred, there is a very strong admixture of Oriental thought and feeling, and the philosopher whom he most deeply reveres, Jamblichus,[2] of Chalcis, was more than half a Syrian. But we must remember that for centuries

the process had been going on by which Oriental
elements were being assimilated into the substance
of Greek thought. The Egyptian Alexandria had
been the great meeting-place of eastern and western
ideas. At one time it may have seemed as if the
Greek mind would perish under the weight of a more
ancient civilisation, as it had in its turn overborne
and diverted the current of culture in Italian lands.
But in the Neo-Platonists of Alexandria the Hellenic
intellect asserted its supremacy and its powers of
receiving and recasting things new and old.

If, however, we desire to leave generalities and to
endeavour to attain some knowledge as to what
Julian's religion actually was, we must study his own
obscure and hastily written but pregnant little
treatises on *King Helios*, and on *The Mother of
the Gods*, especially that on the deity to whom he had
peculiarly devoted himself. The religion of Julian in
his public capacity was Romano—Hellenism. In his
private observances and dominant thoughts he was a
follower of Mithraicism, or the philosophy of Solar
Monotheism. The origin and character of this strange
system need some preliminary explanation before
we see how it was developed in Julian's hands.

The worship of Mithras was, according to Plutarch,[4]
introduced into the Roman world by the Cilician
pirates, who were put down by Pompeius Magnus in
the year 70 B.C. Before that date, Mithraicism had
already passed through many phases. In the simple
nature-worship of the early Aryans, Mithras held a
high place as one of the gods of light and of beneficence. The stern dualism of the Mazdean religion

of the early Persians reduced him to a subordinate station. For them, Ormuzd, the creative god of light and of good, constantly thwarted by Ahriman, the power of darkness and of evil, was separated by a vast interval from the nearest members of the celestial hierarchy. But not even among these, the six Amesha Spentas, did Mithras find a place. He was merely a *Yazata*, a personification of the natural phenomenon of solar light. But the inherent tendency to poly-theistic nature-worships which seems to characterise a certain phase of social and intellectual develop-ment, soon undermined the simplicity of the Mazdean religious system. The early Persian kings ascribe generally their strength and their success to Ormuzd. From the first part of the fourth century B.C., to the reign of Artaxerxes Mnemon, Mithras holds a place of almost equal honour. Ormuzd might still be re-garded as superior Creator, but Mithras ranked as the strongest and the holiest of divine creatures. His qualities of purity and of ubiquity made him the special protector of honest men and guarantor of oaths. Later on, he becomes identified with deities of more distinctly solar character, who had their seats in Phrygia, notably with Atys and Sabazius. Both of these deities were closely associated in their honours with Cybele, the Mother of the Gods. Ac-cording to legend, Atys had been beloved by her, had proved unfaithful, had suffered mutilation and death, had been transformed into a pine-tree, and had finally risen, purified, to a new life. All this story was commemorated in the Mysteries of Cybele and Atys, with hideous orgies, which the symbolic interpretation of the learned might justify, but could never render generally instructive and wholesome. In monumental art, the attributes of Mithras and of Atys are hardly to be distinguished. Sabazius, too, though possibly in his origin a lunar deity, loses his distinctness, and becomes another form of Atys and of Mithras. The connection between Mithras and the goddesses of fecundity worshipped in Phrygia and in Babylon is shown again in the curious confusion made by Herodotus, who identifies the Persian Mithras with the Assyrian Mylitta, a goddess closely analogous to Cybele. But while to the Semitic or partly Semitic races that bowed under the Persian yoke this process of syncretism emphasised the naturalistic side of the early Aryan deity, a somewhat similar process was, in the Persian theology, bringing into prominence the more spiritual attributes of his character. In the Mazdean system, one of the Amesha Spentas[5] called Çaoshyant, was regarded as the redeemer from death, and the giver of immortality. This being likewise seems to have become identified with Mithras, as indeed it is in accordance with the instinct of man all over the world to associate in thought the loss of light and life during the winter and their recovery in the spring with the death of the body and the hope of a resurrection.[6] Thus when the Romans first became acquainted with the Mithraic cult, it had already acquired those characteristics which rendered its appeal to the religious consciousness of Imperial times so forcible and effective.

With the spread of Roman military power all over·

the known world and with the gradual assimilation
by Roman society of all the elements that it could
contain of Greek culture, there set in a current of religious thought and sentiment, which is easily traced
and accounted for, among the uneducated towards
sensationalism, among the educated towards monotheism, among all towards mysticism.   That cosmo-
politan spirit, which had resulted from the conquests
of Alexander and which was among the chief gifts of
Greece to Rome, had so far broken down national
barriers that national religions had well-nigh lost
their *raison d'être.*   Religious observances had come
to be regarded rather as a means of satisfying the
aspirations of the individual than as a compliance
with the requirements of the State.   The highly artificial character of the society in which men and
women of the upper classes lived, the equally artificial and generally precarious life of the lower classes
in overcrowded cities, were favourable to the growth
of self-consciousness and of a morbid desire for novelty.   A reaction had set in against the incredulity
we see in the companions of Cæsar and of Cicero, and
the once widely prevalent scepticism seemed to have
paved the way for a similarly prevalent superstition.
A wider knowledge of nature and of man had led
nobler minds up to the wide and comprehensive
doctrine set forth in the *Hymn to Zeus* of the Stoic
Cleanthes.   For Stoicism, based as it was on the idea
of universal law in nature and of ever-binding duty
among men, was the only form of Greek philosophy
that the narrow, legal mind of the Roman could
adequately grasp.   The later Mithraicism appealed

both to the better and to the worse sides of the religious consciousness of the times. It satisfied the desire for universality, for it was confined to no one nation and to neither sex. It gratified also the longing for mystery and for obscure symbolism. It set forth, when expounded by the worthiest of its professors, the all-importance of moral purity. It supplied exciting and extravagant ceremonies to the morbid imagination of the weak-minded. It had, in its further development, acquired that strong hierarchical organisation which has enabled some religious societies to hold their own through all vicissitudes of fortune. It seemed to point back to those days of primeval simplicity so dear to the fancy of a decadent civilisation ; for is not the sun one of the earliest recipients of religious honours among all peoples, was not all-seeing Helios appealed to alike by the suffering Titan groaning under the tyranny of Zeus, by the heroes swearing solemn oaths under the walls of Troy, and by Greeks and Romans of later times when undertaking obligations under the most sacred, that is, under the most primitive sanctions? And when once the cult of Helios had gained a footing in the Roman Empire, the frequent transfers of the legions were sure to spread it over all the length and breadth of the known world.

The development of Mithraicism after it had become one of the principal religions of the Empire was still in the direction of comprehensiveness, of mystery, and of closer organisation. Mithras became more frankly identified with the sun, and altars to him often bore the inscriptions *Soli invicto*. At the

same time he aggregated to himself the attributes
of almost all the other deities of the pantheon. He
was worshipped in subterranean grottos with mystic
rites, and a whole system of symbolism grew up in
connection with his worship. The most familar
form of Mithras in art is that of a young man, in
Phrygian cap, stabbing a bull. But many other
animals besides the bull—the scorpion, the owl, the
lion, the dog—are regularly found in artistic representations of Mithraic import. The mysteries became more and more severe in their demands on
candidates for initiation, more significant in the
teachings as to immortality and metempsychosis.
Neophytes were admitted by a bath of blood. The
tongue was purified by honey. Severe tests were
applied to those who would join the inner circle of
worshippers, or would rise from a lower to a higher
grade in the society. All members, or perhaps all
who attained to a certain dignity, regarded themselves as soldiers of Mithras, and signified their
relation to him, in one of their rites, by thrusting
aside a proffered garland and grasping a sword,
while uttering the words : " I will have no crown but
Mithras." The passage of the soul from a lower to
a higher state of existence was represented in their
mysteries by a ladder leading from one to another
of the planetary spheres.[7] A strict discipline was
enforced among all men and women who joined the
society. But while the weaker were kept to their
allegiance by the iron yoke of authority, and the
superstitious gratified their cravings by the excite-
ments of a sensational worship, some at least of the

philosophers of the day regarded chiefly the doctrinal side of the religion, and adapted it to the expression of their highest thoughts on the substance and origin of all things, and on the relation of human nature to the divine.

Of this philosophy of sun-worship, Julian is the most notable exponent. In those habits of thought and feeling which had favoured the growth of solar monotheism, he was the child of his age. In his beliefs and philosophic principles he was a disciple of Jamblichus of Chalcis in Cœle-Syria, who had developed and added to the doctrines of Plotinus and Porphyry. In personal character and habits of mind he was, as we have seen, swayed by a passionate devotion to the traditional wisdom of the past, and by the conviction that his great task in life was to restore Greek culture and to save the treasures of old time from the inroads of barbarism and of oriental superstition. And for this mission he nerved himself by constantly thinking that he was bound to the service, and strengthened by the protection of King Helios. In many passages of his work Julian shows by apparently voluntary ejaculations or by express statements how constantly and habitually he regarded himself as the servant of Helios or of Mithras, and the idea of his special mission from that deity is worked out in the form of a fable in one of his *Orations against the Cynics.*

Although single-hearted in his Hellenism, Julian found most of the purely Greek gods, like Apollo and Hermes, too anthropomorphic to satisfy his mystic aspirations. Zeus might be identified with the supreme unity or with the chief creative force. Athene might be regarded as a personification of Divine Providence, but most of the other gods of the Greek pantheon, though always to be honoured and kept in mind, were necessarily relegated to a subordinate position. Nor was the spiritual nature of Julian's theology, any more than his Hellenism, irreconcilable with sun-worship. He always carefully distinguishes, especially when he is controverting the Mosaic story of creation,[8] and again when he is setting forth the nature of King Helios,[9] between the visible solar disc and the real supersensual sun. The compatibility of Mithraicism with Hellenism, with idealism, and with monotheism, can be realised only after a careful study of Julian's oration in honour of King Helios. But in order to grasp, even in slight measure, the meaning and the language of that oration, it is necessary to have in our mind some notions of the theories of Plotinus and his followers as to the divine nature and the divine power and attributes.

Plotinus (who lived from 204 to 269 A.D., and studied and taught at Alexandria and later in Rome), always considered himself a disciple of Plato, and was probably hardly aware of the extent to which he modified the teachings of his master and of the difference in tone which they acquired through his elaborations and interpretations. The splendid Platonic myths hardened, in the hands of the Neo-Platonists, into systems of dogma, whence weapons were often produced for fighting against the doctrines of the Church. The writings of Plato which

they chiefly preferred were the most speculative,
such as the *Timæus*, and they dwelt most willingly
on the most obscure elements of his teaching. Thus,
unlike some followers of Plato, both of ancient and
modern times, who prefer to fix their eyes on
human life, set against a mysterious background of
divine and supersensual existence, and deriving all
its reality and all its nobleness from communication
of the divine energy, Plotinus turned his gaze from
earth to heaven, started from the conception of a
supreme Unity, identical with the supreme Good,
descended thence to the realms of pure Reason, of
$Nοῦς$, comprehending within itself the Platonic Ideas,
the archetypes of all sensible things, and thence
down to the second emanation, $Ψυχή$, the animating
soul of the universe. The chief development which
the doctrine received, at the hands of Jamblichus, was
in the first place the removal of $Τὸ \ ῎Εν$ one step
further from all human thought, the supposition of
a yet more exalted Unity, above that Unity, identical with the Good, which was regarded as the
parent of $Nοῦς$. Of this development, however, I
have not met any trace in the writings of Julian.
The second development in the Plotinic school, important in relation to the philosophy of Julian, is the
separation of $Nοῦς$ into two $κόσμοι$ (orders), the
$νοητός$ and the $νοερός$, the designations of which
have been not quite adequately translated as
the *intelligible* and the *intellectual* worlds. It
seemed to the Alexandrian philosophers that any
act, even the act of thinking, was unworthy of the
denizens of that highest ideal world, who possessed

merely passive attributes, who might be contemplated, but who performed no action save the creation or the generation of an order of intelligent creatures, the νοεροί. These beings, according to the Neo-Platonic system, on the one hand, are ever contemplating the archetypes of the κόσμος νοητός, while on the other hand they create, according to those archetypes, not directly the physical universe, but the psychical, of which the physical is a faint copy. Now to give unity to these conceptions of a primordial divine existence, a world of archetypes, another world of creative agencies, and yet another of generative forces among phenomena, some mediating spirit or agency is required, and this mediation Julian finds in the being and functions of King Helios. He is a perfect manifestation of the Divine Good, whence he has proceeded. He gives being, unity, and beauty to the intelligible or archetypal deities (νοητοί). He rules among the intelligent and creative, whose power is derived from him. He gives form to matter, bestowing at once knowledge and the faculty of knowing, just as from the sun in the heavens are derived both the faculty of vision and the light by which we see. In short, being an exact image of the superintellectual Idea of the Good, the highest being of the intelligible order and the archetype of the great source of light and order in the sensible universe, he stands to the creative intelligence in the relation held by the Idea of the Good to the archetypal principles of being and in that of the solar disc to the creations of the universe of space. Most of the

gods known to the Greeks and the Egyptians may
be regarded as special energies or manifestations of
"Helios, the King of all," though, as Julian sugges-
tively remarks, in treating of a divine being we
cannot entirely separate nature from power or from
functions. It is because of the imperfection of human nature that man often wills to be that which he
is not, and fails to achieve that which he wills. With
the divine nature it is otherwise: "Whosoever he
willeth, that he *is*, that he *can*, that he *doth*." Yet
we who judge of things imperfectly and symbolically
may divide his power, identifying the creative force
with Zeus, the harmonising with Apollo, the life-
giving or healing with Asclepios, the distributive
with Dionysos, the generative and joy-inspiring with
Aphrodite, the soul-liberating with Hades or Sarapis.
Likewise Athene, who has sprung not, according to
the fable, from the head of Zeus, but from the whole
nature of Helios, derives from him her functions as
teacher of arts and of wisdom. By superintending the
mixtures of the four elements, the gods subordinate to
Helios create bodies and souls and give good gifts to
both. From the heavenly motions, men derive their
knowledge of mensuration and mathematics. From
the divine orders upheld by King Helios, Greeks and
Romans have derived their orderly systems of government and all their civilisation. The Romans
show their gratitude to Helios by worshipping him
under the names of Jupiter and Apollo, by rever-
encing as their founder's mother Aphrodite, who is
one of his manifested forces, by their care for the
sacred flame kept up by the Vestal Virgins, by mak-

ing the beginning of their year coincide with the
return of the sun from the south, and by keeping
the festival of Mithras, or Helios, immediately after
the Saturnalia.

From this slight sketch of a very obscure and
difficult treatise may be gleaned some notion of
Julian's use of Greek mythology and also of the
stronger and the weaker sides of philosophic sun-
worship. On the one hand, that worship afforded
sublime objects of contemplation; it left the mind
free to recast the old myths so as to explain away
any ugliness and make them vehicles of sound instruction, it gave a meaning to life and a hope in
death. With one element in some of the oriental
systems Julian had no sympathy, the belief in
metempsychosis. He abhorred the doctrines of the
resurrection of the body and of successive rebirths of
the soul, and regarded it as one of the noblest functions of Helios to deliver the soul after death from
all its bodily fetters. And this freedom from the
body was always associated in Julian's mind with the
conquest of all low and base desires, such a conquest
as might in the present life be attained by those who
endeavour to rise to a state of philosophic calm.
But here we see the weaker side of this religion.
Essentially and apart from strained interpretations
of its rites and customs, it was, if not immoral,
entirely non-moral in character. Not only was its
teaching dark and symbolic;—all religions must deal
largely in symbolism, and any which embraces
various classes of votaries must, in its symbolic
teaching, convey different meanings to different

ASKLEPIOS AND TELESPHOROS.
IVORY DIPTYCH.

types of mind. But in the cult of Mithras or of Helios, there was, we may say, no moral substructure. What moral meaning it was subsequently made to convey was an artificial addition due to conscious adaptation by individual thinkers who had no claim to represent a common tradition, no influence on the life and thought of the common people. A religious enthusiast himself, Julian could not perceive the horrible perversions which must arise where religious enthusiasm is not tempered by respect for the moral law. He felt no fear of familiarising the people with the loathsome stories perpetuated in some of the Mysteries, such as those of the Great Mother. Nay, it even seemed to him a positive advantage that stories about the gods should be strange and monstrous in character. Noble and dignified representations of divine beings give, he said, a lofty but still a purely human conception of their character, while these grotesque myths lead men to think of the mysterious and supernatural. In dealing with the story of Cybele and Atys, both of which deities are very closely associated with King Helios, he guards against any acceptance of it in a literal sense. Since the gods cannot go astray, Atys has never fallen, but rightly interpreted the whole story may be taken as an allegory of the relations between the Supreme Cause and the natural world, of the duty of the soul to moderate its excessive desires and to rise towards the Gods, while from each stage in the ritual celebration, and in each rule of abstinence practised during the ceremonies, may be derived some valuable rule for the guidance of life.

In the treatment of this and of some other myths, Julian shows an eager desire to make the pagan traditions of the Gods a vehicle of moral and religious instruction in rivalry to the teachings of Christianity. The word used for the descent of Atys from the upper world to organise and vivify the world of matter (συγκατάβασις) is the very one sometimes used by Christians to describe the incarnation of their Lord. Again, in his exposition of the Labours of Heracles,[10] he represents him as a divine but suffering and struggling son of man, overcoming the resistance of the elements and of all human woes, through the aid of Athene Pronoia and of his father Zeus, who had brought him forth as a deliverer to the world, and received him home with thunder and lightnings. Julian goes on to contrast Heracles, the hero apotheosised after his human life with Dionysus, who has, if the myths are wisely apprehended, no human side, but is to be identified with certain creative powers of the Divine Intelligence. He refers in another place [11] to Asclepios as a divine messenger from Zeus and Helios, who assumed a human form, walked on the earth, and cured, both during his earthly course and subsequently by special inspiration, the diseases from which men suffer in soul and body.

Thus the habit of meditating upon and of endeavouring to analyse the Divine Power, manifested in nature and in man, made it possible for Julian and other Alexandrian philosophers to keep to a polytheistic mythology, while maintaining a monotheistic position in their serious belief and in their most

HYGIEIA AND EROS.
IVORY DIPTYCH.

cherished religious practices. To Julian, polytheism implied not merely an analysis of the divine attributes. It also supplied a hypothesis for accounting for different races of men and different forms of civilisation. To this point we shall return in considering Julian's controversial writings against the Christians. Here we may remark the unfitness of Mithraicism or any similar system to become in any sense a universal religion. It needed a μεσίτης as powerful as Helios himself, to bring into harmony the minds of the rude soldiers, who raised an altar to the Unconquered Sun, and of the fiery fanatic who exhausted himself in the degrading rites of Atys and Cybele, with the high aspirations of the philosopher, who found in the conception of Mithras a consistent and satisfactory account of the origin of all things, and in the half-orientalised mythology of the late Greek civilisation a source of worthy motives which continually urged him forward in the path of duty. The orgies which had disgraced the reign of Elagabalus, that devoted priest of a solar deity, might have shown how much force the arguments on behalf of moral cleanliness drawn from the veneration of the pure sunlight were likely to exert on a fundamentally unclean mind.

It is possible that some survivals of the old Mithraic worship still linger among us. The pine-tree, once sacred to Atys, is in the form of the Christmas trees still honoured with joyous rites on the day once kept as the "birthday of the Unconquered Sun," although the honour paid to both may date from far earlier days. Some writers are inclined to see elsewhere influences of Mithraicism [12] in Christian ritual. And whether or no this last effort of pagan theosophy had any permanent results on the organisation of the Catholic Church, it has been clearly shown that many Mithraic symbols and modes of thought and worship are to be found among the heretical bodies, especially the Gnostic sects, of the half-Christianised provinces of the East.

But it is time to turn from this twilight of obscure speculations and aspiring dreams, and to observe how Julian contended, in words and deeds, against those religious teachers whose impiety and barbarism, according to his judgment, forced him into action both as a religious controversialist and as a sacerdotal reformer.

Coin of Smyrna. Head of Cybele.

NOTES ON CHAPTER VIII.

[1] Besides Julian's own writings, especially Orations IV.,V., and VII., and the authorities already referred to, among the books which throw most light on this subject are Vacherot's *École d' Alexandrie* (especially the chapter entitled " Successeurs de Plotine"), Jean Réville's *La Religion à Rome sous les Sévères,* which contains a good account of the Mithraic cult, and Maury's *Religions de la Grèce,* vol. iii. ; Ueberweg and the other historians of philosophy give, of course, an outline of the Neo-Platonic system. Since writing most of the above chapter I have read M. Adrien Naville's little treatise on *Julian l' Apostat et sa Philosophie du Paganisme,* which is interesting and appreciative, but does not trace the connection between Julian's doctrine and that of the other philosophers of his school. This would, however, be an almost impossible task, seeing that so much of the work of Jamblichus, Porphyry, and the rest is hopelessly lost. For this reason, we cannot determine how much of Julian's thought is original and how much is directly borrowed from others. But where he borrowed, even, as he said he did, from Jamblichus in the treatise on *Helios,* he probably did not merely copy without rearrangement and adaptation to his special objects. For the influence of classical education on the pagan reaction, I would refer to the interesting work of M. Boissier *La Fin du Paganisme.*

[2] Notably Apollonius of Tyana. See the curious life of this oriental mystic by Philostratus.

[3] There can be little doubt that the letters purporting to be from Julian to Jamblichus are spurious. See Cumont, *Sur l' Authenticité de quelques Lettres de Julian,* also Schwarz, *De Vita et Scriptis Juliani imperatoris.* According to one theory, these letters were written by Julian to the younger Jamblichus (of Apamea), but their style is against this supposition. For the two Jamblichi, see Brucker *Hist. Phil.,* vol. ii., pp. 268, 269. In the new collection of letters attributed to Julian published by Papadopoulos in the *Maurogordateios Bibliotheke,* there is one (No. 4) which mentions both uncle and nephew, and seems to say that the latter excelled in theosophy as the former in philosophy. Probably the works of the two have become hopelessly mixed. See pamphlet by F. Cumont just referred to, p. 4, note 6.

[4] *De Iside et Osiride.* Plutarch mentions a way of regarding Mithras as mediator between Ormuzd and Ahriman. This idea may

be brought into harmony with Julian's if we take Ahriman to represent *matter* and Ormuzd pure spirit.

[5] Or a Yazata?

[6] *De Iside et Osiride.*

[7] Origen *Against Celsus*, vi., 22.   For Mithraic symbols, see C. W. King, *Early Gnostic Gems*.

[8] *Contra Christianos*, 65.

[9] *Oration* iv., 132, etc.

[10] *Oration* vii., 219 *et seq.*

[11] *Contra Christianos*, 200.

[12] Such as C. W. King.

———

A further interesting point in Julian's Oration in honour of the Mother of the Gods is that the allusion in it to the mystic sacrifice of unclean animals (*Or.* v., 176) has led to, or at least assisted, some notable theories on the subject of sacrifices generally. *See* Robertson Smith : *Religion of the Semites, Lecture* viii., *p.* 272.

Coin of Julian and Helena. Heads of Serapis and Isis. Reverse, VOTA PUBLICA.
Isis with sistrum and vase.

CHAPTER IX.

JULIAN AS A RELIGIOUS REFORMER AND CONTROVERSIALIST.

Δίδου πᾶσι μὲν ἀνθρώποις εὐδαιμονίαν, ἧς τὸ κεφάλαιον ἡ
τῶν θεῶν γνῶσίς ἐστι, κοινῇ δὲ τῷ Ῥωμαίων δήμῳ μάλιστα
μὲν ἀποτρίψασθαι τῆς ἀθεότητος τὴν κηλῖδα.
JULIAN, Or. v., 180. (From concluding prayer to the Great Mother.)

"Great God ! I 'd rather be
A pagan, suckled in a creed outworn,
So might I, standing on this pleasant lea,
Have glimpses that would make me less forlorn ;
Have sight of Proteus rising from the sea ;
Or hear old Triton blow his wreathèd horn."
WORDSWORTH.

E have insisted on the necessity for all
those who would attain some insight
into the mind and character of Julian
to study the positive and constructive
elements in his religious philosophy
and governmental policy, before approaching the negative and destructive
parts of his work. But in practice, this course is not

always easy to pursue. True, we can, as a rule, separate his controversial from his didactic or devotional treatises, and distinguish the prohibitory from the regulative orders which he issued on religious affairs. Even here, however, we are not free from apparent interpolations and ill-fitting adjustments in the text, and from the difficulty of deciding how much, in satirical or rhetorical sketches, is meant to be taken literally. And on a nearer view, there appears a conservative tendency in what is most destructive, while in the defence of the old, so much seems to have been borrowed from the new, that the product has the effect of a grotesque patchwork. Julian was too wise to think that he could by a series of enactments make men cease to feel those religious needs which they sought to satisfy in the ways he did not favour. Nay, he was himself in sympathy with those very tendencies towards spirituality in religion and a broader humanity in ethics which were both cause and effect of the rapid spread of Christian doctrine and institutions. Accordingly, he endeavoured consciously and of set purpose, to engraft on the old pagan system all that in the new teaching which most powerfully appealed to the better instincts of man. No doubt it seemed to him that in so doing he was only developing the hidden and neglected meaning of the old poets and sages. And certainly there is much in Homer, not to mention the more didactic writers, which can bear interpretation in a rationalist and moralist sense. Even in our days, a Christian scholar has found in Helen of Troy some features of the Magdalene, and in Apollo and Athene types of the Divine Word. And without soaring so high, we may gather from the Homeric poems both examples of heroic virtue and intimations of the ultimate triumph of the better cause. If such moral instruction is only to be obtained by neglecting other phases of Homeric life and thought which would tend in a contrary direction, we must remember that Julian's eye was less capable than ours of judging works in all their relations, and indeed perhaps few eyes can judge in an impartial and critical spirit any books which it regards as peculiarly sacred. Similarly, no society, and no man deeply imbued with the religious ideas of his society, can judge quite fairly the character and the tendency of the documents and observances of any religion which is regarded as a dangerous rival. To Julian, all the professions and even the practice of active philanthropy on the part of Christians savoured of imposture and charlatanry. Nowhere does he show less practical sense, yet nowhere does the great aim of his life more clearly appear than in his laudable efforts to raise the paganism of his day to a moralising and spiritually elevating power in the world. His aims and methods appear throughout his correspondence and his various writings, but are most clearly set forth in four letters of injunction and exhortation to different officials in the hierarchical system. We purpose therefore to give here a brief sketch of these most interesting documents.

One of them [1] is to a lady named Callixena, who seems to have kept staunchly to her functions as a priestess of Demeter all through the time of Christian domination. In a style of graceful compliment, Julian asserts the superiority of the faithful priestesses to Penelope, whose virtues like theirs bore well the test of time. For piety is an even higher virtue than conjugal fidelity, and again the trial of the priestesses had been twice as long as that of Penelope. In recognition of her merit, Callixena is to receive, in addition to her previous office, that of priestess to the Mother of the Gods at Pessinus.

More important as elucidating all Julian's ideas and plans is a very important fragment [2] addressed to some unknown priest in a high and responsible position. At the point where the extant portion of this letter begins, Julian is in one of those digressions common in his longer letters, and in his treatises, which has led him astray from his main subject—the duties and privileges of the priesthood. He is inveighing against the life of solitary asceticism which he holds to be contrary to the social nature of man.

Returning to his subject, he remarks that as civil rulers have to see that the laws of the State are obeyed, it belongs to those who have authority over priests [3] to cause them to follow the laws of the Gods. The first necessary qualification in a priest is philanthropy. The Gods love those men who love their fellows. Their love is to be shown in divers ways,—it may be even in chastisements. In nature it is like the love of the Gods to men, which love has bestowed all the gifts by which man is superior to the beasts, gifts far richer, and less directly bestowed than the " coats of skin," with which, according to the Jewish story, the Creator clothed Adam and Eve. Men selfishly appropriate these gifts, and cause the poor to blaspheme the Gods. They even ask for more, and if a shower of gold were to fall, they would try to keep it each for himself. Yet if they distributed to the poor, they would not become losers thereby. Julian bears witness that he has never had cause to repent an act of generosity. It was just after relieving some poor people from his scanty means that he recovered the inheritance of his grandmother. We should give more liberally to the good, yet relieve even the bad and our personal enemies, according to their wants, in virtue of their humanity. Prisoners should be treated kindly, especially seeing that they are often innocent. The names by which the Gods are known should be sufficient to inculcate this duty. How can a man less kindly and hospitable than the Scyths dare to approach the temple of Zeus Xenius or of Zeus Hetærius? And how inconsistent it is to worship family deities and neglect the fact that all men are of one family! For this truth stands whether all men are descended from a single pair or whether, as Julian himself believes, men are of divers origins and fashioned by many divinities, but inspired by Zeus with a common life.

Starting them from the performance of their duty towards their brother men, priests should add to their philanthropy piety and purity. The presence of the Gods must by them be ever clearly realised. The images of the Gods should be reverenced, not with idolatrous regard, but as symbols conceded to our fleshly nature, one degree removed from those

visible manifestations of the Gods which we see in
the starry heavens. We may not excuse ourselves
from serving the Gods by saying that they do not
need our services ; neither do they need our praises,
which nevertheless we are bound to render, according to immemorial custom. Veneration for the
images of the Gods is not more idolatrous than is
the affection of a child for the portraits of his
parents. One argument used in disparagement of
such images is that they are perishable. But if they
were not, they would not be the work of man at all.
It is sometimes permitted by the Gods that even
great and good men, those worthier images of God,
may be destroyed by evil men, although the Gods
ever watch over the good.   But the divine vengeance
overtakes murderers ultimately, not always immediately ; and so it is with profaners of temples and
images.   A proof that even sacred things are subject
to irretrievable decay is shown in the failure of
Julian's late attempt (made in all reverence and
sincerity) to restore the Jewish Temple. For Julian
reverences the God of the Jews, though he despises
that race for their want of culture and for their
indistinct ravings, so different from the poetry of
the Greeks.

Everything to do with the divine service should
be respected, and the persons of the priests held
in honour, as was that of Chryses by the host of
Agamemnon.

Julian now returns to the subject from which,
with his usual tendency to fly off at a tangent, he had
wandered, and resumes the consideration of the

duties of priests. He guards, however, against the idea that the reverence due to a priest should depend on his moral character. So long as he performs his functions, he should be respected by virtue of his office. If he is an evil-doer, he should be convicted and degraded, but while he is a priest at all, those who despise him incur the wrath of the Gods, as certain oracular verses plainly teach.

To return then : What should the character of the priest be? The immediate recipient of this letter needs no admonitions, but it may be useful for him to feel the support of Julian's authority as Pontifex Maximus, in his endeavours to maintain discipline among his subordinates. Speaking as a priest to priests, Julian says that he feels unworthy of his office, but he trusts in the Gods, who, even during the life of the body, are able to bring order out of disorder, and yet are more certain to fulfil the hopes of the soul after death. These hopes should enable priests to stand towards the people as sureties on their behalf with the Gods, and as examples of virtuous living. As was said before, piety, a constant recognition of the invisible presence of the Gods, should be found in every priest. Hexameters attributed to Apollo are quoted as showing that the eye of the God penetrates both Olympus and Tartarus, and rejoices in the good deeds of pious men. Surely if the Gods can see through stones and rocks, they can see into our souls, which they are able to deliver from the realms of the dead.

This piety involves purity, in thought, word, and deed. No coarse jesting, no reading of impure poems, can ever be permitted to those of the priestly order. They should study Plato, Zeno, and other philosophers who have taught the existence and the providence of the Gods. Mythological tales, whether of Greek or Hebrew origin, which represent the Gods as envying, fighting, or otherwise acting unworthily of the divine nature, are to be shunned. Histories should be read, but not fictitious love stories. Nor may priests read sceptical works like those of Epicurus and Pyrrho, which, however, have (thank Heaven!) mostly disappeared. For the guarding of the thoughts from evil is even more important than that of the tongue. Hymns in honour of the Gods should be learned, both such as have been composed by the Gods themselves, and such as men have written under their inspiration. Three times, or at least twice a day, the priest should pray and offer sacrifices.

As, however, priests are after all men in the flesh, the nature of their service must depend partly on circumstances. When not on actual duty, the priest should purify himself night and morning. He must dwell in the temple the prescribed number of days (in Rome thirty), and during that time he must give himself to meditation, and not go to his own home nor to the market-place. After he has given over his charge to another, he must still regulate his life carefully. He may only frequent the society of worthy people. He may occasionally go to the market-place, and may hold intercourse with the magistrates, and he must administer relief to the poor. When officiating, let the priests wear splendid vestments, but in private life they should dress as ordinary men, and imitate the modesty of Amphiaraus, which, as Æschylus relates, won the favour of the Gods. Common use of priestly garments brings them into dishonour.

Priests should not go to the theatres, though if the stage could be purified, the case would be otherwise. But such purification, though a noble work, seems impracticable. The company of dancers and actors is to be avoided, as well as wild-beast combats and all spectacles and contests, except those of a distinctly sacred character, at which the presence of women is prohibited,[2] both on the stage and in the audience.

Passing on to the mode of selecting candidates for the priestly office, Julian lays down the principle that men should be chosen according to their merit, and especially their reputation for piety and active benevolence, not for birth or wealth. They should be such as guide their own households in ways of piety, and are also eager to relieve the poor. It is the neglect of the poor by the priesthood that has incited the wretched Galilæans to simulate philanthropy, as kidnappers decoy children with sweetmeats. In the midst of a bitter invective against the Christian love-feasts, the fragment suddenly ends.

It seemed desirable to paraphrase this document at some length, in spite of its fragmentary character and the many imperfections of the text, because it contains several points very characteristic of Julian's mode of thought and schemes of action. It is an example of the rambling style in which he generally wrote, constantly pulling himself up after wide digressions suggested by a passing thought, especially by some allusion to the habits of Jews or of Christians.   There is a striking approximation to the Christian standard of morals, especially in the inculcation of active benevolence and of kindness to enemies, and in the insistence on purity, in thought, word, and deed.   Other interesting points are his justification of Hellenic paganism from the charge of idolatry ; his mention of the attempt (which we shall consider later on) to restore the temple at Jerusalem ; his separation, in thought, of the person from the office of priest ; his remarkable anticipation, in the part relating to the choice of religious officers, of the democratic tendency of the Catholic Church ; and, chief of all, his attempt to derive from the heathen poets and the popular beliefs the same kind of incitement to good works that the Christians found in their Scriptures, combined with the reluctant admission that such motives had not been very successfully applied, and that the hated Galilæans bore at least the semblance of active philanthropists.

The same principles as to priestly duties and a yet more strongly marked disappointment as to what had thus far been accomplished, in comparison with the works of the Galilæans, are to be found in a letter addressed by Julian to Arsacius, high-priest at Galatia,[4] as well as in a very imperfect fragment to Theodorus,[5] who seems to have held priestly authority in the province of Asia.   Arsacius is ordered to enforce discipline among the Galatian priests, and to insist that they with their wives and families frequent regularly the religious services. He is also to see to the maintenance of inns for strangers, for which purpose the Emperor has made special provision.

All people are to be exhorted to kindliness and hospitality by the example of Eumæus in the *Odyssey*. The priests are not to flatter the civil magistrates with unbecoming servility.

The fourth letter⁶ of Julian which we shall cite is addressed to some person, probably in a priestly office, who had been guilty of an assault on a priest. Julian points out the heinous character of the offence, which is not to be excused by any alleged misconduct on the part of the priest who has received the blow. Whatever his actions, his sacred character ought to have protected him. In virtue of his own sacerdotal authority, both as Pontifex Maximus and as custodian that year of the Didymæan oracle, Julian prohibits the offender from undertaking any service about the temple for three months. At the end of that time, if the high-priest gives a satisfactory report of him, the oracle shall be consulted with a view to his restoration. But Julian forbears to curse him, as he disapproves of such a practice, and would rather pray, and exhort him to pray, that his sin may be forgiven.

In all of these letters, we see Julian acting in a priestly capacity, using, for the purposes of religious discipline and reform, those offices which had of old been attached to the Imperial dignity, but not always regarded as an important branch of the Emperor's prerogative, and still less as conveying a far-reaching spiritual authority. It is natural to suppose that the active part taken by Constantius and his sons in assembling church councils and trying to settle ecclesiastical disputes, may have prepared men for the exercise of a similar power on behalf of the ancient institutions and cults. Before we pass on to see the nature of the efforts made by Julian as literary controversialist and as supreme lawgiver, to win men from Christianity to Paganism and to edify pagans in their faith, we may compare with the tone of these letters the general indication of his intentions which caused great alarm among some Christians. The invectives of Gregory Nazianzen are not unexceptionable authority for Julian's motives and actions, but he had some real ground to go upon when he denounced the Emperor's projected reforms. For, as we have seen, one of Julian's chief ideas was to bring about an alliance between a pure and enlightened morality and a devotion to the worship of the Hellenic deities, by infusing into Hellenic education an element of religious instruction, based on the old mythology and literature and designed to train the character and the affections of men up to the purest Hellenic ideal.

Gregory says:[7]

" He [Julian] also, having the same design [as that of Sennacherib], was intending to establish schools in every town, with pulpits and higher and lower rows of benches, for lectures and expositions of the heathen doctrines, both of such as give rules of morality and those that treat of abstruse subjects, also a form of prayer alternately pronounced, and penance for those that sinned proportionate to the offence, initiation also and completion, and other things that evidently belong to our [the Catholic] constitution. He was purposing also to build inns and hospices for pilgrims, monasteries for men, convents for virgins, places for meditation, to establish a system of charity for the relief of prisoners, and also that which is conducted by means of letters of recommendation, by which we forward such as require it from one nation to another,—things which he had specially admired in our institutions." There may be some exaggeration in this statement, but in the main it is probably correct.

We pass on to consider the controversy in which Julian engaged against the doctrine, discipline, and worship, of the Christian Church. This portion of his work has not the unique interest of that which we have considered or of that which will concern us hereafter. Destructive criticism does not require great originality of mind or strength of character, whereas the reconstruction of an ancient system in rivalry to an encroaching new one demands the powers of a philosopher and of a statesman in one. Arguments seldom make converts, and even in their historical aspect they interest us rather in showing what men regarded as the chief bases of their faith than as indicating the ground on which that faith actually rested. It is important for us, however, to observe the nature of the charges brought by Julian against Christianity, since they both illustrate the kinds of proof to which the Helleno-Roman world (here very unlike our own) would submit a religious system, and also help us to understand the attitude taken up in these matters by Julian himself.

A question here meets us to which it is difficult to give a satisfactory answer: How far were Julian's arguments against Christianity original and how far were they derived from previous writers? The chief reason why we cannot arrive at any degree of certainty on this point is that very little of the ancient controversial writings against Christianity has escaped the hands of pious opponents who thought, perhaps rightly, that their best refutation was to be found in the "ordeal by fire." The arguments of the philosopher Celsus have been preserved for us in the replies of Origen. Occasionally they run along the same lines as Julian's, but the resemblances are merely such as one would expect to find between the reasonings of two Hellenes against the new faith. It does not seem probable that Julian studied Celsus. If, as Origen says, that philosopher was an Epicurean, Julian would not have felt much respect for his authority. He is much more likely to have read the works of Porphyry, no longer extant. But even if he borrowed from them, it is not probable that he did so to any large extent. He was no doubt far better acquainted with the Christian Scriptures and Christian usages than Porphyry was. But whether borrowed or original, these arguments represent his own convictions. We see clearly in them, what we have observed already, that Julian's main quarrel with Christianity was simply that it was non-Hellenic, —that it was a barbaric religion which, unlike a national cult like that of the Jews or of the Egyptians, aspired to universality, and that, in spite of any compromise that might be made between lukewarm Christians on the one hand and half-educated Greeks on the other, the two systems of thought and life could not long exist side by side without one of them either secretly undermining or else absorbing the other.

Julian's work against the Christians was probably written [8] during the winter 362–3 A.D. According to Jerome there were seven books, but Cyril, who examined and confuted them, only mentions three. Of these the second was probably occupied with the Gospels and the third with the other books of the New Testament. The first is more general in its scope, and is devoted to an examination and comparison of Hellenic, Jewish, and Christian theology. It has been restored almost entire from the quotations of Cyril, Bishop of Alexandria, who wrote about 432, and has been examined and published in an excellent edition by Dr. Neumann. The general drift is clear enough, though of course we cannot be sure that we have all the thoughts and reasonings in the order and fashion in which they first appeared, and we have probably lost a good many connecting links.

In approaching Julian's objections to Jewish and Christian doctrine, we must not expect to find a similar idea of doctrinal proof to that which prevails in our own age. The modern mind has generally become sceptical by steeping itself in the methods of the inductive sciences, till it has come to demand,

for every theory whether of sensible or supersensuous
things, an absolutely verifiable basis of fact.   Many
of the modern difficulties with which Christianity has
to contend are altogether out of harmony with the
spirit of Julian.   The miracles, for example, recorded
in the Old and New Testaments, are so far from presenting to his mind a stumbling-block to faith that
he speaks scornfully of the small number and unimportant character of the mighty works attributed to
Christ.   But here, perhaps, we may draw a distinction.   Where he is dealing with things that are said
actually to have happened, or to be about to happen,
in the material world, and which are amenable to
the evidence of the senses, Julian argues very much
after the fashion of a modern sceptic.   Thus in treating of the story of the Tower of Babel, he naïvely
remarks that if all the earth were made into bricks,
it would not furnish material sufficient for a tower
reaching only to the orbit of the moon.   Again, he
asks, from what source St. Luke could have derived
his information as to the angel strengthening Christ
in the garden, since the only possible witnesses were
asleep.   He complains of the want of agreement between the pedigree given by St. Matthew and that
in St. Luke, and of the confusions and contradictions
in the narratives of the resurrection of Christ.   In
one passage, too, probably referring to the resurrection of the saints at the Second Advent,[9] he remarks
that not to distinguish, in forecasting the future, between the possible and the impossible, marks the
very summit of human folly.

But in judging of all such matters of religious

belief as lie beyond the regions of observation and experiment, past, present, or future, the proofs which Julian demands are of another character. In his eyes any abtruse religious doctrine handed down by tradition or thought out by a great and original mind is worthy to be received if it be sufficient to acccount for known facts, and if it harmonises with our innate ideas of the character of God and the duty of man.

Thus in combating the Jewish account of the creation of the world, Julian does not ask for evidence or appeal to physical probabilities, but tries to show that the story is inconsistent with itself, that it is insufficient to account for the facts, and that it presents unworthy notions as to the character of the Deity. In Genesis, he says, we have nothing stated about the creation of angels, and certain things "the waters," "the darkness," and "the deep" are left wholly unaccounted for as to origin. Again, the Creator is said to have made some things and simply to have commanded others to be. And how could an omniscient being have framed woman to be a help-meet for man, knowing all the while that she would be the cause of his fall from Paradise? Still more serious are the two objections to the story of the first disobedience ; the notion that God would withhold from man so excellent a gift as the knowledge of good and evil, and the malignant jealousy supposed in the exclusion of Adam and Eve from the Tree of Life. Julian gives no rival theory of the origin of evil. He seems, from some passage in his works, to regard it as an imperfection due to the

14

connection of soul and body, but the absence of belief in an active power of evil is one of the causes or signs of his inability to apprehend thoroughly either the Jewish or the Christian religion. In the Jewish story of the confusion of tongues, again, besides criticising, as we have seen, the possibility of building a sky-reaching tower, Julian objects to the narrow view that must needs account somehow for differences of speech among nations, but sees no need to explain the origin of far deeper distinctions in customs and character. And even if the Babel story be accepted, it is insufficient to account for the facts. Natural distinctions are not to be attributed to an arbitrary fiat, but the commands of God must always be in accordance with the essential nature of things.

For these reasons Julian greatly prefers, as a religious explanation of the origin of man and the world, and of the differences among men and nations, the splendid myth in the *Timæus*, where the Demiurgus is represented as delegating to the inferior and derivative deities, the creation of the various orders of living beings, to which, within certain limits, the divine element or the rational soul is to be distributed. This myth both affords a theory of the differences existing among various orders of life and various races of men, and also shows more clearly than the Jewish story the universal beneficence of the Creator. The point in Jewish theology which most deeply stirs Julian's ire is its exclusiveness, and that in two ways: the supreme God is represented as jealously refusing to share His glory with the inferior deities, whom from the use of the plural number (in Gen. xi., 7, and other passages) the Jews must have supposed to exist; and again, He is supposed to have squandered all His favours on one little race in one corner of the world, to the neglect of the rest of mankind. "I, the Lord thy God, am a jealous God." What more unworthy notion of the Almighty could be formed than this? Jealousy is a hateful passion in man; is it not blasphemous to attribute it to God? And has not Divine Providence bestowed on Greeks, Egyptians, Babylonians, as good gifts as those possessed by the Hebrews? Arts, sciences, politics, all those elements of Greek life and culture which the devout mind associated each with the idea of a particular divinity; were they not a standing protest against all Hellenes who abandoned the faith of their fathers for the worship of an arbitrary and capricious tyrant and of a dead Jew?

Against the Christians, in addition to the objections urged to those points of theology held by them in common with the Jews, Julian asserted that in their interpretation of prophecy and in their elevation of Jesus to the rank of a divinity, they were taking unwarrantable liberties both with the Hebrew Scriptures and with the Gospel narrative. The "Prophet like unto Moses" (of. Deut. xviii., 15), the "Shiloh" (of Gen. xlix., 10), the "Star out of Jacob" foretold by Balaam (Numbers xxiv., 17), the "Virgin-born" (of Isaiah vii., 14) are not to be identified with Jesus, and, even if they were, they would not prove his divinity. This doctrine is entirely contrary to the Mosaic insistence on the unity of the Godhead. He refers also to the passage in which Israel, not Christ, is called the first-born of God (Ex. iv., 22). It is St. John, he says, who first asserts the divinity of Christ, and even he does it in such ambiguous language that we cannot tell whether he entirely identifies the Word of God with the man Jesus. The doctrine of the λόγος was by no means strange to Julian's theology, but the conception of the " Word made flesh " was to him a gross absurdity. He preferred, as we have seen, to regard as the perfect image and the manifested power of the Changeless One, the life-giving and ever-active Helios,[10] whose functions in the world of ideas and among the subaltern gods correspond to those of the revolving sun in the natural universe.

If we proceed next to Julian's views as to Christian practical morality, we find here, as in the theoretical portion of his work, some strictures directed against what is common to the Christian and the Jew, others against what is peculiar to Christians. He regards the Decalogue as unworthy of the high estimation in which it has been held. With the exception of the commands not to worship strange gods and to keep the Sabbath, it contains, he says, no elements which are not to be found in the codes of all peoples, and the exhortation against polytheism is enforced by the assertion of the doctrine, so hateful to Julian, of the jealousy and revengefulness of God. For the rest, the laws of the Jews are far inferior in justice and gentleness to those of Lycurgus, of Solon, or of the Romans. Indeed, the Jewish stories of vengeance taken, or allowed to be taken, on innocent and guilty alike (especially the story of Phineas and the Israelites in Num., xxv.), tend to confuse all notions of calm and deliberate justice.

But to the Jewish law, whatsoever it may be worth, the Christians have not kept faithful, in spite of the saying of their Founder that he came "not to destroy but to fulfil." They have rejected the mild institutions and customs of the Greeks, but they have only learned to combine Jewish presumption with Gentile impurity. With a strange unfairness, Julian tries to prove the loose lives of Christians by citing St. Paul's description of what some of the Corinthians were *before* their conversion (1 Cor., vi.), and when he comes to the words (v. 11), "but ye are washed, but ye are sanctified," he asks, contemptuously, how such washing can have been effected by the rite of baptism, which is unable to cure the diseases of the body, and surely incapable of reaching the soul. This protest must be taken in connection with the fact that, as we have seen, in Julian's day, baptism was often delayed till the last illness, in order that with the prospect of purification before death, the catechumen might feel no fear of free living. Julian's indignation at this pernicious idea is very strongly expressed in a passage at the end of his satire, *The Cæsars* (of which we shall say something later on), where he represents Jesus as standing and crying in words which are a parody on Matt. xi., 28: "Come unto me, all ye that are corrupters, bloodstained, impure, and shameless, and I with this water will make you clean. And if ye again become subject to the same ills, I will grant unto him that beateth upon his breast and striketh his head that he shall be purified."

This passage shows, perhaps, more clearly than any other how far Julian was from recognising in the Gospels any power to reclaim from evil or stimulate to good. He believed, as we have seen, in the possibility of repentance and amendment, even in the case of great offenders, but in the Christian Scriptures he saw nothing which could by any possibility make any man better. If in one or two passages he quotes the authority of Christ against his professed followers, it is merely an *argumentum ad hoc*, and does not show that personally he felt any respect for that authority. When, for instance, he upbraids the Christians for their quarrels among themselves, and says that neither Jesus nor Paul left any rules for persecution, he hastens to explain that fact by declaring that when Christianity was first set on foot, its promoters had no notion that it would ever spread much beyond the miserable little set of fanatics who had first received it. It is not surprising, therefore, that Julian could see nothing but simulation in the apparent virtues of the Christians around him, and that he was but too ready to believe in all the vices attributed to them by their adversaries.

It is in matters connected with religious worship that Julian has the least fault to find with the Jews and the most with the Christians. In all such matters, he always shows himself strongly conservative, and though he is willing to acknowledge the essential identity of the spiritual beings venerated in widely different places and in very diverse forms, he would yet have each nation keep to its peculiar traditional observances. He admires the fidelity with which the Hebrew law and ritual have been maintained. He tries to find traces of augury and astrology in the history of Abraham, and acknowledges himself as a worshipper of the God of Abraham, of Isaac, and of Jacob. But the Galilæans have rejected all the Jewish ritual, and accepted from the Gentiles one thing at least: the license to eat what they will and never to fear defilement. They refuse to sacrifice and to venerate the images of the gods, either those made by man, or those shining upon us from the everlasting heavens. They do not practise circumcision, saying that "circumcision is of the heart," as if, forsooth, they were really separated from other men by superior virtue! Yet by what authority was the Jewish law ever annulled for the followers of the Jews? What right had Paul, that supreme charlatan, ever hovering between a Jewish and a universal interpretation of his doctrines, to declare that "Christ is the end of the law"? But the Galilæans depart most decisively from both Hebrew and Hellenic modes of worship in their degrading reverence for the tombs of martyrs and for dead men's bones. Christ himself spoke of sepulchres with manifest aversion, and bade the dead bury their dead, and Isaiah prophesied against those who "sleep in the graves and in the tombs that they may dream dreams" (Is., lxv., 4. Sept.).

And, again, the worship of Christ seems to him directly contrary to Jewish monotheism.

It will be readily acknowledged that though these controversial writings are not destitute of suggestive thoughts and instructive side-lights, yet in them Julian is not seen at his best, perhaps, indeed, theologians seldom are so seen in their most combative efforts. Yet on behalf of the history of religious thought, we cannot regret that they were written and have been in some measure preserved. For Julian affords a conspicuous illustration of the fact, not easily grasped and borne in mind, that it is possible for a man of devout spirit, subtle mind, and strong love of truth and justice, to fall far short of comprehending the most essential characteristics of a religion in the documents and institutions of which he has been carefully instructed. The question as to what qualities of heart and head are further requisite for such comprehension lies, of course, very far beyond the scope of our present investigations.

Coin of Helena. Head of Isis Pharia. Reverse, VOTA PVBLICA: Isis Pharia on a galley, holding a sail.

NOTES ON CHAPTER IX.

[1] Ep, 21, Spanheim, 388-9.

[2] Sp. 288-305.

[3] This seems to me the natural meaning. Talbot renders it differently.

[4] Ep. 49.

[5] Ep. 63.

[6] Ep. 62.

[7] *First Invective*, c., III, C. W. King's translation.

[8] See introduction to the valuable edition by Neumann. These writings are not to be found in Hertlein, and are not treated of by Mücke. The earlier attempts to piece the fragments together were not quite satisfactory.

[9] Fragment from Suidas referred by Neumann to this connection.

[10] Besides *Contra Chris.* and *Oration in Honour of King Helios*, see *Letter to the Alexandrians*.

Coin of Smyrna. Imperial Times. Cybele in her chariot, drawn by lions.

CHAPTER X.

JULIAN'S POLICY AGAINST THE CHRISTIANS.

" Εγὼ μὰ τοὺς θεοὺς οὔτε κτείνεσθαι τοὺς Γαλιλαίους οὔτε
τύπτεσθαι παρὰ τὸ δίκαιον οὔτε ἄλλο τι πάσχειν κακὸν
βούλομαι, προτιμᾶσθαι μέντοι τοὺς θεοσεβεῖς καὶ πάνυ φημὶ
δεῖν."   JULIAN, Ep. vii.

" In dealing with religious sectaries there is no middle course between the persecution which exterminates and the toleration which
satisfies."   HENRY HALLAM.

IT seemed desirable to make some
study of Julian's religious principles and ideals, his aspirations and
the motives of his efforts in working for himself and for his subjects,
before attempting to understand the
legislative and administrative measures which he used to effect the ends set before
him. It is chiefly through these measures that he
has been held up to the obloquy of all ages, as it

was by them that he incurred the violent hatred of
his opponents and unfavourable criticism from some
who were otherwise favourable judges of his conduct.
Rhetoricians have delighted to point out the inconsistency of a profession of calm and philosophic impartiality with a practice of religious exclusiveness in
bestowal of trust and privileges, and of an insidious
proselytism accompanied by something very like
persecution, in the army and in the State. Sober
men of ancient and of modern times have regretted
that Julian did not maintain the attitude of strict
neutrality which would, they consider, have best become him. Yet if we realise the man and his environment, the inconsistencies seem to explain
themselves, and the strictures, if not wholly unde-
served, to need modification and allowance. Religious toleration, as we understand it now-a-days,
must rest on one or other of two bases : on the opinion that differences in religious feelings and beliefs
are of subordinate importance in the life of individuals and of societies ; or on the experience, which
men in office are ever slow to acquire, that the putting down of error and the establishment of truth
had better be left to other powers than those which
hold supreme authority in the state. The former
ground might be taken by some thinkers and by
some politicians in Julian's day. We have seen that
it was eloquently set forth, in the cause of humanity,
by the philosopher Themistius, and it even finds
expression in the earlier edicts of Constantine, who,
though not quite indifferent himself, yet preferred
that aid should be invoked on his behalf from rival

heavenly powers rather than that a portion of his subjects should cease to pray for him at all. But, as has been already shown, to maintain the position of strict neutrality was found impossible by Constantine himself and by his sons after him. What we have learned of the mind and character of Julian is sufficient to convince us how utterly removed were his thoughts and feelings from everything that savoured of indifference or of an equal regard or non-regard to all religious forms. To him the one thing worth having in life was the consciousness of a close relation to the Divinity. This relation might, of course, be realised in divers forms, but the " Galilæan superstition " tended to obscure it altogether, to give men unworthy thoughts of the Divine, and to cause an ungrateful neglect of all the manifestations of a heavenly presence and power throughout the past life of the Hellenic and Roman peoples. Julian considered, as Libanius says, that " were he to make all men richer than Midas, every city greater than Babylon of old, and overlay with gold the walls of each city, yet should reform none of their errors in religion, he would be acting like a physician who, having taken charge of a person full of maladies in every part of his body, should doctor everything except the eyes."[1]

Nor was it possible for Julian to accept the second basis of religious equality : the strict limitation, in matters spiritual, of any authority that can effectively be asserted by the civil power. He saw, to his credit be it said, that a policy of persecution is worse than useless ; that (to quote again the words of Libanius) " a false belief in matters of religion you cannot eradicate by cutting and burning ; but even though the hand burns incense, the conscience blames and accuses the weakness of the body and holds to the same things as at first." Yet this belief did not hinder him from using the vantage-ground of his Imperial position to counteract the influence and the teaching which he regarded as pernicious. It is a trite saying that autocrats do not easily recognise the bounds which must always exist to their absolute power. And when we consider the exalted position of a Roman Emperor, summing up in his person the authority of all the ancient magistrates, and of the sovereign people as well ; the one head of the civilised world, dispensing mercy and justice to all men, fighting and caring for them in life, and worshipped by them after death, we realise how the only check to his authority that such a potentate could readily conceive would be one of those revolutions that so frequently brought an end to authority, title, and life at the same moment. Julian, with his Greek conceptions of political powers and relations, recognised the supremacy of law as above the individual will of the ruler, and regarded the sovereign as bound to guard and reverence the constitution of the State. Yet finding himself in possession of the helm of the commonwealth, with practically unlimited powers in legislation, administration, foreign politics, and appointment of officials, and accepting these powers as instruments given to him from Heaven, to effect a radical reform in morals and religion, he was not likely to minimise his functions. His high ideal of the kingly office is shown not only in the sentiments attributed to him by Libanius, but in his own writings, especially in *The Cæsars*, the *Epistle to Themistius*, and the *Second Oration in Praise of Constantius*. He likes to dwell on the Homeric idea of kings as " shepherds of the people," and the office of a shepherd does not leave much scope for *laisserfaire*. Nor was it probable that the more zealous among the Neo-Platonic philosophers whom he had called to aid him by their counsels would help him to forget that he was a Hellene and a philosopher while seated on Cæsar's throne. If he had adopted a far more fanatical policy than he did, he would, if we consider both the character of his advisers, and the absence of all reasonable critics, have been entitled to the same kind of excuse as is accorded to more than one mediæval monarch who proved " ane sair saint for the crown." Let him receive due honour in that he not only abjured every directly violent means of action, but also in general strove to follow the lines of a fair and economical policy independently of any religious considerations. This policy we shall see when we consider his general legislation.

That Julian should endeavour, by peaceable means, to lead men to embrace his own views, is what we must naturally expect. But the modern reader cannot but regret that with his intense belief in the pernicious effects of Christianity and in his own mission as philosophic despot, he should have sometimes tolerated or even sanctioned measures which we regard as undignified and unfair. That he was actuated throughout by a radical misconception of Christianity in itself and in its relation to the Hellenic world, must likewise be acknowledged, and need not be excused. The bearing of these considerations will become more evident if we take up separately the chief points in which, as Emperor, he directed his policy against the Christians, their institutions and doctrines.

In trying to understand this policy, however, we meet with difficulties in the documentary and literary evidence before us. Several of his laws are extant, in the Theodosian Code or in the collection of his letters, but many must have been expunged, and of those which we have, investigators are not quite agreed as to how far some of them were framed with directly anti-Christian intentions. A good deal of what has been written on the subject by contemporary churchmen is marked by gross improbability and sometimes by pure childishness. In trying to use both the statements of his enemies and his own professions, we need to read carefully between the lines. In the one case, we have to notice what are the kinds of unfairness and intolerance of which Julian's enemies do *not* venture to accuse him. In the other, we need to reflect on the *indirect* consequences, painful and unjust to Christian individuals and communities, yet very likely to follow the measures which he, acting in all integrity, considered legitimate and reasonable.

In the first place, Julian declared his intention not to persecute anyone for religious opinions. So far, he seemed to go back to the principle of the Milan decree. There is something almost *naïf* in the indignation expressed by the leading Christians at his adoption of a course which allowed no scope for honourable suffering on the part of confessors. " He begrudged the honour of martyrdom to our combatants," wrote Gregory Nazianzen, " . . . that we might suffer, and yet not gain honour as suffering for Christ's sake."² There certainly was an irritating contempt in the manner in which the boon of religious liberty was granted. There might even seem an element of superstition in his fear lest sacrilege should be committed, if unwilling persons were dragged to the temples and altars of the gods. Two of his letters show how he understood and interpreted the grant of liberty he was making. One is directed to a certain Artabius, and runs thus. " In the name of the gods, I do not desire that the Galilæans be killed or beaten contrary to justice, or that they suffer any other evil, but I emphatically assert that god-fearing persons are to receive greater honour ; for it is through the Galilæans' folly that all things have been well-nigh overturned, but it is by the favour of the gods that we are all preserved. Wherefore we should honour the gods and god-fearing men and cities."³ The other letter, which we shall have to cite again, is to the people of Bostra (probably the Arabian city of that name), and contains these words : " We do not permit anyone of them [the Galilæans] to be dragged unwilling to the altars, but we expressly command them, if anyone wishes to partake with us in purifications and libations, first to offer the expiatory sacrifices and to supplicate the gods who avert evil. So far is it from us to desire or dream that any of the impious should ever desire or dream of sharing in our holy sacrifices, before he have purged his soul with supplications [λιτανείαι] to the gods, and his body with the appointed offerings." Further on, after complaining of the presumption and unruliness of the clergy and their partisans (to which we shall recur), he says that he has given them public permission to meet as they will, to offer what they are pleased to call prayers on their own behalf, but that they are not to abuse the privilege by deeds of violence and sedition. He has already held up his own policy in contrast to the partiality and persecution of Constantius, and we cannot wonder that some of the Christians while accepting the grant of toleration, felt no great thankfulness, but were inclined to attribute it less to any really liberal policy on his part than to a hatred of his predecessor combined with a desire to sow dissensions among themselves and to deprive them of the prestige of dignified suffering. The typical agitator of all times will " prefer the grievance " to its removal.

With the edicts of toleration there went a number of arrangements by which Christian symbols were removed and pagan ceremonies restored in all public places and functions. Not that the extirpation of all signs of paganism had been as yet accomplished. Some tokens, however, especially the Labarum which was borne before the army, had publicly signified that Christianity was the religion of Emperor

and Empire. These were of course, removed. Public
sacrifices were again offered and temples everywhere
reopened, though, as we have seen, no one was compelled to take part in the worship of the Gods.   An
exception is mentioned by Gregory Nazianzen[4] which
may possibly be due to a voluntary or involuntary
misunderstanding.   Julian seems to have restored
the *thuribulum* or incense altar which had previously
been one of the Imperial insignia, and to have expected every soldier (or perhaps only each member
of his own guard) who was entitled to receive the
Imperial donative, to throw a few grains of incense
on the fire.   The ceremony implied little more than
the kind of reverence which kneeling to perform
homage used to betoken in feudal times, or bowing
towards the mace in our House of Commons.
There can be little doubt, however, that such an act
could not have been performed without qualms by
conscientious Christians, and Gregory relates how
some soldiers, who had fallen into the snare, on discovering that some of their messmates regarded
the act as a renunciation of Christianity, rushed in
horror to the Emperor to implore the honour of
martyrdom which, of course, though he banished
them for their sedition, he had no desire to confer.
Among the pagan symbols which replaced the
Christian, the most remarkable are the heads of
Egyptian deities, or his own head with divine symbols, on some of his coins.   These coins, are, however, considered[5] to belong to the later part of his
reign.

Another and very important part of his religious

policy consisted in the withdrawal of a good many privileges that had of late come to be enjoyed by the Christian clergy. The cutting down of immunities by which an important part of the well-to-do classes escaped their obligation to contribute towards the expenses of the government, is part of the system of finance reform which we shall consider hereafter. Other provisions follow from his idea of entrusting to pagan officials the administration of public doles, and from his principle of recognising no official rank among the different classes or orders of Christians.

On this part of his action, the testimony of his laws and letters and of the writings of pagans and Christians is tolerably consistent. We have a letter of his to the Byzantines[3] in which he orders that no man who ought to discharge the duties of a senator shall be excused by reason of "the superstition of the Galilæans." Again in the letter to the people of Bostra, he declares that the liberty granted to the clergy does not mean that they may exercise special judicial functions or draw up wills. He naturally associates this latter power with a desire to secure to themselves the wealth of the superstitious. In the Theodosian Code[6] we have special orders that Christians who are trying to escape from the charges to which they were liable as Decurions are to be recalled to their duties, and if they have sought refuge in the houses of powerful persons, such persons are to be heavily fined, while slaves or clients who, unknown to their masters or patrons, have aided and abetted such evasion, are to suffer capital punishment. Sozomen[7] says that he "compelled the virgins and widows, who, on account of their poverty, were reckoned among the clergy, to refund the provision which had been assigned them from public sources." This demand cannot possibly have been made from the poor who were recipients of charity, and seems to point to a politic restriction of " benefit of clergy " as well as to a design for withdrawing the monopoly of charitable relief from the Christian communities and officers. Another of the advantages now withdrawn from the clergy was that of the frequent use of public means of conveyance. Ammianus[8] mentions the journeys of the clergy to their synods as sometimes, in the reign of Constantius, entailing serious damage to the finances of the state. The retrenchment might be commendable, yet we cannot wonder that it was felt to be hard, especially as free use of the public post was accorded by Julian to many of the philosophic friends whom he summoned to his court.

Few things, perhaps, caused more intense dissatisfaction, or led to more of the violent local tumults in which some enthusiasts sought and found the glory of martyrdom, than the Emperor's orders for the restoration of the temple property of which the Christians had taken possession and the rebuilding of temples that had been destroyed. It is not easy to determine with accuracy the limits of the process of refunding, which, as is natural, some of Julian's enemies represent as a case of shameful spoliation. That what had been unlawfully seized should be restored does not seem unreasonable. That no new endowments should be made from the Imperial treasury, is what we must necessarily expect. How far recent gifts were to be resumed, our authorities do not agree in telling us. The Emperor's wish to be fair is shown in the fact that not only heathen temples, but churches belonging to sects that had been recently oppressed were to be rebuilt, as was especially the case with a church of the Novatians at Cyzicus. This had been destroyed by the Arian bishop, Eleusius, who was now compelled to rebuild it, within two months, at his own expense.⁹ Any such orders, were, of course, attributed by Julian's detractors to his eagerness in sowing dissension among the Christian parties. With regard to the pagan restoration, it seems most probable that no uniform rule was followed, and that the execution of the Emperor's orders was modified by the discretion, or indiscretion, of the various provincial governors. Probably the very divers degrees in which the different regions were by that time christianised made the task much easier of accomplishment in some cities or districts than in others. On one point, however, we can have no doubt : that neither Julian's officials, nor Julian himself (who had not personally, before the days of his freedom, been withheld by conscientious scruples from assisting at rites which he hated), could quite understand, or see the justice of tolerating that compunction which made it impossible for some fiery souls to do or help to do anything that might tend to encourage or promote the " worship of devils." Hence the cases of persecution and martyrdom which must wear in the eyes of the civil government the appear-

ance of just punishment necessitated by obstinacy
and insubordination. One of the sufferers on whose
treatment the church historians and the orator
Gregory chiefly dwell, was Bishop Marcus of Arethusa. He had, says Sozomen, demolished a costly
and magnificent temple, and was now ordered to
rebuild it. Difficulty in raising the funds, combined
with religious scruples, induced him to fly. On
hearing, however, that his friends were suffering on
his account, he returned, and allowed himself to be
brutally lynched by the mob which, by a refinement
of cruelty, anointed his bruised body with honey,
and exposed him, in a rush basket, to the stings of
bees. His fortitude is said to have moved the admiration of the Præfect. A small amount would
have at the last been accepted in commutation of
the penalty, but he persisted in refusing even a
penny to what he considered the idolatrous cause.

In Arethusa, we see, the people were fanatically
pagan. In Cæsarea of Cappadocia,[10] situated in the
regions where Julian had spent many dreary years
of boyhood, it was the inhabitants of the city that
had themselves been guilty of wholesale iconoclasm
and sacrilege. Here, as was not unnatural, strict
inquisition for the stolen property was made among
the citizens, orders for rebuilding were peremptorily
issued, and meantime the fiscal privileges of the city
were reduced.

Elsewhere the orders for temple restoration led to
iconoclasm and to consequent suffering for conscience' sake on the part of zealous persons of private station. Thus, at Merus, in Phrygia,[11] three

brothers broke into a temple at night, and destroyed the newly polished statues. We are told that they were tortured with a view to compelling them to offer sacrifice, and that they perished in agony rather than soil their consciences by complying. But if this is true, the governor of the province must have been acting on his own responsibility, and contrary to the Emperor's declared and customary policy.

The point, however, about Julian's behaviour towards the Christians which is of most importance in its results on ecclesiastical history, is the equal indulgence accorded to the representatives of jarring sects, which led to changes in the balance of ecclesiastical parties. We have already seen, that, in the Arian reaction, the party opposed to the Nicene creed acquired the ascendency which it held to the death of Constantius. This party, however, was by no means united in itself. Arius, and his statesman supporter, Bishop Eusebius, had both been long dead, and while the Nicene party formed a tolerably compact band, their adversaries were divided into theological factions, which local jealousies, personal differences, and the rancour excited by Court intrigue and backstairs politics, had greatly emphasised and embittered. Without going minutely into differences of creed, we may broadly distinguish three principal factions :—that of the semi-Arians, not in all respects incapable of reconciliation with the Nicenes, though dissatisfied with the Nicene formula : the Anomœans, who stood on the left wing of Arianism : and the Homœans, whose main principle was the rejection as unscriptural and superfluous of all such terms as " of the same essence," " of like essence," and so forth.   In 359 some of the leaders of the semi-Arian and Homœan parties had drawn together and issued from Sirmium a somewhat ambiguous formula[12] to which, as they believed, or as they sought to persuade the Emperor Constantius, most men might assent without violating their principles. A council of bishops of the West was held at Ariminum and one of eastern bishops at Seleucia. Neither assembly was entirely favourable to the proposed compromise, but after a conference held at Constantinople, late in the same year, the influence of Acacius, bishop of Constantinople, and not a little pressure from the Emperor Constantius, who was eager to bring about some kind of harmony, and was easily swayed by some intriguing prelates who had secured his ear, forced a somewhat reluctant assent.   This brought about a victory of the Homœan party, and the exile of some prominent members of other factions.

To all these disputes, Julian was, of course, profoundly indifferent. As we have already seen, he had no more sympathy with one form of Christianity than with any other. If Arianism seemed to harmonise with Platonic doctrines of emanation, it deprived King Helios of his glory to give it to one who had assumed the semblance of a man ; and between the various shades of Arianism, Julian probably took no pains to distinguish. The Nicene persuasion, on the other hand, was closely identified with the one man whose energy and single-heartedness Julian had most reason to regard with aversion and dread, the exiled patriarch of Alexandria. The Emperor's first decided step in these matters was to order the recall of all who had been exiled for religious reasons. He seems next to have held a conference at Constantinople in which he vainly hoped to bring about some compromise[13] and a general toleration. "Hear me," he cried, as the voices of the disputants drowned his arguments, "the Franks have heard me, and the Allemanni." But the words, adopted from the saying of his hero-model, Marcus Aurelius, fell to the ground. If he were to establish a *modus vivendi* among Christians, it was not to be by means of any concessions drawn from the hostile camps.

Among the prelates recalled from banishment, two may be especially noticed, the one for his curious personality and wandering life, and for his friendly relations with the Emperor, the other for his commanding influence and the strength of his opposition to Julian's aims,—these are Aëtius of Antioch and Athanasius of Alexandria.

Aëtius[14] seems to have been an Anomœan, of the class of Arians furthest removed from catholic orthodoxy. Certain expressions of a different tendency attributed to him are probably less due to vacillation or to self-interest than to the delight often taken in paradoxical and sensational statements by a mind more subtle than deep. He had worked his way up from the ranks, having been left by his father, an army contractor who had failed in his business, in a state of extreme destitution, with a widowed mother to support. According to one account, he became for a time a household slave, and after he had recovered his liberty, a working tinker. The craft of a gilder seems to have been that by which, when grown up, he supported his mother and himself, till her death set him free to follow his own intellectual bent, though he returned to his gilding when more congenial work failed. His quick intellect, which shone in the logical and rhetorical disquisitions so much practised during that age, attracted the attention of certain teachers, Christians and pagans, under whom he studied at Antioch, Tarsus, and elsewhere. He seems to have acquired an ardent passion for controversy, and on being once worsted in a disputation with a heretical teacher, felt that life was no longer worth living, till, as Philostorgius says, a vision appeared to comfort him, and " from that time forth Aëtius had a special gift from God which saved him from defeat in his disputations." Subsequently, at Alexandria, he confounded a leading Manichee so completely, that the unfortunate heretic sickened and died in a few days. He had received ordination from the Arian bishop of Antioch, and seems to have used his clerical status as a means of exercising more actively his power of disputation. When the Homœan party obtained the ascendency, he was banished, and now by Julian's order he was recalled. The Emperor must have been personally acquainted with him during some period of his life, possibly when Aëtius was living in Constantinople, or else in Asia. According to one account, Gallus had employed Aëtius in a fruitless attempt to make Julian a good Christian. Julian was probably attracted by the versatile intellect of the man, and by his skill in logic and dialectic. Or there may have been another reason for showing him especial favour. Aëtius, in addition to his other occupations, had studied and practised the art of medicine, and Julian, who was very desirous of maintaining the high status of physicians, may have hoped to win over Aëtius from less fruitful fields to the useful art of healing. Accordingly he wrote to invite him,[15] in the name of old acquaintance, to come to Court, and invited him to make use, for the purpose, of the public post. He bestowed upon him a landed estate near Mitylene, in Lesbos, to which he was forced to retire when the time of persecution returned for him on Julian's death. He was, however, pursued thence, and finally closed his varied career in an intimate circle of like-minded friends at Constantinople, in the reign of Valens.

Widely different were the character and fortunes of the great Nicene champion, whom Julian's mandate recalled from his third exile. Athanasius had been violently, even treacherously ejected from Alexandria in 356, and had since that time kept up from his Egyptian retreat, by secret means, the influence which he had so powerfully exerted over both men and women who had fallen under his personal sway. Meantime, the bishopric was held by George of Cappadocia, a violent man who showed no tact in conciliating parties. While severely prohibiting the worship and usages of the Nicene party, and even, according to Athanasius, persecuting the private members of the party with a refinement of cruelty,

George enraged the pagans by parading, with ceremonies insulting to their feelings, the purification of
the temple of Mithras, and won over the governor
of the province to lend the secular arm to the execution of his religious policy, and to allow of certain
financial claims which the archbishop asserted over
the Alexandrians.[16]   This governor, Artemius, who
was in Constantinople at the time of Julian's accession, suffered the capital punishment which he seems
richly to have deserved.   George experienced a yet
more cruel fate.   He became the object of the summary justice of an infuriated mob, and his mutilated
corpse was then burned along with that of the camel
on which he had been exposed to the popular vengeance.   On hearing of this event, Julian wrote a
letter to the Alexandrians in terms of reproof tempered by compliments.   He acknowledges the great
provocation they had received from the impious man
on whom summary justice has been inflicted, but
blames them for not ridding themselves of the grievance by lawful and regular means.   He forbears to
punish them, however, in consideration of his respect
for their tutelary deities, and also his regard for his
uncle who was at one time their ruler.   At the same
time, he wrote to the Præfect Ecdicius, to cause a
careful search for all George's books lest any should
be destroyed or lost in the general plunder.   Many
of them only contain the doctrines of the impious
Galilæans, but there are also works of philosophy and
rhetoric, which Julian had previously borrowed in
order to have copies made, and he does not wish the
good to perish with the evil.

Meantime, Athanasius returned, resumed his episcopal functions, and was soon as powerful as ever in the great city itself and in the whole Eastern Church. He took prompt measures to heal old breaches and to secure common action against the danger which threatened all Christians alike. A synod of twenty-one bishops was held at Alexandria in the summer of 362, in which rules were passed for facilitating the accession of Semi-Arians to the Nicene party, and for permitting a few differences that seemed to be merely verbal. But the action of Athanasius was not within the limits assigned by Julian to the principle of religious liberty. His indignation was deeply stirred by the news that Athanasius had been baptising some high-born Greek ladies. Accordingly he wrote a very sharp letter to the Alexandrians, explaining to them that recall from exile did not involve resumption of episcopal functions, still less liberty to pursue a course of action hateful to god-fearing citizens. The offender must again be banished forthwith. The Emperor's desire was complied with, and Athanasius withdrew. " Let us retire for a little while," he said to his friends, " it is but a small cloud, which will soon pass away." While he in Upper Egypt resumed his life of dangerous adventure and of underground influence, his friends in Alexandria petitioned for his recall. This request led to another letter from Julian to the Alexandrians which displayed, yet more clearly than the previous one, his sentimental regard for the historic greatness of Alexandria, his detestation of the archbishop, and his total incapacity of recognising anything of real religion in the attachment of the Christians to their faith and to its champions. He appeals to them by the memory of their pious founder, Alexander; by the honour ever shown to Sarapis and to Isis in this their chosen city; by the ancient lordship of Egypt over Israel, which should shame them out of their adhesion to a sect sprung from the Jews; by the glories of the Eternal Sun, so vastly more to be admired than those of a mortal man; by the prosperity which the city had enjoyed under the institutions it now would fain destroy; and his appeals become threats as he insists on his determination never to recede in this matter. He wishes that all the new doctrine were embodied in Athanasius, that it might be crushed at one blow. A letter like this showed the Alexandrians the futility of halting between two opinions. It gives plausibility to the view that if Julian had lived much longer, his reign could never have been held up as one of religious toleration.

Another of Julian's acts which has met with severe criticism both from friends and foes, seems on nearer view to be logically and necessarily connected with his idea of his own mission and of the corruption of the times,—I refer to his edict prohibiting Christians from giving instruction in the public schools.

This edict we possess in two forms. In the Theodosian Code[17] there is a provision that no man shall be suddenly appointed public lecturer, but that a decree of the members of the Curial Order in each city must be obtained, the final approval being reserved to the Emperor himself. It is not certain, however, that this law was designed especially against the Christians. It might still stand under Christian emperors as a guard to public morals. Much more explicit and definite is a document published among his letters. In this he starts from certain undeniable propositions, as to the importance of good principles and right opinions in those who have to superintend the education of youth, and consistently deduces from them a system of prohibition which everyone would now stigmatise as persecuting, and which even the favourable and sober-thinking Ammianus blames as " inclemens." He states clearly that whereas teachers of rhetoric and philosophy have to expound the ancient classics, they cannot do so adequately and honestly if they consider these classics to have been utterly misguided even in all those points as to which right belief is most important. Such teachers ought, if they are honest, to give up their emoluments and confine their expositions to Matthew, Luke, and other writers whom they really reverence. They are not to be compelled to attend the temple services, but they must make choice between their educational profession and their Christianity.

What we have observed in preceding chapters on the general character of education at this time and on Julian's way of regarding Greek letters and Greek religion as indissolubly bound in one, furnishes abundant comment on this enactment. We may perhaps conclude that Julian was here more far-sighted than his critics, that whole-hearted loyalty to the philosophers and poets of old was impossible to those who studied their works merely for the form and disparaged all the underlying ideas. Had he been a little more far-sighted still, he might have discovered that by means of a classical education, however maimed and one-sided, elements of old-world culture would gradually filter into the Christian Church, and in time effect a combination of many Hellenic elements with the primitive data from Palestine. He wished, however, for no such combination, and with the hopefulness known only to a religious enthusiast, he trusted by means of sound and appreciative instruction in the great thoughts and the manifold life of the Greeks of old, to undo all the work of the centuries during which more potent influences had been undermining the Hellenic. It is possible to disapprove his policy without condemning his generous indignation against that ingratitude which would turn to account the work of philosophers and orators for purposes of Christian apology and pulpit eloquence, while reviling the memory of the great minds and characters whence that work had proceeded. Some feelings of gratitude to the teachers of old are certainly to be found in some of the broader Christian minds of the school of Origen, and even in the works of a few leaders like Augustine, but they are ever mixed with a pitying or contemptuous disparagement which might, to their enthusiastic devotees, seem more insulting than hatred.

It is not easy to say how much practical effect this edict produced. Proæresius, of whom mention has already been made, and who was personally on friendly terms with the Emperor, resigned his chair at Athens. A certain popular instructor in rhetoric at Rome, Victorinus,[18] who had been slow and reluctant in avowing his faith, but was now staunch in abiding all its consequences, also gave up his profession. A curious countermove was begun by some educated Christians who wished their children to receive a literary education without coming under anti-Christian influences. A certain Apollinarius,[19] a Syrian by birth, with his son of the same name, took upon themselves, with the approval and admiration of their contemporaries, to compose a Christian literature free from the barbarism of the canonical books. They produced a " grammar consistent with the Christian faith," a version of Bible History in epic and dramatic forms, and a Gospel improved into would-be Platonic dialogues! It was well that the Christian youth for whom this fare was produced speedily recovered permission to browse in more wholesome pastures. The genius of the vigorous barbarian races might one day be strong enough to cast into new form some part of the sacred matter brought from the East. But it was not a task to be safely attempted by the decrepit intellect of Asia or Greece.

Apart from the direct action of Julian, by laws and other acts of government, much was done in indirect ways that aroused the discontent of many Christians and challenged the criticism of the indifferent. It must have been annoying to see turncoats, like the sophist Hecebolius, who was only too ready to turn again directly after Julian's death, received

into high favour. It is melancholy to find a man
generally enthusiastic for truth and earnestness,
admiring the conduct of a pagan who had received
and held a bishopric in order to save the temples of
his diocese from spoliation.[20] Still worse was it to
see an advocate of civilisation and courtesy insult to
the face an old bishop who had come to reproach
him, even though the old man escaped with im-
punity.[21] It was a sad but undeniable fact that
city mobs when they inflicted outrages on the pagan
side, as we have seen happen at Alexandria and
Arethusa, and as was also the case at Gaza and
elsewhere, received far less castigation than turbu-
lent Christian communities, like those of Cæsarea
and of Edessa.[22] Whether it be possible for a
religious man, in possession of far-reaching authority,
to try to serve the cause of religion without ever
being guilty of any acts of unfairness or of unreasonable violence, it is hard to say. Certainly such
a height of impartiality combined with zeal was not
attained by the Emperor Julian.

Coin of Julian.   Reverse, VOTA PUBLICA: Isis suckling Horus.

NOTES ON CHAPTER X.

[1] Libanius ; *Epitaph ;* King's translation, p. 160.

[2] *First Invective*, 58 ; King's translation.

[3] Ep. 7, I subjoin a list of the principal letters of Julian on matters relating to the Christians, as chronogically arranged by
Schwarz :

Ep. 31, Recalling Bishop Aëtius, Jan., 362.

Ep. 10, To the Alexandrians, on the murder of Abp. George,
Jan., 362.

Ep. 9, To Ecdicius respecting George's books, Jan., 362.

Ep. 7, To Artabius on the meaning of toleration, between Feb.
362 and Jan. 363.

Ep. 26, To the Alexandrians, ordering the expulsion of Athanasius, March, 362.

Ep. 11, To the Byzantines, on duties of Christian senators, etc.,
May or June, 362.

Ep. 36, To Porphyry (probably treasurer) concerning George's
books, May or June, 362.

Ep. 78, Story of pagan Bishop Pegasius, between Feb. 362 and
Feb. 363.

Ep. 52, To the people of Bostra (in Arabia) Aug., 362.

Ep. 42, Edict against Christian schoolmasters, between Aug.
and Nov., 362.

Ep. 6, To Ecdicius, respecting Athanasius, Oct., 362.

Ep. 51, To the Alexandrians, reproaching their desire for Athanasius, Nov., Dec., 362.

[4] *Invective*, i, 83.

[5] By Schiller.

[6] Especially xii., tit. i., 49, 50, and xiii., tit. i., 4.

[7] v., 5 ; Bohn's translation.

[8] xxi., 16.

[9] Soz., v., 5. Socrates (iii., 11), says that the church had been destroyed by Euzoïus, the Arian bishop of Antioch.

[10] Soz., v., 4.

[11] Soc., iii., 15 ; Soz., v., 2.

[12] Τὸν υἱὸν ὅμοιον τῷ πατρὶ κατὰ πάντα, ὡς αἱ ἅγιαι
γραφαὶ λέγουσί τε καὶ διδάσκουσί.

[13] Ammianus, xxii., 5. He attributes Julian's policy, as do the
Christian writers, to a wish to increase disaffections, but the explanation seems superfluous.

[14] He bears a very bad character in the writings of the orthodox historians, but Philostorgius (iii., 15, *seq.*) gives a more favorable and interesting account of his career.

[15] Letter xxxi., (Aëtius is styled *bishop* in the heading to this letter, but he seems not to have had any particular see.)

[16] Besides the ecclesiastical historians, see Ammianus, xxii., 11.

[17] Bk. xiii., tit. iii., 5.

[18] See an interesting account of Victorinus in the *Confessions of Augustine*, book viii.

[19] Socr., iii., 16 ; Soz., v., 18.

[20] For the story of the pagan bishop Pegasius, see Jul., Letter 78.

[21] The blind Man of Chalcedon, see Socr., iii., 12 ; Soz., v., 4.

[22] See Ep., 43.

Coin of Helen: Mother of Constantine.
Reverse, SECVRITAS REIPVBLICAE.

Coin of Tarsus: Head
of the Tyche of the city

CHAPTER XI.

LEGISLATIVE LABOURS AND ADMINISTRATIVE REFORMS.

" Ἔστι γὰρ ὁ νόμος ἔγγονος τῆς δίκης, ἱερὸν ἀνάθημα καὶ θεῖον ἀληθῶς τοῦ μεγίστου θεοῦ, ὃν οὐδαμῶς ὅ γε ἔμφρων ἀνὴρ περὶ ὁμικροῦ ποιήσεται οὐδὲ ἀτιμάσει ἀλλὰ ἐν δίκη πάντα δρῶν τοὺς μὲν ἀγαθοὺς τιμήσει προθύμως, τοὺς μοχθηροὺς δὲ ἐς δύναμιν ἰᾶσθαι καθάπερ ἰατρὸς ἀγαθός προθυμήσεται."
JUL., Or. II., 89.

" Princes are like to Heavenly Bodies which cause good or evil times, and which have much veneration but no rest."　BACON.

HEN we turn from our attempt to follow Julian's ideas and course of action, in religious affairs, to inquire into his general policy of government as shown in legislation and administration, we have indeed to contemplate another side of his activity, but we do not find ourselves, as in the study of some theorist-politicians, introduced

245

to him in a new character. Julian was, as we
have seen, a highly-idealistic philosopher, called, as
he believed, to effect a reactionary reform in religion
and to direct the affairs of a vast empire. Yet he
does not appear before us in a three-fold character.
His principles of religious reorganisation were, as has
been shown, an essential part of his speculative and
practical philosophy. And his statesmanship was
entirely that of a philosophical reformer. Not that it
was visionary and unpractical, but rather it was as a
rule based upon general principles which there was
no attempt to disguise. These principles are, of
course, only such as are compatible with enlightened
despotism. Julian's Hellenism was not of the kind to
make him long to go back to the republican glories
of the Greek states in their golden days. In his letters
to great cities of old, notably to Athens, Argos, and
Alexandria, he shows, it is true, what we might
regard as an exaggerated respect for their ancient
prestige, but this respect is not accompanied by any
grants of actual power. There may have been political as well as financial objects in Julian's attempts
to encourage municipal life and prosperity. There
may be something more than mere sentiment in the
deference which he paid (as already narrated) to the
Roman Senate and to old Roman republican usages.
But republicanism in its essential principles was at
that time so far beyond the range of practical politics, that no man of sense could dream of restoring
it. It is possible that Julian scarcely knew that it
had been destroyed, or realised how much the world
had changed since the days of Aristotle's Politics,

just as few people of our day distinguish the difference between our government and that which existed at the passing of the Bill of Rights. As "shepherd of the people" he aimed at the general prosperity, not at the extension of political freedom. Liberty might still furnish themes for rhetorical exercises. The politician, whether philosopher or not, had very little concern with it except in the universally undesirable form of rude license in city mobs.

In one sense, of course, every man who engages in public life and in abstruse speculation at the same time must feel that he is leading two lives. Action and thought must ever call forth different faculties and necessitate the contemplation of life from different stand-points. This contrast was very strongly felt by Julian himself.[1] But the nature of public affairs in his day was such as to make the contrast less conspicuous than at most times and places. Firstly, there was little scope in the Empire at that time for anything like state-craft. There were no rival foreign powers to be dealt with by skilful diplomacy, unless we may regard the relations of the border states between the Roman and the Persian Empires as furnishing a field for that art. If they did, the field was not skilfully cultivated by Julian. And in domestic affairs, there were no distinct political parties to be balanced against one another, and dealt with by measures of compromise or of subjugation. There were, of course, ecclesiastical parties, but Julian would have disdained to steer between them. The favour he showed to the Jews was due, in all probability, to a certain limited sympathy with them and a hatred for those that rivalled them, rather than to any scheme of balancing their influence against that of the Christians. Then again the character of all legislation and of administrative orders under the Empire had been imposed on it by juristic theorists who loved order and elegance, and liked to give reasons for every step that was taken. Vested rights and interests and considerations of temporary expediency might be lightly set aside. On the whole the task of legislation might seem to a philosophical prince one well worthy of his best efforts.

Under the term *legislation* we must include much that was of the nature of temporary enactment. The commands which were issued by Julian, and against which there was no appeal, have generally come down to us in the form of instructions issued by him to Prætorian Præfects, Governors of provinces, and other officials. Many of these were afterwards admitted into the Code published by Theodosius II. in the year 438, although even among these a large number must before that time have ceased to be operative. Others we find interspersed in the collection of his letters public and private. Of others again we know the general purport from statements made by the historians and orators. Many must have perished, and with regard to many more our indications are slight and indefinite. Yet enough remains to enable us to discern generally the difficulties with which any ruler of the Empire had to contend, and the ways in which Julian endeavoured to meet them.

The two great and cognate evils which seem to have been felt through the length and breadth of the Empire were the uncertain and imperfect administration of justice and the crushing and unequal weight of the public burdens. These diseases were too deeply seated to be amenable to satisfactory methods of cure. But palliative measures might be devised, and such measures we see in Julian's legislation. The object everywhere seems to be to tighten the control exercised by the central authority over all public officers, judicial, financial, and military. An attempt is made to alleviate undue pressure in some quarters, even at the risk of offending powerful persons; temporary distress is met by measures of temporary relief, and economy is sought in Imperial and public expenditure.

The historian Ammianus [2] describes Julian's regard for equity and right as being such as to fulfil his aspiration of restoring to mankind the goddess of Justice, who had been banished afar by human vice and iniquity. Ammianus goes on to say that in his legislative policy, at least, there were exceptional cases in which he was inconsistent with himself. These were such as concerned his religious measures, in which, from our point of view, not much inconsistency appears, and also those wherein he showed himself indifferent to certain class-privileges, as to which the views of Ammianus may seem to us less enlightened and impartial than those of his master. Libanius is less reserved in his laudations, and he states very emphatically that the actual business of jurisdiction was to Julian not only a serious duty but a keen pleasure. And when we consider what the law-courts were, and in what direction Julian's education and temperament had directed his tastes, we can readily believe that listening to disputations was often to him a refreshing amusement after military and financial business. Libanius says [2] : " Though he had it in his power to leave this fatigue to the most learned and incorruptible of judges, he nevertheless offered himself for one of those that try causes, and stripped himself for the combat—unless anyone objects to the word and says that law-cases were no *combat* for him, but rather a diversion and a rest ; so easily did he repel the deceptions of the advocates and seize upon the right thing in each affair, testing false arguments by true ones with incredible quickness of wit, refuting and baffling quibbles by means of laws." [3] He goes on to describe Julian's conduct in a way that would make him guilty on one occasion of something very like a quibble. A plaintiff was using papers which the Emperor strongly suspected of being forgeries. Nevertheless, as the opposite party had not detected or proved the deceit, the Emperor, "as slave to the law" gave his decision in favour of the forger, along with a reprimand for his crime. " In this way he contrived not to infringe the law and yet to punish the culprit." But the justice to be obtained from the Imperial court was usually of a more substantial and less pedantic kind, or it would hardly have happened that, as the orator subsequently relates, the court was flocked to by suitors of all kinds who sought refuge from oppression and wrong.

There were three ways in which the judicial action of the Emperor might be applied to the settlement of individual cases.[4] By means of a *supplicatio*, one party to a suit could, before the trial, request from the Emperor either a personal hearing, or a letter of instructions to a special or to the ordinary judge. As a rule the rescripts in accordance with the *supplicationes* were drawn up by secretaries, and the decisions pronounced by *judices* without any personal intervention of the Emperor. But Julian, as we have seen, enjoyed the hearing of causes, and probably many more were judged by him in first instance than by his predecessors and followers.

It is the maintenance of the two other methods of Imperial intervention, however, that is the object of special precaution in Julian's legislation : the *appellatio* and the *relatio*. The *appellatio* was the process by which recourse was had *after* the decision of a case by any magistrate under the rank of a Prætorian Præfect, to the judgment of the Emperor himself. Such final judgment might be delegated to a special commissioner, or might be pronounced by the Emperor in his *consistorium*, which was a kind of State-Council comprising the chief officers of the Imperial household. Or he might settle the matter personally in the Senate of Rome, or in that of Constantinople, which received from Julian powers and privileges equal to those of the Roman Senate. In the Theodosian Code, we have laws of Julian's second year, to facilitate and regulate appeals from lower judges to higher, and from the higher to the Emperor himself.[5] Such appeals must be made within thirty days from the passing of the sentence, the necessary written statements must accompany the appeal; and the arrangement of such cases must be consigned by the provincial *Vicar* to some specially appointed official. If such appeal has, by means of terrorism, been hindered within the legitimate period, it may, on cause shown, be still held valid.

The third method was that of the *relatio* or *consultatio*. In some difficult cases, the judge, after hearing statements and evidence, was expected to send the information to the Emperor and await his decision. In one of Julian's laws,[6] complaint is made that many *Rectores* have failed to do their duty in this respect, and such as shall offend again are sentenced to a heavy fine.

Besides hearing and providing for the hearing of difficult cases, both in first instance and on appeal, Julian exerted himself to facilitate the administration of justice generally, to correct anomalies, and to deliver those seeking redress from the chicanery of the unscrupulous advocates who, if the descriptions of Ammianus are to be trusted, constituted the bane of the whole system.[7] An inscription of his reign has been found at Amorgos, containing provisions for the hearing of petty cases.[8] He made it impossible to claim back money that had been paid for unlawful purposes, especially for that of bribery.[9] He repealed a law of Constantine allowing married women under age to sell their property.[10] He put an end to the system by which litigants postponed the day of trial, while they summoned as parties to the suit men living at great distances.[11] He made it un-

lawful for a commission to expire with the death of
a principal party to a suit. It seems strange that
laws should have been needed to assert that in ordinary cases long custom should be followed, but two
of Julian's laws make this provision against arbitrary
innovations.[12]

More important, perhaps, in his own eyes and in
those of his contemporaries, were the measures he
adopted for moderating and equalising the public
burdens.[13] We have already seen that the population
of the whole Empire was heavily taxed, and taxed
in a way that seemed to cause the maximum of suffering and discouragement with the minimum of
substantial advantage. The land, industry, and com-
merce, were subject to heavy dues, and in general
the responsibility for regular payment, both of Imperial and of local taxes, rested with the body of
leading and well-to-do citizens of every community
who constituted the body of *Curiales* or *Decuriones*.
This system was fatal to enterprise and to local patriotism. Those concerned with the assessment of
taxes naturally endeavoured to restrict individuals
within the hereditary industrial corporations from
which payment could be most effectually levied.
And the citizens who from wealth and status should
naturally have been the leaders and protectors of the
people came to have no more eager desire than to
escape from a dignity of which the obligations were
so much more conspicuous than the privileges. In
these circumstances, Julian's objects, as those of any
serious financier in like case, were two-fold: to diminish, by economical government, the amount re-

quired to meet demands, and to prevent, by very strict enactments, the evasion of burdens by those on whom they would naturally fall.   He also endeavoured on some occasions to act directly on the immediate causes of local distress by issuing directions to merchants and tradesmen.   In this last expedient, as we shall see when we come to narrate his dealings with the people of Antioch, he was not eminently successful.   Here we will consider chiefly his broader lines of economic legislation.

Julian's prompt and decisive measures of palace reform, which have been already described, were probably dictated as much by philosophic aversion to luxury as by maxims of financial policy.   Important as an economic reform, however, was his regulation of the number of Imperial guards.   He prescribed the rations to be allowed to those that attended his person, and stopped the distribution of supplies to those who ranked as supernumeraries.[14] He issued a decree as to the distance from their quarters at which the pay of the soldiers on march was to begin.[15]   But the economy which he seems to have most earnestly and effectually endeavoured to achieve was in connection with the *Cursus Publicus* or Public Post.[16]

From the early times of the Roman Empire, the maintenance of a good system of communication between the distant provinces and the capital had been a most essential requisite of orderly government.   This necessity had led to the laying down of those magnificent roads which still seem to testify to us more powerfully than anything else which survives,

of the resolution of the Romans in their undertak-
ings, and their persistency in accomplishment. But
if our imagination would recall the appearance of
these roads in the fourth century, it must people
them with parties of travellers, hastening to transact
their own business or that of the State, riding or driv-
ing the animals most suited to the locality and to the
object of the journey: oxen, horses, mules, camels,
or asses; and we must furnish those roads with
convenient stages, some being mere halting-places
for the change of beasts (*mutationes*) others accommodated with everything that a wearied or a luxurious
traveller could desire to lighten the fatigues of his
journey and ensure the comfort of his rest (*man-
siones*). Now the maintenance of these halting-places,
the constant supply of carriage-animals, of beasts of
burden, and of food and drink for man and beast,
necessarily involved very heavy expenses, which
fell on the heads of the luckless *Curiales*. In earlier
times, some of the stronger and more statesmanlike
Emperors (notably Hadrian) had endeavoured to
relieve the provinces of so intolerable a burden by
ordering that the expenses of the *cursus publicus*
should be defrayed from the Imperial *fiscus*. Before
the time of which we are now treating, however, the
burden had been relegated to the provincial authorities, and the testimony of historians and orators alike[17]
shows us how they groaned under it. It was felt to
be the more galling in that those who were locally
responsible derived little if any benefit from the
arrangements they had to keep in working order.
The postal system was, in the Roman Empire, not

designed to facilitate the journeys of private persons, or the conveyance of their goods and letters. It was reserved for the use of those who held high positions under the Imperial government and also, especially after the time of Constantine, for the rapid transfer of military bands and of all that appertained to the soldiery, including even wives and children. At the same time, the higher officials had the power, extensively used also by the Emperors themselves, of issuing free passes (*evectiones*) for distances of a certain length, which sometimes (*tractoriæ*) even included free and comfortable accommodation at the halting-places. When synods of bishops were frequently held, their use of these free passes was an object of bitter complaint. At the same time the Imperial agents who travelled to-and-fro on their journeys of inspection were often hated as spies, whose visits could well be dispensed with on other than economic grounds. And it is evident that under an emperor as easily swayed as Constantius, rapacious officials had ample opportunity both of obtaining means of travelling free of expense for themselves and their friends, and of diverting to private uses many of the provisions of animals, carriages, and various necessaries, destined to public purposes.

This abuse of the public post-system, Julian, according to the testimony of both friends and foes, set himself energetically to correct. True, he continued to grant free passes to the philosophic and other friends whom he invited to his Court, but this seems a legitimate and not excessive use of the Im-

perial right. The historian Socrates says : " The
mode of public travelling and conveyance of necessaries he also reformed, abolishing the use of mules,
oxen, and asses for this purpose, and permitting
horses only to be so employed. These various re-
trenchments were highly lauded by some few, but
strongly reprobated by all others, as tending to bring
the Imperial dignity into contempt, by stripping
it of those appendages of pomp and magnificence
which exercise so powerful an influence over the
mind of the vulgar." [18] Libanius [19] after drawing a
hideous picture of the sufferings of overtaxed cities,
delayed and angry travellers, and overworked beasts
that fell dead when taken out of the yoke, says :
" This disorder, also, Julian put a stop to, by prohibiting all posting that was not absolutely necessary, and by declaring licences of this kind equally
dangerous to grant and to receive ; as well as by
instructing his officers, some to keep beasts of their
own, others to hire them when wanted." He goes
on to say that from this time forward those who
kept the public animals were obliged occasionally to
give them exercise,—a proof of the cessation of over-
work.

But our best evidence of what Julian did to reform
the system is to be found in those of his laws which
afterwards formed part of the Theodosian Code.
One of them, after complaining of the sufferings en-
tailed by the frequent grants of *evectiones* by those
who held the position of *Vicar* or of *Præses* of a province, withdraws the power of granting such privileges from the lesser officials and restricts it to the

17

Prætorian Præfects. The minor magistrates may
have a limited number of *evectiones*, signed by the
Emperor's own hand, but all use of the public conveyances shall be strictly in pursuit of necessary
business. The way in which provincial magistrates
shall arrange for the transport of military stores is
provided for, and care is taken that the extent of the
license granted in an *evectio* shall not be widened
through ambiguity in terms. The *mancipes* or contractors for public work, may use the *cursus* with the
consent of the proconsul, but any use for private
buildings is very strictly prohibited.[20]   In Sardinia[21]
where the use of horses was not generally profitable
and convenient, the provincials need no longer keep
such in readiness, though vehicles for transport of
stores must still be held at command. Those who
want to ride must use their own horses. It is perhaps but fair to Julian's predecessors and successors
to say that many of their laws seem to have been
directed to the same objects. But his were so dras-
tic in character, so numerous considering the short
period of his rule, and apparently so effectual for a
time, that we are justified in noting the reform of the
postal system as a specially characteristic part of his
domestic policy.

The construction and maintenance of roads was
not regulated on exactly the same principles as the
public post. They existed for the benefit of the
public, not of the government only. There were
no tolls on the Roman roads, and the work of construction and repair seems to have been apportioned
by lot to certain private persons, probably the land-

owners of the districts through which the roads passed. A law of Julian's demands such apportionment, and pronounces the responsibility to lie with the individuals to whom each part had been respectively assigned.[22]

But even when public works constructed on the scale of those of the Roman Empire are managed with a view to securing economy and good order, they must still require vast sums for their maintenance, and the demands on some classes are apt to become ruinously heavy. Julian's policy in assigning financial duties involved three principles of action: liberal concessions of immunity in case of real poverty: the granting of exemptions only to such persons, or classes of persons, as were most to be encouraged: and the strict insistence that none should escape such duties who could have fulfilled them, but who preferred to shift them off on to the shoulders of their neighbours.

Among the concessions was one made to the Thracians, in answer to a petition from them. The Emperor in reply[23] explains that it would not be fair to the public that he should grant entire remission, but he promises that part of the tax shall go to maintain the military force which guarantees to the Thracians peace and security, and that for two periods, nothing shall be levied at all. He remits the excessive tribute demanded from the Jews,[24] and promises to try to induce their patriarch to lessen the burdens which his authority imposed upon them. The customary gift of golden crowns is no more to be demanded. The province of Africa is excused

from the payment of arrears,[25] except such dues as
consist of the precious metals. In one document[26]
the nature of the exemption granted is liberally
defined. Those that were excused from the land-tax
were also to be free from the payments in kind
which went to make up what mediæval lawyers
called *purveyance*. The mutual claims of separate
cities received the Emperor's attention ; thus Corinth
was forbidden to gather unauthorised tribute from
Argos.[26a]

Among the classes that received special exemption
from ordinary payments were the highest, or official,
who had long enjoyed it,[27] the physicians,[28] to whom,
following here the footsteps of Constantine, he
wished to accord special favour, and those government
secretaries or clerks who had served in the offices
for fifteen years, with the semi-military *agentes in
rebus* who had accomplished a certain length of service, also citizens who had reared thirteen children,
and soldiers who had served in ten campaigns. In
general, however, Julian was most anxious to prevent the curial duties from becoming confined to an
ever-diminishing class. His law forcing the Christian clergy to fulfil their duties in this respect has
already been cited. Honorary citizens who had
accepted the franchise while still owing curial duties
in other cities are not to be excused from the burdens of their new citizenship except under special
circumstances. Particular care is to be directed to
the nomination of substantial persons. It may be
that in this way Julian aimed at the improvement of
the municipal administration as well as at the regular

and equitable provision of funds. Libanius says that the desire to escape from municipal duties had made the governing bodies of some cities to resemble ragged and decrepit old women.

A difficulty of another kind attended the apportioning and levying of taxes in country districts. Julian had to provide, as many mediæval and even modern legislators have had to do since, that when land is sold or sublet, the State loses none of its dues. No man is allowed to contract himself out of payment of the land-tax.[29]

We have a good many laws on various matters which do not come strictly under the heads of justice or public finance. We have the appointment of a tester to guarantee the quality of coins, where disputes arise as to buying and selling. There is also a law to give security to land-occupiers who have enjoyed possession for four months,[30] and one regulating the force of marriage contracts.[31] A curious law about funerals[32] might be regarded as belonging to his religious legislation. Funeral processions in the daytime, and the disturbance of graves or removal of ornaments therefrom are strictly forbidden. We have already seen, and we shall have to observe again, the disgust and contempt that Julian felt for the custom of translating the bones of martyrs, and of making their shrines a kind of temple. The edict as to the appointment of professors and schoolmasters, as we have it in the Code, is not specially directed against the Christians, and might be used by the Emperor to ensure the appointment of men of good character.

In general we may say of Julian's legislation that although, in its main objects, it resembles that of such of his predecessors and successors as aimed at the alleviation of the evils from which the whole Empire was suffering, and to which it was doomed finally to succumb, yet it is notably distinguished by a very vigorous effort in the direction of retrenchment and reform, an evident desire both to do justice and to let it appear clearly that justice is being done, and a conscientious regard for the people whom he regarded as committed to his care.

As we have mentioned Julian's measures for alleviating the oppressions felt by the Jews, we may here consider his general policy towards that people, with a very curious episode in his life, his attempt to restore the city and temple of Jerusalem, and its remarkable frustration. Although we have references both to the enterprise and to its failure in the writings of Julian himself and a narrative of the affair in Ammianus, and in the Church historians and orators,[33] yet some points require to be cleared up. According to Ammianus, he undertook the rebuilding of the Temple at great expense, and gave the conduct of the scheme to his learned and trusted friend Alypius of Antioch, who had formerly superintended the government of Britain.[34] But although Alypius set vigorously to work with the assistance of the *Rector* of the province, the operations were speedily hindered by alarming globes of fire, which burst out close to the foundations of the building, rendering the prosecution of the work impossible and killing some of the workmen. The attempt was therefore

Coins selected as illustrations for Chapter V.

Coin of Constans I.
Reverse, FEL IX TEMPORUM REPARATIO.
Constans and Victory on a ship.

Coin of Antioch.
Time of Diocletian.

Coins selected as illustrations for Chapter XI.

Coin of Smyrna.
Cybele on her throne.

Coin of Tarsus. Imperial Times.
Obverse, Tyche of city. Reverse, seated Zeus.

Coins selected as illustrations for Chapter VII.

Head of Isis.
Pharia.

Coin of Nisibis.
Tyche of city.

Coin of Tarsus.
Victory.

abandoned. When we compare this meagre account with other references or narratives, we see that very various views may be taken as to Julian's motives in the undertaking, the share of the Jews themselves in the enterprise, and the nature of the final catastrophe.

Julian's enemies saw in his attempt a blasphemous endeavour to prove the nullity of certain passages in the Prophets and the Gospels which would seem to imply that the restoration of the Temple was never to be accomplished. It seems, however, that only a very forced interpretation of those passages is consistent with this view, and that any such predictions if drawn from the Old Testament might have condemned the enterprise in the eyes of the Jews as well as in those of Christians. Nor can Julian have been actuated by any great affection for the Jews themselves or any hope of "making them pagans" as one of the Church-historians says. But when we consider the light in which (as already shewn) he regarded the Jews and their religion, we seem to find a clue to our difficulty in the statement of Socrates: that he asked the Jews why they did not offer sacrifices according to the Mosaic ritual, and on being told that this ritual could only lawfully be followed at Jerusalem, he ordered them to set about rebuilding Solomon's Temple, and promised to defray the expenses himself. Now as we have seen, Julian objected to Judaism as a universal religion, but thought it respectable and even admirable as a national cult; it was inferior to Hellenism, of course, as Jews were inferior to Greeks, but if it was suited to the genius of the Jewish people, they were right in maintaining their traditional loyalty to it. Now if Judaism were once again localised and nationalised, it would take its proper place among the religions of the world.   There need be no more fear of proselytism among the adherents of more civilised and enlightened systems, nor would the religion of Israel figure any longer as the forerunner of the religion of Christ.   To restore to it those national and ritual accompaniments of which it had lately been deprived would make it cease to be a rival force against the new and purified Hellenism, while the difference between Jews and Christians would tend thereby to be accentuated.

If this was Julian's idea, was the first attempt to realise it made by the Jews themselves, or how far did they co-operate?   The answer to this question is differently given in different accounts.   It is certain, however, that there had been a good deal of uneasiness and disaffection felt among the Jews. Very severe laws had lately been passed against any attempt at proselytism on their part, and they may well have hoped for some relief from an Emperor whose views differed so widely from those of Constantine and his sons.   We know, too, from the letter already cited, that Julian had corresponded in a friendly way with the Jewish patriarch, whose name of Hillel he hellenises into Ἰουλος, and of whom he speaks as "my brother"—probably in reference to his own office of *Pontifex Maximus*. Most of the authorities tell us that the Jews were eager to help, both with labour and money, and if this is so, the statement that the whole undertaking was to be at Julian's own expense needs some modification. In his letter to the Jews, Julian says that he hopes, on his return from the Persian Wars, to see the holy city which will have been restored by his labours, and there, with them, to give thanks to the Most High. Meanwhile, he asks for their prayers.

With regard to the catastrophe, the most probable hypothesis is that there was an earthquake, similar to many of which we read in not very distant regions about this time, with some kind of conflagration. As to the nature and also the exact place of the fire, our authorities are confused. The narrative of Gregory represents the flames as issuing from a sacred place to which people had fled in alarm at the tempest and the earthquake, and this has led to a conjecture[35] that in the confusion, a mob of Jews assaulted the Church of St. Helena, and were repelled with burning brands. In any case events and circumstances were eminently favorable to the growth of an impressive and harrowing tale. Probably Julian was somewhat easily led to believe that the Powers were against his proposal. He referred to the event afterwards as an illustration of the mutability of earthly things. It were idle to speculate as to what might have been the result if he had persevered. But we cannot believe that the alliance between neo-Hellenism and reactionary national Judaism could possibly have been very firm, or of long duration.

(For designs of coins selected as illustrations for this chapter, see page 262.)

NOTES ON CHAPTER XI.

[1] See especially his Letter to Themistius.

[2] xxv, 4.

[3] c., 583 ; King's translation, pp. 178-9.

[4] See Willems, *Le droit publique Roman*, pp. 611, 612, and authorities there cited.

[5] Cod. Theod., xi., 30.

[6] Cod. Theod., xi., 31.

[7] See his description of these vampires in xxx., 4.

[8] See Haenel, *Leg. Imp.*

[9] Cod. Theod., ii., 29., *cf.* Ammian., xxii., 6.

[10] Cod. Theod., iii., 1., 3.

[11] Cod. Theod., ii., 5., 1.

[12] Cod. Theod., v., 12., and xi., 16.

[13] See Schiller, iii., i. Sec. 6.

[14] Cod. Theod., vi., 24. 1.

[15] Cod. Theod., vii., 4.

[16] For the Roman system of Public Post, see Dr. E. E. Hudemann's excellent little treatise *Geschichte des Römischen Postwesens während der Kaiserzeit.*

[17] See especially Ammianus, xix., 11, xxi., 16 ; Libanius, *Epitaph.* 569, etc.

[18] iii., 1., Bohn's translation. Hudemann (p. 144) thinks that this regulation tended to limit the use of the *cursus velox* as distinct from the *cursus clabularis.*

[19] viii., 5., 12., *et seq.*

[20] This explanation of viii., 5., 15., has been kindly given to me by Dr. J. S. Reid, who considers *canalem* to mean here a trench from which marble is cut. He suggests that the public contractors were often also engaged on private buildings, so that it would be hard to stop irregularities ; but commentators seem to take *canalem* as meaning a cross-road.

[21] viii., 5, 16. This law is sometimes attributed to Jovian. The change, as Hudemann shows, is to abolish the *cursus velox*, retaining the *cursus clabularis.*

[22] xv., 3., 2. But the text is here doubtful and obscure.

[23] Ep. 47.

[24] Ep. 25.

[25] Cod. Theo., xi., 28.

[26] xi., 12., 2.

[26a] Ep. 35 : but on the authenticity and probable occasion of this letter, see Cumont, p. 21.

[27] xiii., 3., 4. ; vi., 27, 2.

[28] xii., 1., 55., 56. See xii., 1., 50, 56.

[29] xi., 3., 3.

[30] Symmachus 10. 39. (*apud* Hænel)

[31] Cod. Theod., iii., 13. 2.

[32] ix., 17, 5.

[33] For Julian's dealings with the Jews, and attempt to rebuild the Temple see Ep. 25, Fragm. Ep. 295, *Am. Mar.* xxiii., 1., and all the Church historians, especially Socrates, iii., 20 ; Sozomen, v., 22, and (the marvellous element increasing like a snowball), Theodoret, iii., 20. Also Gregory Nazianzen, *Second Invective*, 4.

[34] Epp. 29 and 30 are addressed to Alypius.

[35] Of Mr. C. W. King. *Julian the Emp.* p. 88. Julian's relations with the Jews and his attempt or project to rebuild the Temple are discussed in an able and interesting article by the Rev. Michael Adler in the *Jewish Quarterly Review* for July 1893. With regard to the general subject, Mr. Adler shows clearly that Julian must have been intimately acquainted with Jewish institutions and with the Hebrew Scripture, though not with the Hebrew language. He also shows, by quotations from the Talmud, that some of the arguments used by Julian against the Jews, formed part of the stock-in-trade of controversial Greek philosophers. As to the Temple : Mr. Adler's conclusion is that the rebuilding was merely contemplated, never actually taken in hand, and that the whole miraculous story (missing from contemporary Jewish writings, and from the Syriac account written in the sixth century) was a fiction of Gregory Nazianzen. The question is certainly a difficult one, but though the passage in Julian's writings is interpreted by Mr. Adler consistently with his hypothesis, it is difficult for us to allow that Ammianus copied from Gregory. The absence not only of any record of the enterprise, but of any grateful recollection of Julian himself from contemporary Jewish writings is a puzzling fact, and some writers, *e. g.* (Prof. Gwatkin) have thought they have found such recollections. We might suggest that the same historical conditions which, on Mr. Adler's theory, nipped in the bud the good-will and gratitude felt by the Jews towards Julian may also have silenced their tongues as to the unfortunate issue of his well-meant attempt on their behalf.

Medal of Maximian.
Obverse, Head of Maximian with attributes of Heracles. Reverse, three female
figures with cornucopiæ, signifying wealth.

CHAPTER XII.

LITERARY RECREATIONS.   CONTROVERSY WITH
THE CYNICS.

δίδωσιν ὁ θεὸς παίζειν.
Convivium, 306, A.

" Or let my lamp at midnight hour
Be seen in some high lonely tower,
Where I may oft out-watch the Bear,
With thrice-great Hermes, or unsphere
The spirit of Plato."   MILTON, *Il Penseroso*.

I N studying Julian's relations to the
philosophical and religious parties of
his time and his labours in the camp
and council-chamber, we become
impressed with three facts as to his
enterprises in the world of literature:
first, that all through his life, and not
much more at one period than at any other, he is to

be regarded as a most industrious and prolific man of letters; second, that all his literary labours were closely associated with the projects and the accomplishments of his active life ; and third, that from the day on which he left Athens for Milan, literature was regarded by him as a recreation, noble and elevating it is true, and even worthy of great sacrifices of time and ease, but still as subordinate to the main business of his life. His delight in books and in literary controversies seems to have been gratified chiefly during the hours that he stole from sleep. This fact, though creditable to him as a conscientious ruler, is not without some undesirable effects on his literary works. To most readers, they may smell of the lamp, and they certainly bear marks of haste. When we read that the *Oration in Honour of Helios* was composed in three nights, that the *Oration against the Cynics* was the work of two days, and that the *Oration in Honour of the Mother of the Gods* and that *Against Heraclius the Cynic*, were each finished in one night, we are astonished at the swiftness of his powers of thought and utterance. A calm and thorough treatment of his subject we cannot, under such circumstances expect to find. Perhaps we may console ourselves for the hastiness of the composition by reflecting that more time might have given scope for a more elaborately artificial style. Orations composed as a labour of love, and amid the stress of serious occupations, bear at least the trace of not having been produced by a *mere* orator.

Considering the rapidity with which Julian wrote

or dictated, we can easily believe that many of his writings have not come down to us. Besides those that we possess, there are said to have been, along with other treatises, a narrative of his wars in Gaul,[1] and a *Cronica*[2] which some would identify with *The Cæsars*. Those which we have cannot all be precisely assigned to accurate dates.[3] There is little doubt, however, that it is to the period of his life with which we are now concerned, that we may attribute the most finished and elaborate of his works: *The Cæsars*, the *Oration in Honour of the Mother*, and most likely one at least of the orations against the Cynics.[4] It was probably during the next year, at Antioch, that he wrote the other oration against the Cynics, as well as the anti-Christian writings already considered, and the *Misopogon*, which we shall naturally consider in treating of his relations with the Antiochenes. His *Oration in Honour of Helios* may belong to either year. As we have already examined Julian's religious and philosophical opinions as indicated in his theological writings, we may now look at some of his writings on their literary side, though, as we shall see, morals and religion figure largely in all that we have from his hand.

Besides his prose writings, we have a few little pieces of verse generally attributed to Julian, of which two only are of some interest. These two represent the Greek mind contemplating for the first time two institutions destined to become important in western civilisation, beer and the manual organ. Julian seems to have made the acquaintance of the

favourite barbarian beverage during his residence in
Gaul. He dislikes the smell of it, regards it as a poor
substitute for the noble gift of vine-growing lands,
and is inclined to attribute it to Demeter rather than
to Dionysus. The wonder which he feels on behold-
ing a musical instrument the pipes of which are
metallic and the wind of which is supplied from
leather bags instead of coming from a human chest,
is significant and has afforded some light to the historians of the musical art.[5]

The Cæsars is a satire in prose written for the Saturnalia of the year 362. Its object is professedly
playful, though to the modern taste the jesting may
seem a little heavy, and the interest lies chiefly in
the dramatic way in which the scenes and the persons
are brought before us, and in the light thrown on
Julian's views as to history, and his judgment on his
predecessors on the Imperial throne.

He imagines that Romulus or (to call him by his
name after deification) Quirinus, when celebrating
the Cronia, summons all the Gods to a banquet, and
likewise all the Emperors of Rome. The Gods seat
themselves on their resplendent thrones on Mount
Olympus. The Cæsars have their feast prepared in
the regions about the moon. The Gods sit and observe the Cæsars as they enter. Silenus places himself next to Dionysus, to whom he acts as a peda-
gogue, and makes jocular remarks throughout. In
fact he is represented as a kind of court-jester to the
Gods, and his fooling constitutes the comic element
of the piece.

The Cæsars approach one by one. First comes

Julius, whom Silenus taunts with an ambition that would fain dethrone Zeus himself, and with a boldness equal to the jester's own. Next Octavian, changing colour and demeanour like a chameleon, and trying to captivate Aphrodite and the Graces, till Apollo turns him over to the typical Stoic philosopher Zeno, to be made into a sensible man. Then Tiberius, fierce and foul, before whom Silenus brings up some of his evil deeds. Caligula wears the aspect of a wild beast, and is seized by Diké and given over to the Furies for punishment. Claudius is twitted by Silenus as being a nobody without his freedmen and his wife. Nero comes in imitating Apollo with cithara and laurel, but is speedily disgraced by that indignant god. Vindex, Otho, Galba, and Vitellius rush in amid wild confusion, thickening the air with the smoke of burning temples and cities, till Zeus and Sarapis order Vespasian to go and quench the conflagration. Of Vespasian's two sons, Titus is allowed to sport with Aphrodite ; Domitian is chained with a collar as a dog. Against Nerva, Silenus has no objections to make, but he grumbles at the Gods for allowing to so good a ruler such a short reign. Zeus, however, promises a succession of better emperors. Trajan enters, carrying his trophies. Then Hadrian playing the lyre and busying himself with many things. Antoninus Pius is rallied by Silenus on his stinginess. Marcus Aurelius and Lucius Verus enter in fraternal harmony. Even Silenus is moved with respect, though he has a word of criticism for the indulgence shown by Marcus to his wife and his son. Commodus stumbles and

PRIMITIVE ORGAN.

falls, unable to follow the path of the heroes. Pertinax enters bewailing his sad fate. Diké bestows her pity on him, but blames his share in the conspiracy against the son of Marcus. It is noteworthy that the next Emperor, Didius Julianus, receives no mention. His name was one that the present Emperor had no wish to preserve from. oblivion. Severus comes in looking so fierce and stern as to crush all the mirth out of Silenus. His sons are summoned to justice by Minos. Geta is admitted, but Caracalla sent away to punishment. The blood-stained Macrinus and the effeminate Heliogabalus are forced to fly. Alexander Severus seats himself apart and laments his misfortune, while Silenus rallies him on his leaving everything in his mother's hands. Valerian enters with his prison-chains about him, Gallienus luxurious in apparel and effeminate in countenance. Both of these are prohibited by Zeus from coming to partake of the banquet. Claudius (who, as we have seen, was Julian's ancestor) is received with acclamations, and the throne is promised to his posterity after him. Aurelian appears flying from those who would have him tried for his severities before the tribunal of Minos, but Helios (who had been a special object of his veneration) interposes, declaring that he has sufficiently expiated his violent deeds. Probus receives honour as a builder of many cities, but Silenus reads him a little lecture against over-harshness. Carus and his sons are driven away by Diké. Diocletian comes in attended by Maximian and his son, and by the older Constantius, who treats him with a

reverence which he declines to accept. He gives all
his baggage, however, into their hands, that he may
walk unencumbered. The Gods approve the harmo-
nious union of the company, but Maximian is
chased away on account of his impurity. Licinius
is turned out by Minos, Constantine seats himself
and keeps his throne for a long time, and his sons
come in after him. Magentius is rejected because
what good he has effected has not been done from
good motives.[6]

On the completion of the company, Hermes pro-
poses, and Zeus approves, a trial of strength among
the Cæsars. Romulus is anxious to have one of
them selected to receive divine honours. At the
request of Heracles, Alexander the Great is admitted to the competition. As no one makes way
for him, he takes the vacant seat of Caracalla. A
discussion thereupon arises between Silenus and
Romulus as to the relative merits of this one Greek
and of all the Romans. Romulus asserts that his
descendants honour Alexander above all other strangers, but not above all their own heroes.

The method of the trial is next discussed, and it is
decided that, as in ordinary Greek sports, the prize
shall be adjudged to the victor of those who have in
their turn vanquished the others, so that not all need
contend in one heat. Accordingly chosen champions are called out. Alexander has been already
summoned to the contest. Hermes calls up three
other great conquerors, Julius Augustus, and Trajan. At the request of Cronos, Marcus Aurelius is
added, to represent philosophy. He obeys the call,

approaching with dignified mien, his personal beauty undiminished by the traces of his heavy labours or by the simplicity of his attire. Dionysus would also admit a man of pleasure. Zeus will not allow such an one to enter the sacred precincts, but Constantine is allowed to come to the entrance. These champions are now called upon each to make a speech in his own behalf, after which the Gods, who love truth above persuasiveness, are to submit them to a more searching examination. A water-clock is to limit the time allowed to each one's oration. Finally Hermes utters a metrical summons to the lovers of glory, of wisdom, and of pleasure, the lots are cast, and Julius Cæsar begins the day. Cæsar seems to regard Alexander as his special rival. Accordingly he boasts the superiority of his conquests, showing especially how much more formidable a rival was Pompeius than Darius. He compares his lesser wars with the great ones of Alexander, and contrasts his own forbearance with Alexander's violence. Alexander retorts angrily that though Cæsar disparages him, it was from him that example had been taken in Cæsar's career. He speaks slightingly of Pompeius, shows how *he* had not, like Cæsar, taken up arms without cause against his country ; proves the superiority of Greeks to Romans by pointing to the embarrassment caused to Rome by Ætolia ; taunts the Romans with not having conquered the Persians ; claims for himself the honours of a follower of Heracles ; and justifies his severities in the camp except in a few cases of violence where the deeds had been followed by " the saving goddess " Repentance.

Augustus, against whom Poseidon bears a grudge, and who is consequently stinted of water for his time-measure, extols, when his turn comes, his conclusion of the Civil Wars, his friendship for philosophers, his restorative measures in the State, and his moderation in keeping the Empire within its due limits, and in withstanding temptations both to ambition and to self-indulgence. Trajan, blustering in speech (since he had been accustomed to leave oratorical displays to others), points to his Getic and Parthian Wars, the latter of which time had not permitted him to finish. Silenus reminds him of the length of his reign in comparison with that of Alexander. Stung by his jest, Trajan makes a fresh start, and appeals to the fact that his most vigorous actions have always been tempered by clemency. This is allowed to be in his favour by the opinion of the Gods. When Marcus begins to speak, Silenus prepares to hear some sophistical quibbles, but in this he is disappointed. The philosophic Emperor makes no speech, but commends himself to the judgment of the Gods, as to those who are already entirely acquainted with all his actions. Constantine, knowing himself to have preferred, in life, the allurements of ease and pleasure to the claims of justice, is for a while afraid to compare his deeds with those that have just been recited. On being obliged to speak, however, he boasts the superiority of his achievements over those of Alexander, in that he has fought against nobler races of men, over those of Octavian because of the more pernicious character of the tyrants he has destroyed, and over those of Trajan

since he has again subdued the lands that Trajan
had conquered. The silence of Marcus he interprets
as giving consent to those claims. Silenus puts him
to the blush by comparing his accomplishments with
the artificial basket-gardens that were carried in procession at the festival of Adonis, but had no permanent root or vitality.

In order to eliminate the effects of fortune from
the achievements of the Cæsars, the Gods institute
an inquiry into the ruling principles of the lives of
each. Alexander confesses that his object has been to
conquer all, but Silenus accuses him of having fallen
a slave to wine and to his own passions. The hero
vainly tries to save his reputation by logical quibbles.
Cæsar's object was in all things to be first. But he
failed, Silenus says, in gaining the love of the people.
That of Augustus was to rule well, which he explains, on being pressed, as meaning to rule for-
tunately. Silenus taunts him with being a great idol
manufacturer, in that he had begun the apotheosis of
the emperors. Trajan's aim in life had been the
same as that of Alexander; but he had suffered himself to be overcome by pleasures. That of Marcus
was to imitate the Gods; not, as he is made to explain, by living on nectar and ambrosia, but by following the divine reason, by contenting himself with
little, and by doing good to as many as possible.
When Silenus brings up his unwise treatment of his
wife and son, he appeals to the authority of Homer
as to the kindness due to a wife and the indulgence
shown by Zeus to his son Ares; he adds that he
could not tell what an evil disposition Commodus

would develop, and that the honours conferred on him and on Faustina were merely customary. The object of Constantine had been to obtain for himself and his friends as much enjoyment as possible. Silenus accuses him of wishing to become a money-changer and ending in the trade of a cook and barber, and he is again put to a shameful silence.

After deliberation, the Gods award the palm to Marcus, but all the Cæsars are to be honourably dismissed, and each may choose a tutelary deity as his special protector. On hearing this, Alexander chooses Heracles, and Trajan runs after him; Octavian turns to Apollo, Marcus to Zeus and Cronos. Cæsar, vacillating, is chosen and patronised by Ares and Aphrodite. Constantine fails to find in any of the Gods the image of the life he desires. He follows after Wantonness, who leads him to Intemperance, and, followed by his sons, he seeks from the Founder of the new religion the purification which the older and sterner Gods would deny. The Gods would persecute him, but Zeus spares him, in consideration of his ancestors Claudius and Constantius, and grants to Julian himself the perpetual protection of Mithras.

A sketch like the foregoing gives an inadequate notion of the character of this little piece, which shows considerable dramatic power, besides spirit in conception and facility in expression. The bitterness against Constantine, as well as the somewhat unkind treatment of some previous emperors, is an indulgence allowed under the satiric form of the composition, yet it cannot be regarded as creditable to Julian's fairness, especially as Constantine does not figure in history as a mere votary of self-interest and pleasure. There can be no doubt, however, that Julian regarded the recognition of Christianity as the opening of a door to all manner of licentiousness, and his severity towards the memory of his uncle is due to this opinion. The idea of the whole and the way in which it is executed shows a remarkably vivid realisation of history on the part of Julian, who always felt, so to speak, on close and familiar terms with great men of bygone days. Another characteristic feature is the modern, almost Christian standard of virtue acknowledged in the stress laid on the clemency of Trajan, the philanthropy of Marcus, and the penitence of Alexander. The point which naturally surprises us, in relation to the known views of Julian on such subjects, is the liberty taken with the names and even the personalities of the Gods. That Silenus should be made to act as a buffoon, and that Dionysus should not always appear dignified, is no matter for wonder, but though certain of the Gods, especially Zeus and Cronos, are treated with some respect, yet at least one jest is levelled at the " father of gods and men." This attitude of men towards the pagan pantheon is, of course, familiar to us in satiric and comic writers of the best classical period, but it is not in accordance with Julian's views as expressed elsewhere. We must not, however, regard the power of jesting with sacred symbols as inconsistent with respect for their authority. There was much fooling with the conceptions of sacred lore in the mediæval " ages of faith." Of all the faculties and proclivities of the human mind, none vary so much from age to age in their quality and mode of expression as do the sense of reverence and the sense of humour. If some of Julian's jests seem to us ponderous, it does not follow that he entirely lacked Attic salt. And if his treatment of divine beings would seem to us irreverent, we may not conclude that he had not a profound respect for the objects of his worship.

As to the source whence Julian derived the plot of his little play, Dr. Mücke would regard the first part as suggested by the wall-scene of the Third Book of the *Iliad*, and the second part by the competition between Æschylus and Euripides in *The Frogs* of Aristophanes. But the plan of introducing historical personages into rhetorical compositions and moralising under cover of their names, was, as we have seen, a favourite one among the literary men of that age, and one to which Julian was likely to feel attracted.

The two orations against the Cynics, while bearing marks of hasty composition, and of some bitter feeling against opponents whose influence seemed detrimental to the interests of religion and philosophy, are full of interest, both in showing us Julian's attitude of mind towards various philosophical sects and practical questions of his day, and in throwing some light on a curious and little-studied school of thinkers and moralists.

Julian's seventh oration *Against the Cynic Heraclius*, deals with the question " Is it consistent with Cynicism to make use of allegories or myths?"

From his own account, Julian had felt his indignation aroused in listening to a discourse from a wandering Cynic teacher, who was telling stories of a kind that tended to diminish the reverence in which the names and persons of the Gods were held among men. He consequently examines into the uses and abuses of the parabolic or allegoric method of treating religious and moral subjects, showing how such a concession to human weakness is contrary to the original idea of so stern a system as that of the Cynics, and how, when it is used, it should always be as a means of religious education. Some of the principles he lays down are hardly in accordance, at first sight, with his own practice in the composition of *The Cæsars*. But, as we have said, it is difficult for us to judge of the feelings towards the Divinity expressed in that piece. It is evident that what Julian most dreaded and disliked was the representation of the Gods under a purely human form, or the assumption on behalf of actual known men of the attributes and names of divine beings. And in *The Cæsars* the all-seeing, superhuman powers of the Gods are exhibited, as far as is possible, in the form of a tale. The oration against Heraclius contains a model-story by Julian himself, setting forth his own mission as he conceived it, a story that is written in pleasing and tasteful style, and that one may imagine to have been produced earlier, for a private circle of friends, and brought in here by way of illustration. He describes the estate of a rich, avaricious, and careless land-owner, on whose death there had been a general scramble for his possessions, disgraced by

bloodshed, marriage of near relatives, and spoliation
of temples. In this grievous state of things, which
represents, of course, the Empire after the death of
Constantine, Zeus appeals to Helios, and they call
the Fates to take counsel with them. It may be
noticed that Julian here makes the Fates subservient
to Zeus, while Helios is almost equal to him, and
acts as a ready executor of his decrees. The decision
is reached that a little neglected nephew of the rich
man shall be rescued from the general destruction,
and placed under the special charge of Helios and
Athene. But when this child is grown to early
manhood, he is overpowered by the sense of the
family miseries and longs to hide himself in Tartarus. Now, however, Athene and Helios cause a
deep sleep to fall upon him, and in a vision Hermes
conducts him by a rugged path into a fair flowing
plain, and thence to a high mountain where dwells
the Father of the Gods. Hermes then vanishes,
and the boy beseeches Zeus,—whether that name or
any other is best pleasing to him,—to show him the
way to himself. Helios then appears, and the youth,
in an ecstasy of joy and devotion, vows that he will
ever follow the service of that deity. He is found
to be but imperfectly armed, yet Helios and Athene
tell him that he must return to earth, to accomplish
the task assigned to him. He is prepared for the
task by initiation, and by a vision of his kinsman
indulging in ease while his possessions are being
wasted by knavish herdsmen. Helios prepares to
set the boy in his kinsman's place. At first he en-
treats to be spared the labours of such a position,

but on being threatened with divine displeasure, he promises loyal obedience. Hermes returns to act as his homeward guide. Athene gives him three parting counsels: never to prefer a flatterer to a friend; to be watchful against hypocrites; and to honour the Gods and godlike men. Then Helios comes forward with a final exhortation. He enjoins the boy to use his friends as friends, not as mere servants; to love his subjects as the Gods love him; to trust in the divine power always working with him; and never to minister to his own fleshly desires or to those of other people. He is to receive a torch from Helios, so that the divine light may keep him from desiring the things of earth; a helmet and ægis from Athene, and a golden staff from Hermes. After a last injunction to be faithful, Helios dismisses him with the promise that if he is true to his purpose, and uses his body as an instrument to that end, respecting his soul as immortal, he shall at last become as a god, and be admitted to the vision of the Father.

The last part of the oration, which is very rambling in style, is devoted to the same object as the sixth oration *To the Unmannerly Dogs*, wherein he tries to convict the Cynics of his own day of a falling off from the moral greatness of the founders of the sect.

The philosophers whom Julian attacks might be called Neo-Cynics, as others of the day are Neo-Platonists and Neo-Pythagoreans, for Cynicism, like other philosophical systems, had taken a new lease of life, and tried to adapt itself to changed condi-

tions, when Greek thought and life had interpene-
trated the moral and intellectual organisation of the
Roman Empire.[1] Originally, the sect was Pre-
Socratic, but though the founder of the School,
Antisthenes, had struck out his particular line of
thought before he became acquainted with the great
Athenian, yet he seems to have discerned in the
teachings of Socrates all that he had taught and
more besides, and to have been ready to merge his
pupils and his doctrine in those of a nobler and
wider teacher. But the phase of Socratism which
he represented was distinct enough to form the
nucleus of a special school, and the remarkable personality of Diogenes emphasised yet more strongly
its peculiar practical characteristics. Of these two
and of Crates, the third among the leaders of the
early Cynics, Julian speaks with great respect, and
in order to understand his relations to them and to
their degenerate successors, we may trace very
briefly the character of their doctrine in its origin
and its decline.

Unlike other schools of Greek philosophers, the
Cynics had no theory of nature or of human life,
and they despised all thought that did not bear
fruit in action. Their root-idea may be summed up
in one word: self-sufficiency ($\alpha\dot{v}\tau\acute{a}\rho\kappa\epsilon\iota\alpha$). In Greek
history we are constantly familiarised with the polit-
ical principle that each state should be able to provide its own necessaries, luxuries, and means of
defence. This idea of self-dependence, transported
from the sphere of politics to that of individual life,
becomes the corner-stone of Cynic morality. If

analysed, it is found to involve several far-reaching consequences. It reduces to a minimum the goods to be considered necessary for life and happiness. The Cynic can dispense with a comfortable home and warm clothing, and all but the simplest food and drink. He must be free from all the vices that tend to weaken mind and body. Again, Cynicism involves independence of the ties of nationality and of social conventions. Diogenes, who first adopted the designation κοσμοπολίτης, said boldly that the wise man was not bound by the laws of the state but by those of virtue. His motto, many times cited by Julian, παραχάραξον τὸ νόμισμα ("forge" or probably "countermark money"), is a pregnant one, and it is natural to suppose that these words, imperfectly understood, may have given rise to the whole story of the forgery and punishment of Diogenes in his early days.[8] It has been conjectured[9] that they may refer to the practice of striking afresh with the proper die of a State the coins brought into it from abroad, in order to proclaim their legal value. This signification would agree excellently with the interpretation given by Julian,[10] but whether the literal application is to the coining, the forgery, or the countermarking of money, the meaning evidently is that no established usages, however high their traditional authority, are to be accepted as binding on the philosopher until they have obtained his individual assent and received the stamp of his approving reason and conscience.

As might be naturally expected, the Cynics cared little for art and literature and still less for meta-

physical speculations. Books were worthless to
them in comparison with the principles stored in the
mind; difficult questions were best solved by practice; abstruse terms had no significance to those
who cared only for practical life. Their contempt
for tradition and authority extended to matters of
religious belief and observance. The early Cynics
were not atheists, but they ridiculed the popular
mythology, held aloof from national rites, and denounced prophets and soothsayers as contemptible
charlatans, while they received with a scornful scepticism all suggestions of a world after death. Thus
Diogenes, in words quoted with approval by so religious a Hellenist as Julian, asked a youth who desired initiation into the mysteries: " Thinkest thou
that in Hades the initiated publicans will enjoy
bliss, while Epaminondas and Agesilaus are wallow-
ing in the mire?" The idea that righteousness of
life is necessary in a man who would enjoy the Divine favour is strongly maintained by the leading
Cynics, and it may have disposed many noble-minded
men to regard them with indulgence while feeling
both repugnance and fear at their general destructive tendencies. Their chief merit is their respect
for reality and hatred of cant in every form. Antisthenes, like Socrates, insisted on definitions of terms
in common use, and ridiculed some of the extrava-
gances of popular democracy. In their dealings
with their neighbours, the influence of the Cynics
tended to sweep away unmeaning distinctions and
to clear up the mists of prejudice. They despised,
or affected to despise, the verdict of the vulgar, yet

A POET, OR PHILOSOPHER.
IVORY DIPTYCH.

respected human nature as capable of achieving the highest excellence. Diogenes declared that virtuous men are the best likenesses of the Deity.

The third of the Cynics, Crates, though by no means an attractive character as depicted by Diogenes Laërtius, seems to have been a man of singularly noble and upright life, if we may judge by some details given by Julian [11] as well as from some verses of his, cited both by Julian and by Clement of Alexandria.[12] His prayer was that he might have enough of the necessaries of life to be free from servile anxiety, that he might be useful, not merely agreeable, to his friends; and that his treasure might not be of material things, like that of a beetle or an ant, but of righteousness, from which he might offer sacrifices to Hermes and the Muses. He had given up all his property, and passed his time in trying to reconcile enmities and feuds among his friends.

Few, however, of the Cynics of the succeeding generation approached within a measurable distance of the moral elevation of Crates. For a considerable space of time, there seems to have been no men of note belonging to the school, and meantime what was most admirable in their teaching had become the possession of another sect, that of the Stoics. The doctrine of the Porch strongly resembles that of the Cynosarges, but toned down, and made more compatible with social order and intellectual culture. Not that the Stoics confined their efforts to a mitigation of Cynic doctrine by the negative process of eliminating its harsher elements. Rather may they be said to have penetrated to its central idea and to have given it a wider and grander significance. The aim of both sects was the same : " to live according to Nature"; but while the Cynic referred all things to his own individual nature, his wants, preferences, and idiosyncrasies, the Stoic rose to the conception of a universal nature embraced by one undeviating law, to the authority of which all individuals, whether Gods or men, must be subservient, save only the supreme law-giver Zeus. And while cosmopolitanism in the Cynic sense probably meant little more than a capacity for living under very diverse conditions and for regarding men in general apart from their nationality, the genuine Stoic felt his citizenship with all men on earth who were with himself mutually dependent on the kind offices one of another, and bound with him in obedience to the common law of Nature.

Accordingly when Cynicism again lifts its head in the first century of our era, it appears as a kind of left wing of Stoicism. The *raison-d'être* of Neo-Cynicism is to be found in the need of a practical protest against the novelties and the follies of a superficial and highly conventionalised society. The best representative of the school (who, however, is not mentioned by Julian), Demonax the Cypriote,[13] was a friend of Epictetus, and the Cynic Deme-trius was friendly with Seneca. One of the disserta-tions of Epictetus [14] shows the very respectful attitude towards Cynicism taken by the best of the later Stoics. The philosopher is here arguing with a youth who, in his enthusiasm for the Cynics, thinks

of adopting their mode of life. The tone of Epictetus is like that of a pious Catholic towards an eager
aspirant after the monastic life. He tries to show the
young man how great is the honour at which he is
aiming, and induces him to think well before com-
mitting himself to a course which may prove beyond
his moral strength to attain. For a Cynic who has
no dark corners in his life should be as pure as sunlight in all his thoughts and ways, and his function
towards his fellow-men is to act as a messenger sent
from Zeus to guide them into the paths of virtue.

Now between the time of Epictetus and that of
Julian, Cynicism had had about two and a half centuries in which to degenerate. The whole system
lent itself with peculiar ease to caricature, and it was
ever likely to attract followers from among those
who regarded it chiefly as a means of emancipation
from social restraint and who developed to a high
degree its most repugnant features. And these certainly were very unamiable. As Julian well says,[16]
Cynicism is like a noble city, abounding in sacred
temples and stately houses, whence everything that
might excite disgust or suggest meanness and squalor
had been ejected without the gates, so as to greet
the traveller on his approach. And apart from the
essential ugliness of their system, Julian had some
special grounds of dislike against the Cynics of his
day. Heraclius, against whom he wrote *Oration VII.*,
seems to have shown a servile deference to Constantius and an absence of regard for Julian himself.
He had also, following the fashion of the Cynic
Œnomaus, controverted the religious beliefs of

19

those who adhered to the Hellenic worships, and used scurrilous language on subjects that lay very near to Julian's heart. He regards the Cynics as playing into the hands of the Christians, and as following the fashion of those Christian ascetics who had won glory for themselves and support from their co-religionists by affecting a mode of life superior in sanctity to that of the vulgar. At the same time, he regards this assumption as a mere pretext to hide luxurious and unrestrained habits indulged in private. And finally, as a Neo-Platonist, Julian felt no sympathy with the Cynic tendency to depreciate all culture and to set aside all traditions of the past. But since his own morality was, as we have seen, entirely of the Stoic type, he shows the same reverence as does Epictetus for the pure and uncorrupted principles of the original Cynic code, and for the characters of the three great Cynics. The special function of Cynicism is, he says, to teach by deeds, as other philosophers did by words, how it is possible to scorn convention and live according to the simple dictates of Nature. But the Cynics of his day are false to their mission. They keep the outward garb of the sect, yet they indulge their lowest appetites, truckle to those in power, use smooth words to captivate the vulgar, instead of giving the warning bark of the watch-dog, and, worst of all, they speak with impious license against the Gods. In vigorous and earnest language, Julian exhorts them to examine and see whether they have sufficiently overcome the " many-headed monster " within to be able safely to set all human conventions at defiance. If they have a hankering desire after the good things of this life, they should avoid touching them even with the finger-tips. Let no one be so bold as to neglect outward decency, as Diogenes did, till he has shown himself equal to Diogenes in all his nobler qualities. For it is not the coarse cloak, the wallet, and the staff that make the Cynic, but rational discourse and a well regulated life.

In the course of his discussion, Julian dwells on certain principles which have been already shown to lie at the basis of his whole system of thought and morals—the essential unity of all philosophy ; its practical aim ; the obligation to live above-board and to have no secret corners in the soul wherein unworthy desires and thoughts may lie concealed [16] ; and beyond all, the need of an infinite aspiration after a Divine life to enable men to live purely and bravely on this earth.

Although Julian regards the Cynics as leagued against him with the Christians, we find, in the Christian Fathers the almost unanimous expression of a sentiment closely corresponding to that of the Emperor, as to the disgusting boldness and contemptible charlatanry of the wandering Cynic teachers. True, the Fathers themselves many of them forged weapons against pagan superstitions from the material provided by the destructive works of Œnomaus and others. Yet Justin,[17] Chrysostom,[18] and Augustine[19] cite the Cynics as examples of shamelessness and hypocrisy. In times a little later, we find them associated, in the minds of a few writers, with some early Christian communities of ascetics, nor is it impossible that there may have been some intercourse between such Christian communities. But to trace the subsequent history of Cynicism, and the relation of Pagan to Christian asceticism lies far beyond our present task. The controversy between Julian and the Cynics illustrates the many varieties of schools and intellectual tendencies with which the Emperor was at various times brought in contact, and also his worthy ambition, in the case of all non-Christian sects, except perhaps the Epicurean, to do justice to the elements of truth contained in their teaching, while guarding against all dangers of extravagance and one-sidedness in thought and action.

Reverse to medal of Constantine.
Seated figure receiving a trophy
and gifts.

Constantine the Great.
Bronze medallion.

NOTES ON CHAPTER XII.

[1] Zosimus, iii., 2.

[2] Or. iv., 157, C.

[3] For the chronology of Julian's writings, see the pamphlet of Schwarz which I have frequently cited, pp. 6–15.

[4] See Libanius, *Epit.*, 574. Schwarz thinks that Or. vi. must have been composed at midsummer, and so before he left Constantinople, from a reference to the solstice in p. 181. But the proof does not seem to me conclusive.

[5] Version of Julian's epigram on the Organ (given by E. A. G.) :

> Strange reeds are these ; surely it is a crop
> Wild-springing from another " brazen field."
> No human breath that shakes them, but the blast,
> Springing from leathern cave, is led along
> Beneath the roots of various piercèd reeds.
> And a skilled player, nimble of his hands,
> Touches the rods that commune with the pipes
> And lightly dance and so press out the tune.
>
> (*Cf.* Hopkin and Rimbault, *History of the Organ*, p. 15.)

[6] It seems rather strange that there should be no mention of Galerius, and that Magnentius should be placed among the lawful Emperors.

[7] See an interesting monograph by Bernays, *Lucian und die Cyniker*, published as an Introduction to his translation into German of the *Death of Peregrinus*.

[8] See his biography, by Diogenes Laërtius.

[9] For this suggestion I am indebted to Prof. P. Gardner, who was led to the supposition from his studies of numismatics.

[10] Especially in Or. vi., 188 ; and Or. vii., 211.

[11] Especially in Or. vi., 201.

[12] *Stromata*, ii., 492. Jul., Or. vi., 199.

[13] See the very charming life of Demonax, attributed to Lucian, but probably not from the same pen that wrote the *Death of Peregrinus*.

[14] III., 22.

[15] Or. vi., 186, 187.

[16] For the idea as to the absence of all need for secrecy in a well

regulated life, compare the first of the new letters in the Μαυρο-γορδάτειος βιβλιοθήκη.

[17] See his *Second Apology*. He calls the Cynic Crescens, φιλόψοφος, φιλόκομπος, and φιλόδοξος.

[18] Homily xvii.

[19] *De Civ. Dei*, (lib., xiv.).

Coins of Antioch.

A Goddess in her Temple.   Tyche of the City.

CHAPTER XIII.

JULIAN AND THE ANTIOCHENES.[1]

362–3.

μήποτε οὖν, ὦ φίλε, νομίσῃς εἶναι ἐλεύθερος, ἄχρις οὗ
γαστὴρ ἄρχει σου . . . οἵ τε τοῦ παρασχεῖν τὰ πρὸς
ἡδονὴν καὶ ταῦτα ἀποκωλῦσαι κύριοι, καὶ εἰ τούτων δὲ
γένοιο κρείττων, ἕως ἂν δουλεύῃς ταῖς τῶν πολλῶν δόξαις,
οὔπω τῆς ἐλευθερίας ἔθιγες, οὐδὲ ἐγεύσω τοῦ νέκταρος.

JULIAN, Or. vi., 196, C.

> How happy is he born and taught
> That serveth not another's will—
>
> . . . .
>
> Whose passions not his masters are,
> Whose soul is still prepared for death
> Untied unto the worldly care
> Of public fame or private breath. —WOTTON.

HILE planning and executing the various administrative reforms and the literary works, controversial and playful, which we have just been considering, Julian was engaged, throughout the year 362, in preparations for a renewal of the Persian War. He must indeed have regarded the prosecution of that war as

one of the duties involved in the acceptance of the Imperial dignity. Nor, considering the ruined state of the frontier provinces, and the constant danger of a serious invasion, can we regard that view as in any sense unreasonable. Whether, as some of the Church-historians say, the death of Constantius encouraged the Persians to attempt more daring enterprises, or, as seems more probable, the accession of a prince who had already won great military fame in the West, led Sapor at once to desire negotiations, Julian must have felt sure that he could only win a secure and honourable peace by forcing the Great King to feel more respect for the Roman arms. It seems, therefore, hardly reasonable to charge him with rushing needlessly into war,[2] still less are we to regard his Eastern campaign as part of a great plan for crushing the Christians everywhere. Doubtless, a successful war would have done much to increase his authority, and so would have facilitated many of his projects of reform. But apart from any such consideration, the continuation of the Persian War was inevitable. And Julian determined that, if he led an expedition at all, it should be on a grand scale.

The length of time which elapsed before the campaign was actually begun, and which is rather remarkable, considering the usual celerity of all Julian's enterprises, is to be accounted for partly by the Emperor's anxiety to set on foot the reforms we have been considering, and partly by the extent of the preparations required. These preparations were carried on first at Constantinople and then at

ANTIOCH AND THE ORONTES.
STATUE IN THE VATICAN.

Antioch. Early in the year 362 he received ambassadors from many Oriental states, including Armenia,[2] and probably discussed terms of co-operation in the war. It was most likely in the early summer[4] that he left Constantinople for Antioch. He had named as officers of the army Victor and Hormisdas, the Persian fugitive whom we have already seen in the company of Constantius. They probably had to direct the muster of troops and the gradual transference of the various companies from Europe into Asia.

Julian and his immediate attendants did not pursue the most direct route into Syria. He seems to have chosen to visit those cities which most required his presence or which were most interesting to him from considerations of religion or of old acquaintance. He stayed on his way at Nicomedia, a city familiar to him in his younger days, which had lately suffered from a terrible calamity: a great portion of it had been shaken down by an earthquake. Julian explored the ruins, exchanged greetings with those of his old acquaintances who remained in the reduced and impoverished city, and contributed a considerable sum of money towards the work of restoration. After proceeding to Nicæa, he turned southwards to visit Pessinus in Galatia, in order to do honour to the famous abode of the Great Mother. He then went on to Ancyra, the inhabitants of which seem to have been of litigious nature, for they overwhelmed him with complaints and difficult questions, of a public and of a private character. Here, as elsewhere, Julian sought to show the dif-

ference in his disposition from that of his predecessor, by treating with scorn all accusations based on
an interested sycophancy. On hearing that a rich
citizen had ordered a purple robe, he ordered that
his accuser should convey to him a pair of purple
shoes. In examining into claims of exemption from
public duty, he showed that stern determination to
let no man off too easily, of which we have seen
abundant traces in his legislation.

On his way from Phrygia to Cilicia, through Cappadocia, Julian wrote a pleasing letter [5] to a certain
philosopher named Aristoxenus, whom he did not
know personally, bidding him come to him at Tyana,
and show that there was at least one pure-blooded
Greek dwelling in those lands. He is not to hesitate
to place himself among the Emperor's friends. All
are naturally friends to one another that have the
same aspirations towards what is best. Similarly at
Pylæ, on the Cilician frontier, Julian welcomed an
old philosopher-friend, Celsus by name, now acting
as *Rector* of the province, and took him up into his
chariot. Wherever Julian went, he was likely to
pick up philosophers by the way and add them to
his cortège, as Frederick William of Prussia picked
up giants for his guards. He passed on through
Tarsus, and arrived at Antioch just as the inhabitants were celebrating the festival of Adonis. The
sounds of mourning which accompanied the doleful
ceremonies seemed to betoken an unhappy issue to
the sojourn thus inauspiciously begun.

It needed, however, neither omens nor prophet to
predict that Julian's relations with the Antiochenes

THE CILICIAN GATES.

were not likely to continue easy and cordial. The
physical and moral atmosphere of the voluptuous
city which Ammianus calls " Orientis apicem pul-
chrum " was almost as dangerous to Julian as it had
proved to his brother Gallus. He might be proof
against its enervating influences, but the contentious
spirit which ran riot among the people was not so
easy for him to withstand. The great drawback to
his achieving any measure of success was that while
the city was divided into numerous factions, not
one of them seemed to the Emperor deserving of
sympathy, and his conduct ended in setting them
all against him and in wellnigh uniting the seldom
unanimous city in a common aversion to himself.
The Christian majority was divided into three parties, to all of which he desired to do justice as he
considered it, without feeling the slightest interest
in the points at issue. At Antioch, while Arianism
or Semi-Arianism had of late been dominant, the
section which held the Nicene creed was again divided, on what seems to have been a purely personal
question, into two factions that could never worship
together. The Pagan minority, while not very
zealous for their religion, loved dearly everything
of the nature of games and shows. The contempt
of amusements and the ascetic mode of life always
exhibited by the Emperor were not likely to com-
mend his creed to those whose chief associations with
the Pagan deities were of luxurious and indecent
oriental rites practised in the temples and groves of
Daphne. The sober and moral element among the
people to which, in the next generation, John

Chrysostom could appeal, was equally incapable of appreciating his anti-Christian zeal and enthusiasm for sacrifices. The sect of Pagan-Puritans with whom he might have expected to feel some sympathy, the Cynics, were not unrepresented here, but, as we have seen, he disliked them as depreciators of culture and as unfaithful to their original principles. He felt no sympathy with the cry of the lazy mob for bread and games, still less if possible with the covetous eagerness of the rich to profit by the necessities of the poor. He was anxious to reduce public expenditure, but had no toleration for the lazy longing to escape all public burdens. And a series of events occurred which speedily brought into play all the latent causes of mutual disaffection.

There was, however, one man in Antioch who enjoyed the esteem both of Julian and of the Antiochenes, and who seems to have tried, with some measure of success, to mediate between them. What Libanius tells us in his autobiography[6] and his orations is certainly to be taken with a grain of salt, and it is by no means always consistent with itself, but his account of his relations with the Emperor at this time seems in the main fairly in accordance with what we know of the characters of both. Libanius thought it beneath his dignity to wait on the Emperor before he was specially summoned. He desired that the Emperor should miss his presence and inquire after him. Julian did so, at a sacrifice made in the temple of Zeus Philios, and sent him a message on a tablet which gave the sophist an opportunity for repartee. Libanius continued to absent

himself, considering, apparently, that the Emperor
had not been sufficiently cordial in his advances.
But by waiting he obtained his reward. Julian sent
for him, made what Libanius interpreted as an
apology, and invited him to the mid-day meal.
When Libanius replied that he could only eat late
in the day, Julian asked him to come in the even-
ing. Even the excuse of chronic headaches did
not make the Emperor impatient. Libanius finally
promised to come when invited, and from that time
forth the two had many " feasts of reason " together.
Libanius refused, he says, all offers of offices and
emolument, and the Emperor was delighted to find
a man who cared more for his friendship than for
his power of rewarding his friends. Consequently,
when Julian had quarrelled with the Senators, Libanius spoke on their behalf without incurring the
Imperial displeasure. He was chosen to make an
oration when, at the beginning of the year 363,
Julian entered on the consulship in company with
Sallust. The Emperor seems to have bestowed on
the sophist compliments to his heart's content. He
corresponded with him after leaving Antioch for
Persia. He promised, Libanius says, to receive
favourably communications from the offending citizens if uttered by their illustrious representative. If
all the Antiochenes had been of the mind of Libanius, the months which Julian passed among
them would have been pleasanter and more peaceful
for both parties.

At first Julian won favourable opinions from the
common people by his assiduous and strict adminis-

tration of justice, though they probably felt more
puzzled than pleased when he prevented them from
wreaking their wrath against Thalassius, a former
opponent of Gallus, by saying that the quarrel belonged primarily to himself, and by settling it without
delay.   In a similar spirit he accorded full pardon
to one Theodotus of Hierapolis, who grovelled before him as he went to sacrifice on Mt. Casius, and
confessed, what Julian had already heard, that he
had petitioned Constantius, on his last march eastwards, to send Julian's head for exhibition in his
native town.   Such men were scarcely worth pun-
ishing.   Others of more formidable character received harsher measure.

But the favour he might win in the law-courts
was lost again in the temples and the senate-house.
The extravagance of Julian's sacrifices might constitute a real grievance in a time of scarcity, and sensible men were provoked by spectacles of gorging
and drunkenness resulting from the festivals among
the soldiery, especially the Petulantes and Celtæ,
who often had to be carried home incapable to
their quarters.   Julian boasted of his barbarian
fighters that the mimes and other amusements of
the refined Antiochenes seemed to them utter mad-
ness.   Yet he felt obliged to indulge some of their
grosser proclivities if he would retain their allegiance
and keep them well affected to the Gods of Greece.
Some of his measures, however, were of a kind not
only to arouse disgust among the right-minded, but
to stir up a fiery fanaticism among the vulgar.

Antioch stood almost above all other cities of the

time [7] in the magnificence of her buildings,—the
palace of kings and emperors, the baths, race-course,
theatre, and aqueducts, with the shady porticoes
running along the evenly laid streets, delightful to
the ease-loving citizens, and the temple and statues
of the Gods.   Here, as elsewhere, the honours paid
to royalty, to the people, and to the Divinity were
closely associated in thought and deed, for some of
the emperors who had been benefactors of the city
received in it Divine honours, and the races which
delighted the citizens were run in honour of the
Gods.   In fact, Daphne, a beautiful suburb some
miles from Antioch, had been made by the successive benefactions of Seleucid princes and Roman
emperors, into a little Elis, where stood a noble
temple of Apollo, built by Seleucus, and one of
Zeus, the foundation of Antiochus Epiphanes, each
containing a colossal statue of the God.   Here at
the traditional seasons were celebrated races and
other contests modelled on those of Olympia, and a
temple dedicated to Nemesis was supposed to indicate the severity of the contests and the justice of
the awards.   There were other sacred places in the
neighbourhood, to say nothing of numerous temples
in Antioch itself.   There was a celebrated temple to
Zeus on Mt. Casius, where a sacrifice by the Emperor Hadrian (a great benefactor of the city) had
been miraculously consumed.   But the choicest
abode of the tutelary gods of Antioch was Daphne,
where they declared their will by means of sacred
streams. One of the most famous of these Castalian
wells had long ago been closed, it was said, by the

prudence or the superstition of the Emperor
Hadrian. This Julian determined to reopen, and
accordingly he issued orders for its purification, by
the removal of all bodies that had been buried in
the vicinity. Now during the rule of Gallus, a protest had been made against the Pagan orgies which
at times defiled the Daphnic groves, in the shape of
a transference to that spot of the bones of the martyr Babylas. Julian naturally resented this, and he
also felt disgusted at the neglect into which some of
the sacred rites had fallen. In the late summer, on
the occasion of a great festival, he went to celebrate
it in the temple, and was met—not, as he expected,
by jubilant crowds with incense and victims, but by
a priest with one goose provided at his own expense.
This led the Emperor to address a strong remon-
strance to the Senate. He upbraided the Antiochenes
with being more chary in their gifts on public occasions than any petty Pontic village, though he finds
them profuse enough in their private festivities and
in letting their wives bestow gifts on Galilæans pro-
fessing poverty. Through their fault, he said, the
God had forsaken his temple. But unfortunately
for Julian, both the zeal and the numerous con-
course of people which the festival of Apollo failed
to call forth were ready enough to appear in honour
of St. Babylas, as his remains were conveyed back
from Daphne to the place in the city which thenceforth became their shrine. Men, women, and children helped in the sacred task, singing as they
marched the words of the psalm : "Confounded are
all who worship graven images, who boast them-

selves in idols." This ebullition of enthusiasm for
the popular martyr and of spite against the unpopular Emperor gave colour to the suspicion that iconoclastic zeal was the cause of the subsequent catastrophe. On the 22d of October, the temple in
Daphne, the joy and pride of the city, was destroyed by fire. It was but natural that suspicion
should fall on the Christian zealots, especially as
some had expressed dissatisfaction at recent addi-
tions to the temple. Inquiry was made, perhaps
aided by torture, yet no satisfactory solution was
obtained. It was asserted that a devout philosopher, Asclepiades by name, had been burning wax
candles before a silver statuette of Cybele, which he
had placed at the feet of the colossal Apollo of
Daphne, and that an accidental conflagration had
occurred therefrom in the night, when there was no
help at hand to extinguish the flames. If this story
were accepted, the Antiochenes might be convicted
of gross negligence, but of no wanton destructive-
ness, and the retaliatory measure taken by Julian,
the prohibition of services in their principal church,
would appear somewhat harsh and unjust.

But the purses of the Antiochenes were probably
at least as dear to them as their religious principles,
and in this region also they were subject to Julian's
attacks. We have observed his determination to
allow no qualified person to escape the pecuniary
and other burdens attached to membership in the
Senate. The illegal and corrupt way in which the
senators recruited their members was one of his
grievances against them, and he set his face against

20

what he regarded as insufficient claims of exemption, on the ground of clerical profession, half-birth, or recent domicile. But more serious than even these regulations was his attempt to regulate the price of corn,—a rock on which his brother Gallus had made shipwreck many years before.

The autumn of 362 was marked by great physical calamities. So great was the drought that many springs were dried up. The city of Nicæa and the remains of the unhappy Nicomedia suffered severely from another earthquake. A general scarcity of provisions set in, and, as usually happens in such cases, the rich were accused by the poor of hoarding their supplies in order to obtain a harvest for themselves from the general disaster. The people of Antioch, assembled in the circus, besieged the Emperor's ears with the cry : " Plenty of everything ; everything dear." As to the course taken by Julian in this emergency, some of his bitterest foes give him credit for good intentions, while some of his staunchest supporters acknowledge his want of discretion. Yet, according to his own account, he did not proceed hastily. He summoned a meeting of the chief people, and ordered them to find a remedy for the prevalent distress. During three months, however, their deliberations led to no effect. At the end of that time, Julian took the matter into his own hands, and drew up a list of prices, by which corn was to be sold at a moderate rate. This step naturally led the dealers to restrict their sales still further, and when the Emperor procured for the people quantities of corn from Chalcis, Hierapolis,

and afterwards from Egypt, the proprietors naturally
felt the cheapness as a grievance. As the hoarding
continued, and in all probability the wealthy citizens
set themselves to buy up the stores so liberally provided, in order to sell again at the most profitable
time and place, Julian had another and a stormy
meeting with the Antiochenes, which ended in the
whole body of senators, over two hundred in number, being ordered into custody. True, they were
liberated before supper-time, and an orator like
Libanius might descant on the mildness of the vengeance taken by the autocrat whose benevolent
intentions were ever thus perversely opposed. But
in later days it seemed to Libanius that the senators
had not been much to blame after all, and he took
pride in the thought that he had defended them in
the Emperor's presence. It was not, however, the
wealthy only that felt dissatisfaction with Julian's
tariff. To some of the people it seemed desirable
that the price of some of the minor luxuries, as well
as the necessaries of life, should be reduced. But on
this point Julian felt no obligations. He considered
himself bound to provide the poor with bread, but
not with superfluities, so that here again he failed to
obtain the approval and gratitude of any of the conflicting classes and interests. When, in order to
render the relief permanent, he made a grant to the
town of three thousand lots of waste land, he found
that they were not being distributed to the most
needy and deserving, and felt it necessary to burden
them with obligations towards the State in order
that private individuals of the wealthier classes

should not be able to appropriate the whole advantage. Class privileges, the commercial advantages of the wealthy, the love of the common people for races and shows, the attachment of the many to the martyrs who were ousting the prestige of the ancient Gods,—all these things he not only discountenanced, but attacked with a virulence that led those who were deprived of more potent means of resistance to have recourse to the last resort of the weak,—a sarcastic and spiteful tongue, and to calumniate his name with reproaches, while they ridiculed his appearance and habits in biting comic verse.

It would certainly have been better for Julian's reputation if he could have shown himself as clement and humane towards those who laughed at his beard as he did towards those who desired his head. If he had already shown that a controversialist on the throne must needs descend from the sphere of dignified impartiality which best becomes a far-ruling sovereign, he was now to prove that a satirist on the throne loses yet more of that personal dignity which should strike respect into his subjects of all degrees. Perhaps Julian's reputation has suffered more from the *Misopogon* among later generations than among his contemporaries, seeing that many commentators, wanting in sense of humour, have taken *au sérieux* many of the unpleasant statements he ironically makes against himself, and so presented us with a representation of his person and manners disgusting in itself and inconsistent with what we read in other authors. The object of the satire is to ridicule the Antiochenes under cover of ridiculing himself from

the Antiochian point of view. In the character of
an Antiochian "beard-hater," he ridicules his own
personal appearance, especially his ragged, unkempt
beard, his excessive plainness of living, and his want
of taste to appreciate games, dances, and all spectacles. From the same point of view he ridicules as
boorish and inhuman the σωφροσύνη, which the
Emperor puts first of all things, and which the Antiochenes entirely fail to comprehend. It seems to
them to consist in such a slavery to the Gods and
the laws, with rigid rules of abstinence and self-
control, as must lead to the destruction of the city,
with its love of liberty in all things. Then there are
his tiresome habits of always going to the temples,
and his harshness in reproving the people who would
applaud him in the sacred places where he insists on
reverent silence.[8] The Antiochenes, faithful to the
memory of their founder, Seleucus, are self-indulgent
in love and in diet, but Julian inherits all the rough-
ness of his Thracian ancestors. His justification lies
in his early education, especially in the narrowing
influence of his pædagogue Mardonius, and in the
stern moral maxims from the philosophers which
have been impressed on his mind. The Antiochenes
allow much license to their women. They care only
for the K and the X (Κωνστάντιος and Χρίστος),
from whom the city has never suffered such annoyance
as from Julian. But he has made himself obnoxious to
the people because of his adhesion to the religion of
his fathers and his little care for the theatre and for
pleasures. They had shown their mood in old times
by preparing a splendid reception for Demetrius,

the wealthy freedman of Pompeius, which, by a
ludicrous mistake, was given to Cato the Stoic, a
man by no means delightful to them. Julian's life
among the Gauls, who have no taste for Antiochian
entertainments and refinement, and whose barbarous ways has made them feel loyal to him as to a
congenial spirit, has further removed him from all
sympathy with civilised people. He goes on to express the difference between himself and the citizens
in their ideas as to the relative scale to be observed
in private and in religious festivities, and the impossibility of co-operation against the disastrous results
of the famine. He acknowledges that he has failed
with them and that he had better go. If he tried
to reform his manners, he would but be as the kite
that tried to copy the neighing of a horse, and so
lost his own voice without acquiring the other. His
benefits have aroused no gratitude, and he has only
brought trouble to himself and to them.

The tone of the whole piece is very bitter, especially towards the end, and it concludes with something very like an imprecation. True, what Julian
denounces is only what deserves the strongest de-
nunciation : the wanton, frivolous, covetous tone of
a luxurious and unprincipled community. Before
long, the Antiochenes were to receive more lashes
for the same offences, at the hand of one of the
noblest of eastern Bishops. [9] Julian's governmental
system would hardly have afforded scope for a
censor in the position of Chrysostom, yet moral
denunciations may seem to us more becoming in

the mouth of a spiritual than in that of a temporal ruler.

While at Antioch Julian lost one of his nearest and strongest supporters, his uncle Julian. Church writers see in his painful end a judgment on his co-operation in the anti-Christian measures of his nephew. The elder Julian seems to have been popular among some of the Oriental communities over which he had ruled, and his death must have been greatly regretted by the Emperor on public as well as on personal grounds.

When he left Antioch, Julian declared his intention, on his return, of staying at Tarsus rather than at Antioch. These words must have seemed afterwards a melancholy forecast as to the place which should afford him quarters for more than one winter. Meantime, he appointed to the government of Syria a Hierapolitan named Alexander, known to be of a severe and violent disposition. If this appointment was made chiefly with a view to harass the Antiochenes, as Ammianus seems to imply, Julian must indeed have allowed personal feeling to move him from the path of rectitude. A letter of Libanius,[10] however, will show that Alexander, though unpopular, was able to maintain his authority and keep order, and thus his policy may have been more successful than that of Julian himself. The Emperor was certainly right in discerning a mutual incompatibility of temperament between himself and the people of the great Syrian city. According to his principles of morality, he was justified in making no secret of his feelings. What, if he had reigned longer, the ultimate result might have been of this abandonment of self-control, so different from the dissimulation in which he had passed his youth, must remain a matter of conjecture.

Coin of Antioch.
Obverse, Head of Tyche of city. Reverse, a spray of laurel. (?)

NOTES ON CHAPTER XIII.

[1] The chief authorities for this chapter are: Ammianus, xxii., 9 *ff.*; Julian's own account in the *Misopogon*, Zosimus, iii., 11; the *Orations* and *Autobiography* of Libanius; and the Church historians, especially Socrates, iii., 17, 19, and Theodoret, iii., 21 *ff.* See also Mücke, ch. 6, 7. Schwarz is always useful for chronological data.

[2] As Schiller would seem to do, iii., 3, 26.

[3] Ammianus, xxii., 7.

[4] Zosimus says that he spent ten months in Constantinople, but this is probably an error. See Schwarz, p. 18.

[5] Ep. 4.

[6] Autobiography, 82 *ff.*

[7] See two papers, *De Antiquitatibus Antiochenis*, by K. O. Müller, published with his lesser works in German.

[8] It is interesting to compare what Julian says of the irreverent behaviour of the Antiochenes in the Temple services, with the very similar reproaches made by St. Chrysostom in his sermon to them on Christmas day. See W. R. W. Stephens' *Life and Times of Chrysostom.*

[9] See a bright little sketch called *St. Chrysostom's Picture of his Age*, published in 1876 by the Society for the Propagation of Christian Knowledge.

[10] Libanius, Ep., 722.

Coin of Sapor II. of Persia.
Reverse, Fire Altar with worshippers.

CHAPTER XIV.

JULIAN'S PERSIAN CAMPAIGN.   HIS DEATH.[1]

363.

" The end of life is the same as if a prætor who has employed an
actor dismisses him from the stage.   ' But I have not finished the five
acts, but only three of them.'   Thou sayest well, but in life the three
acts are the whole drama.   For what shall be a completed drama is
determined by Him who was once the cause of its composition, and
now of its dissolution ; but thou art the cause of neither.   Depart
then satisfied, for He also who releases thee is satisfied."

Meditations of Marcus Aurelius, xii., 36.
(Long's translation).

Y the 5th of March, 363 (the year of
Julian's fourth consulship, in which
he was associated with Sallust, Præfect of the Gauls), the Emperor's
preparations were sufficiently advanced for him to be able to begin
his Eastern campaign.   He probably
felt much relieved in departing from the city in
which he had experienced so much of disappointment and failure.   The fickle people of Antioch

were profuse in their demonstrations of good wishes, and the senators accompanied him on the first stage of his journey, after which they were dismissed with a hortatory and not very condescending address.

It is not certain whether at this moment Julian had either arranged a detailed plan for the campaign, or decided as to his ultimate course with regard to Persia in case he should prove successful. He certainly meant to strike at the heart of the kingdom, but was as yet unaware at what points he might expect to encounter resistance from the enemy. The comparative ease with which, in the great days of Greece, armies from the West had penetrated to the neighbourhood of Babylon, may have rendered him insufficiently regardful of the vastness of his enterprise. The thought of Alexander was ever with him, and many ages seemed to witness his deeds, as forty centuries looked down from the Pyramids on the armies of Napoleon. At the same time, he did not neglect the less encouraging memories,—those of Cæsar, of the younger Gordian, of Valerian. Critics have remarked that he relied too much on the kind of experience he had gained in the Gallic wars, whereas that which he was now undertaking required greater forces and more circumspection. Even at that time, warning voices were heard. The Greek oracles which he consulted (of Delphi, Delos, and Dodona)[2] seem to have given favourable responses. But the Sibylline Books, and various omens, as well as some purely human warnings, such as those of Libanius and of Sallust, Præfect of the Gauls, were strong on the other side. However, Julian's piety never prevented him from interpreting oracles and omens in his own sense, nor did his loyalty to his friends ever lead him to subject his judgment to theirs.

It is probable that from the first, Julian had conceived a plan for avoiding future dangers on the side of Persia.[3] This was to dethrone Sapor, and to replace him by the fugitive prince Hormisdas, whom we have already seen in the company first of Constantius and later of Julian. The parentage and history of this man is not related alike by the different historians, but, according to a not improbable account,[4] he was an elder brother of Sapor, who had been excluded from the kingdom in consequence of a quarrel with the Persian grandees. In any case, he had incurred the enmity of the existing government and fled, first to the Armenian and then to the Imperial Court. The conspicuous position which he holds in Julian's army, the frequency with which he is employed in negotiations; and the enmity which is shown towards him by his fellow-countrymen, are in favour of the supposition that the prospect of greatness had been held out to him.

We have already seen that Julian had received embassies with a view to alliance. Some of these he declined, probably because he did not wish to be burdened with the task of supplying provisions to an unwieldy host. He built some hopes, however, on Arsaces, King of Armenia, who had been, as just stated, the protector and friend of Hormisdas. This king had received in marriage, at the hand of Constantius, a lady of high birth, and he and his people regarded themselves as hereditary allies of the Romans.[5] Some Saracen tribes were inclined to support the Emperor if he would pay them sufficiently high subsidies. As he deemed such a course derogatory to the dignity of Rome, certain of them stood aloof or took the part of his adversaries, though, on his demand, some joined him before he had gone very far.[6] Some Goths also joined him after a few days' march.

A fleet was meantime prepared on the Euphrates, to join the army on its march down that river. The number of the vessels, as of the entire army, is differently given us by our different authorities. If, according to Zosimus,[7] Julian had with him a force of 83,000 horsemen and foot together, it was a powerful army for attack, but not sufficient to garrison all the strong places that he must capture on his way.

On the 10th of March, Julian arrived at Hierapolis, a city about twenty miles to the west of the Euphrates. Thence he sent an interesting and characteristic letter to Libanius, describing the journeys of the last five days and his present occupations. His style is terse and vigorous. He knew that the recipient of the letter would supply ample adornment to the material given, before it should be published to the world. The places at which he had lodged were Litarbæ, Berœa, and Batnæ. At Berœa, he had held a meeting of the senators, and tried in vain to impress on them the duty of piety towards the Gods. He had found the Berœans more ready to applaud him than to follow his exhortations, except such as were already of his way of thinking. From another source,[8] we hear of his endeavouring, while in this city, to mediate between a father and his son whom he had disinherited for going over to the Hellenic worship. After vainly trying to move the old man by setting forth the injustice of using compulsion in matters of faith, Julian turned to the younger, and offered to bestow on him the care which his parent had denied him. From Berœa, he had proceeded to Batnæ, a charming place which reminded him of Daphne. It was Hellenic in character, though barbaric in name. But the worship of the Gods was practised in too sensational a style, and without sufficient reverence. In Hierapolis, Julian had been delighted to find a son-in-law of Jamblichus, a staunch Hellene, whom neither Constantius nor Gallus had been able to induce to forsake his religious principles. Julian was now actively occupied in conducting trials in the camp, superintending sacrifices, negotiating with the Saracens, organising a system of scouts, and collecting provisions for the army, so that we may thank the fulness of his hands for the business-like character of his communication.

After a three days' stay at Hierapolis, the army marched on eastward, crossed the Euphrates by a bridge of boats, halted for a day at another Batnæ (in Osrœene), and proceeded to Carrhæ,[9] a place memorable as the scene of the disastrous defeat of the Crassi. Here Julian held a great review of his troops. Thence two courses were open to him by which to reach upper Asia. He might strike across Mesopotamia eastwards, past Nisibis to the Tigris,

or he might march southwards to Callinicus on the
Euphrates, and then down that river to Circesium
and so onwards.   The former was the route once
followed by Alexander, the latter that of Xenophon
and the Ten Thousand.   While he was deliberating,
news came that the Persians were making raids on
the peoples subject to the Romans, apparently in
the neighbourhood of Nisibis.   This decided him to
adopt a plan to which he was already inclined, and
to despatch a considerable force eastwards, that
might hold the brigand bands in check, effect a junction with Arsaces, ravage the provinces on the As-
syrio-Armenian frontier, and subsequently join the
main body in Assyria.   This detachment was placed
under the command of Sebastian, formerly *Dux* of
Egypt, and Procopius, a relative of the Emperor,
and in the eyes of some his probable heir.[10]   With
the main host, after a feigned movement towards
the Tigris, Julian proceeded south, and reached Callinicus on the 27th of March.   Here he celebrated
the festival of the Mother of the Gods, and was rejoined[11] by his fleet.   He then proceeded, in hopeful
spirits, down the Euphrates to Circesium.   This
town possessed a considerable garrison, which Julian
is said[12] to have strengthened.   He seems not yet
to have abandoned the plan of keeping a line of
communications behind him.   Or it may be that the
last important place on Roman soil seemed specially
worthy of defence.   A few days' march, past
Zaitha, near which lay the tomb of the Emperor
Gordian, and Dura, brought the army into the regions called by the vague name of Assyria, which

owned the Persian supremacy. The first hostile demonstration to be made was against an island fort variously called Anatho and Phathusa. The commandant, however, capitulated and was received into Roman employ, the lives of the defenders were spared, and the army had the satisfaction of restoring liberty to a number of prisoners, including an old man who had been captured in the expedition of Galerius, more than thirty-six years before, but had always kept up a hope of being buried in Roman soil. The fortress was burned down, and the country that the army passed through was ravaged. Some fortresses were left untaken, on a promise of adopting the side of the Romans should their expedition prove successful. The army marched so as to cover a large space, the baggage in the centre, while the Emperor rode actively from company to company to avoid disorder and straggling. A large number were told off to act as scouts,—a necessary precaution, seeing that small detachments of Persians were hovering in the neighbourhood, from one of which Hormisdas had once a narrow escape. They had further difficulties to encounter, as they proceeded southward, from the canals and marshes which the dwellers by the lower Euphrates, like the Dutch in later times, could render useful allies against an invading army. When the waters had been crossed by swimming, or on improvised bridges, a serious resistance was encountered from the strongly fortified town of Pirisabora. His first assault having failed, Julian ordered a wooden turret to be applied,—the *helepolis*, first famous in the sieges of Demetrius Poliorcetes. This led the commandant to propose a capitulation. Quarter was given to the inhabitants, but the town was utterly destroyed. The stores of arms and provisions were gladly appropriated by the Romans.

The discipline maintained in the Roman camp was strict, not to say harsh. When three squadrons were overcome by a body of Persians under command of the *Surena*, and a standard taken, the Emperor, by a daring and swift attack, recovered flag and honour, and inflicted death ("according to the ancient laws," as Ammianus says) on ten of those that had been guilty of cowardice in flight. The donatives given to the soldiers after the capture of a town did not satisfy their expectations, and Julian could only restrain the tendency to mutiny by assuring them, in a vigorous speech, that more could not be spared for them at present, though abundant wealth lay before them if they were only courageous, and trusted in God and in himself. He meant to carry on this enterprise as long as he lived and reigned, and he appealed to their loyalty to support him. His exhortation was well received, and his spirit communicated to the whole host, which knew his readiness to take his full share in all labours and privations.

The abundant produce of the land through which they now had to march, especially the dates and vines, afforded some compensation to the soldiers for the annoyance of having to cross more sluices and canals on palmwood planks, swollen skins, or whatever else could serve the purpose. They had

21

now left the main stream of the Euphrates, and were approaching the Tigris. Another important siege had to be undertaken, that of Maogamalcha, while the trusted commander Victor, with a body of reconnoitrers, went on towards Ctesiphon to see if any enemy were to be encountered. While surveying the fortifications of Maogamalcha, Julian was personally attacked by some Persians who had observed him, and only escaped after a hand-to-hand conflict with his foe. The city did not yield to the first assaults. Recourse was had to mining, and a simultaneous attack from without and from below led to surprise, confusion, and a ghastly massacre. Women and children seem never to have been spared in these assaults. Libanius says that Julian would have preferred to take prisoners rather than to slay, but he could not restrain his excited soldiery. He specially ordered, however, that the King's guards should be spared with their leader, who was, nevertheless, put to death soon after for insulting Hormisdas.[13] For his personal share in the abundant spoils, he took only three pieces of gold and a deaf-and-dumb child, whose pantomimic gifts had struck his fancy. Some Persians who had taken refuge in a subterranean passage were suffocated by a fire made at the entrance. The terror spread by the Roman successes was so great that a Persian prince who had lately sallied forth from Ctesiphon to oppose Victor and his forces, thought it best to desist from his attempt and beat a retreat.

Not far from Maogamalcha, the army arrived at a magnificent park and hunting-ground belonging to

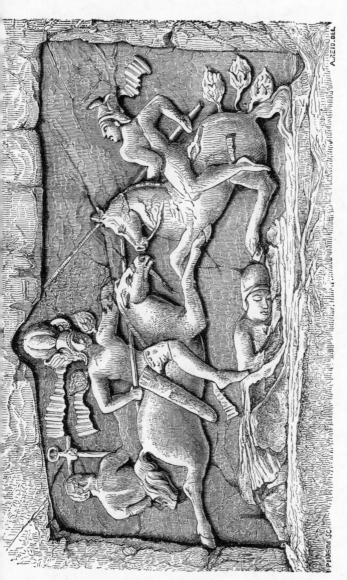

PERSIAN BATTLE-SCENE.
FROM A BAS-RELIEF.

the King, with a palace built in Roman style. Julian
ordered the enclosure to be destroyed, and the men
enjoyed some sport of an exciting character, since
lions and wild boars were among the game preserved
for the royal amusement. The palace he ordered to
be spared, but if Libanius is right, it was fired by
the soldiers. The army was allowed a halt for repose, but difficulties and the need for watchfulness
by no means diminished as it proceeded. On one
occasion, the Persians made a successful assault on
the Roman baggage. On another, a sudden sortie
from a fort led to the flight and seizure of several
Romans, though this was followed by the disgrace
of some cowardly horsemen, and the subsequent
capture of the place. Meanwhile, the fleet had to
be brought from the Euphrates to the Tigris. From
books, and from the testimony of the natives, Julian
had learned of a canal, called the "Royal River"
(Naargamalcha), which formerly flowed from the one
to the other, but was now choked up with rubbish."
He ordered it to be cleared, and the ships were safely
conveyed into the waters of the Tigris. Before proceeding he roused the spirits of the men with games
and races, in preparation for the next step on which
he had decided. This was to transfer his forces to the
other side of the great river. It seemed a hazard-
ous proceeding, as a Persian host was already mustered on the opposite side, strong in missile weapons,
in horse, and in elephants. Several of the generals
to whom Julian made known his design remonstrated. But the Emperor was quite determined on
the matter. The heavier transport ships were un-

laden and filled with men, and five of them were
entrusted to Victor, with orders to effect a crossing
under cover of the night. But the enemy on the
high bank opposite perceived them, and hurled burning brands which set the ships on fire. The Roman
host felt alarmed, but Julian had the presence of
mind to resort to a pious fraud, such as he had
probably learned to use in interpreting oracles. He
declared that the flames which the soldiers saw were
the prearranged signal of the successful landing of
their comrades. All were now eager to embark, and
the night together with the day following were
occupied in the crossing and in desperate fighting on
the eastern bank. In the end, thanks in great measure to the personal activity of the Emperor, the
troops were transferred, the half-burned ships recovered, and the enemy driven back with great loss.
The way now seemed open to Ctesiphon, and but
for the opposition of Victor, who had been wounded,
and felt unequal to any further enterprise, an attempt would have been made on that city, into
which the Persian generals with the fugitives effected
a retreat.[16]

The army had now penetrated into the neighbourhood of those ancient cities, the centres of several
civilisations and capitals of successive empires, which
had from of old dominated the great river-basins
north of the Persian Gulf. Julian was within about
fifty miles of Babylon, on the Euphrates, now no
longer a place of importance. Close at hand on the
Tigris was Seleucia, great in the days of Alexander's
successors, long since reduced to almost nothing by

the arms of Verus, and now commonly known as
the village of Coche. Opposite to it was Ctesiphon,
the capital of the Parthian empire, now occupied by
the Persian forces. Great as had been the success
of the army hitherto, its position was still critical.
The force which had harassed it on the Euphrates
was by no means annihilated. A strongly fortified
city dominated the river by which the fleet must
pass if it were decided to advance in a north-easterly direction to meet the force sent on before and
the Armenian allies. To the East lay a comparatively
unknown region, with a terrible possibility of en-
countering the Great King and all his host. To the
West, along the route by which it had come, was
a devastated land through which retreat was impossible.

Julian halted, awarded prizes for valour to the soldiers who had distinguished themselves, offered sacrifices, the victims of which gave unfavourable signs,
and held a council of war as to the step to be taken
next. The most natural thing to do, it seemed,
would be to lay siege to Ctesiphon. To leave so
strong a place in one's rear was against all the rules
of prudent warfare. Yet, strange to say, the opinion of the officers, to which the Emperor acceded,
was that, under present circumstances, and considering the probable nearness of the King, the siege had
better not be undertaken. Ctesiphon had not proved
impregnable in by-gone days, but probably Sapor or
his predecessors had lately strengthened its fortifications. In any case, the idea was abandoned. Another course, which some of Julian's modern critics

would have advised, was to wait for Arsaces and the forces sent by way of the Tigris to join him. Julian was anxiously looking out for these troops, and different causes are assigned for their non-appearance. But whether the generals had quarrelled among themselves, or turned aside to make war on the natives, or whether Arsaces had found it inconsistent with his Christianity to support an apostate emperor, the forces did not appear. It would, perhaps, be unfair to reproach Arsaces with treachery. He suffered in after times for his fidelity to the Roman cause. And it seems, after all, not improbable that, if sufficient time had been allowed, he would not have missed his appointment.[16]

Again, it might have been possible to accept the overtures of Sapor and enter into negotiations with a view to an honourable peace. According to some accounts,[17] Hormisdas was himself desirous of such a course. But Julian was anxious lest the news of any such suggestions might damp the ardour of the soldiers, and ordered the messengers to be sent away secretly. What he personally intended to do was to follow in the footsteps of Alexander and to strike out eastwards.

The rashness of this course is evident to us. Julian can only have hoped to justify it by some brilliant success. It is not easy, however, to form a clear notion as to his plans at this moment. He cannot have been unaware of the difficulties in the way, from the enemy, the climate, and his own ignorance of the country. The Persian guides whom he had with him soon proved themselves utterly untrustworthy. It was now the middle of June, and the burning sun, with mosquitoes and other pests, were peculiarly trying to men accustomed to the snows and the winds of the far West. And if he had had Alexander's army, and Alexander's genius, the example of his hero could hardly have been appealed to here. For when he advanced towards India, Alexander did not leave Susa or Persepolis untaken in his rear, nor was Darius then at large with a great army. Julian might also have remembered that Alexander's career was at last checked by the refusal of his soldiers to go further. Such an event might soon be looked for in his own camp.

The determination on an eastward march involved a most momentous step—the destruction of the fleet. It was of no use to leave it there to fall into the hands of the enemy; the army could not be thinned so as to leave an adequate guard; and the ships, even if sufficiently manned, could not force their way up the Tigris, in the teeth of the garrison of Ctesiphon. Even if they did so, they would be of no service to the army in its farther progress or on its return. It was decided to set fire to all the ships, except a few small vessels, suitable for bridge-making, that could be conveyed inland on waggons. These were before long captured in an attack of the enemy. The loss of the fleet was felt bitterly afterwards. Even before the conflagration was completed, Julian is said, on discovering the treachery of his spies, to have revoked his decision. But it was too late to extinguish the flames.

Now began a time of greater sufferings and disasters

for the Romans than they had as yet experienced. The Persians had destroyed all the provisions in the country through which their road lay, so that famine was added to the other terrors of the midsummer march. Julian did what he could to encourage the men. On one occasion, remembering probably the example of Agesilaus, he displayed before them the puny forms of their oriental captives, and asked what they could dread from such men. It was not, however, so much the Persian army as Julian's patron King Helios above and the trench-divided land below that hindered progress and made the men insist, tumultuously at last, on a retreat homewards. Most reluctantly, Julian was obliged to consent. The question now was whether to march westward through Assyria or to go in a northerly direction, and occupy Corduene, the frontier province between Armenia and Media. Sacrifices were made. The victims gave no decided response, and it was resolved to proceed towards Armenia. In that direction, an unravaged country might be hoped for ; there was a chance, too, of hearing of Arsaces. And might not Julian also have had in mind the retreat of the Ten Thousand ?

Before long an ominous cloud of dust suggested anxious questions in the army. Was it a flock of wild asses, or a body of Saracens, such as were now proving very formidable to the retreating host, or might it be the great host of Sapor himself ? After an anxious, sleepless night, the most serious alternative proved the true one. The Persians were seen, clad in well-fitting armour, and backed by their formidable elephants, the sight and odour of which terrified both man and horse. Nor was there a chance that, as in many battles of old, the great beasts might be driven back so as to prove more fatal to friends than to foes. For we are told that each driver carried a short knife with which to stab in a mortal place the elephant on which he rode as soon as it should show dangerous symptoms.

Formidable as the aspect of the army was, however, the Romans greeted it with joy. Fighting was more to their mind than painful marching. But Julian was unwilling to bring on a general engagement without due preparation. A stream separated the hosts, and for a time there were but skirmishes and partial encounters in which some deeds of daring were performed.[18] The Romans were even able to halt and rest for two days at a place called Hucumbra. During the succeeding days, we have the old stories of attacks on the baggage, of alarms, of degradations for cowardice, of distressing efforts to secure the burning harvests. At a place called Maranga, the Romans found the foe drawn up in battle array, and a more serious engagement was fought. The battle seems not to have been decisive, but the loss was much greater on the Persian side. In fact, the Persians proved themselves far less formidable in hand-to-hand fighting than in sudden charges and flights with missiles, and this discovery was an encouragement to the Romans.

A three days' truce followed, for the recovery of the wounded and the repose of the exhausted. But the want of provisions prevented the men from de-

riving much benefit from the rest. Julian himself
could live on thin broth, and was ready to give to
the most needy any extra portion supplied for him.
But his men were not all accustomed to Stoic training, nor admirers of the life of Diogenes.

Even at this time, Julian used to spend most of
his time at night in writing and meditating. On
one occasion, according to a story which his friends
said they had received from himself, he saw, perhaps
in a vision induced by weariness and anxiety, the
Genius of the Roman People, moving sadly away,
with head and cornucopia hidden in his robe. Longing to see a more favourable sign, Julian came out to
look at the starry heavens. A brilliant meteor met
his glance. Next morning, he asked the Etruscan
haruspices who accompanied his army how they
would interpret the sign. They answered that no
military operation should be attempted at present.
But Julian, whose pious regard for omens was rather
that of Hector than that of Nicias, gave orders that
the camp should be broken up at daybreak.

The Persians had returned to their old tactics.
Avoiding any direct encounter with the infantry,
they remained on the high ground at a little distance, watching the Romans, in readiness for any
opportunity of a sudden and partial attack. Julian
tried to keep the flanks firm and the squares solid,
but the nature of the ground was such that occasional gaps were inevitable. Always foremost in
making surveys, the Emperor, without shield or
breastplate, was occupied in the van, when tidings
were brought to him that the enemy had attacked

the rear. Seizing a shield, and without waiting for
other accoutrements, he hastened towards the point
in danger, but was speedily recalled by the news that
the van was now experiencing a like assault. He
returned to find that it was indeed so, but, heedless
of showers of missiles, of elephants, of terror all
around, he restored the spirit of his men and the fortune of the field. The enemy fled, and Julian was
foremost in pursuit. He might have remembered,
even now, the old device of the foe, to hurl missiles
backward while in full flight. As he pursued the
fugitives, the javelin of a flying Persian pierced his
unprotected side, and being double-edged, cut his
fingers, and thus rendered vain his manful efforts
to draw it out with his hand.[19] He fell from his
horse, and was at once carried from the field. A tent
was immediately pitched to receive him, since the
Romans had not been able to make an entrenched
camp this harassing day. There surgical aid was at
once applied.

For a while Julian did not realise that he had
received his death-wound. When clear consciousness returned, he asked for horse and armour, that
he might return to the field and encourage the soldiers whom his disaster was already stimulating to a
desperate valour. But loss of blood had weakened
him. When he asked the name of the place where
he lay, and they told him "Phrygia," his hopes
waned yet more. For he had been told that
Phrygia should be the place of his death, and, like
Henry IV. in Jerusalem Chamber, he heard his
death-warrant in that word. He had doubtless

thought to die near the sacred precincts of the
Mother of the Gods.

When he realised that the end could not be far off,
he ceased from further effort to continue his active
course, and endeavoured, while physical and mental
strength remained, to comfort and encourage his
friends and himself by falling back on those main
principles of life which no press of active duties or
of manifold cares and considerations had ever obscured in his mind.[20]   He had always believed, he
said, that the soul was nobler than the body, and
that death was not an evil, but rather a special favour
from the Gods.   Nor had there been anything in his
life which, at this moment, could fill him with
anxious thought.   He had been faithful in his task
as ruler.   As to success, that was not within the
power of man to achieve ; the event must ever be
determined by the Supreme Powers.   He was thankful that death came to him in fair fight, not by
treachery, nor by lingering disease.   He forbore to
express any wish as to his successor.   His choice
might not be the best, or it might bring trouble on
the man chosen.   He could only hope, for the sake
of the whole State, that a worthy man might be
appointed to rule over the people.

Thus calmly, without remorse and without sense
of failure, he set about the arrangement of his private
affairs.   Not that he was indifferent to the fate of
the Empire, but that he had too much confidence in
his cause to believe that it must perish with him.
Nor did his clear conscience imply that he acknowledged no higher standard than that to which he had

always conformed. But to a man of his habits of thought it seemed that all human imperfection was due to the connection of the soul with that fleshly envelope, from which he was presently to escape.

One little touch of nature, however, affected the by-standers more than all this expression of lofty sentiment. He asked for his friend Anatolius, the Master of the Offices, probably in order to give him a last token of esteem. The Præfect Sallust, who had himself narrowly escaped the sword of the enemy, replied that Anatolius was "beatus,"—in plain words, that he had been killed. On hearing this, Julian showed bitter grief. The sight of a dying man lamenting one who had preceded him but a few hours, in its pathetic inconsistency, brought tears to the eyes of those who had known them both. The Emperor reproved them. It was weakness, he said, to grieve for their prince as he was being taken up to the starry heavens. He then turned to the philosophers Maximus and Priscus, who stood by his bed, ready to confirm his faith and strengthen his parting spirit. Breathing became difficult. He asked for a draught of water, and quietly expired at about midnight.

Christian legend [21] soon began to busy itself in weaving strange tales around the Emperor's death-bed, for which we have no foundation in any trust-worthy authorities. They need no disproof. But perhaps more importance should be attached to the notion which early gained ground, that the hand whence the weapon came by which Julian died was that of a Christian traitor in his own camp.

The story as told by Ammianus, whom we have followed in our account, is consistent, probable, and apparently based on first-hand knowledge. The notion that things might have been otherwise would doubtless be suggested by the known fact that there were Christians who desired his death, and by the equally patent and very disgraceful fact, that grave writers were afterwards found who applauded such a supposed deed of murderous treachery. Countenance was certainly given to the opinion by a writer who loved not the Christians, and deplored the Emperor from the depth of his heart,—the orator Libanius. He is not quite self-consistent in his accounts, but argues that Julian must have fallen by treachery, since no Persian claimed the price which Sapor had placed on the Emperor's head. Even if Libanius were well informed on this point, the argument is inconclusive, for how, after the confusion of the battle, could any soldier present proofs as to the effect of his own special missile? Or, if the slayer of Julian were a Christian, why should he not still claim reward from the King? Some said that it was a Saracen that did the deed. The character of the weapon would have been the only evidence, and of that nothing conclusive is related. In any case, however Julian had died, men would have seen something portentous and supernatural in his end. Hermits and saints would have seen visions at a distance, and men would have tried to find in the last words of him they hated and feared an acknowledgment that the Galilæan had conquered, that Helios had rejected his devotee, and that the

Carpenter's Son had prepared a coffin for the scorner.

Julian may be said to have slain many in his death as in his life. The immediate result of his removal from the field was not a panic, but a more determined attack on the enemy. Fifty distinguished men among the Persians are said to have fallen in the field. But the Roman loss also—apart from the greatest loss of all—was considerable. Some bands of the soldiers took to flight. One gained possession of a fort in the neighbourhood, and held it till, after three days, it was enabled to rejoin the main body of the army.

But, after all, the death of Julian was a far greater calamity to the Romans than would have been the loss of many battles. For long, no tidings of him had reached the frontier. Libanius, in Antioch, was hoping to hear of fresh victories, when the disastrous news arrived. The earthquakes which were again working havoc in Asia Minor seemed a fitting presage of the dire event. Superstition might express in fantastic forms the sense men had of a far-reaching occurrence. It could hardly exaggerate the importance of what had actually happened.

Coin of Jovian.

NOTES ON CHAPTER XIV.

[1] Besides the already-mentioned authorities, I have found two treatises very useful as to the subject of this chapter : Sievers' *Studien zur Geschichte der Römischen Kaiser : Julian's Perser-Krieg*, and Reinhardt's *Der Tod des Kaisers Julian.*

[2] Theodoret, iii., 22.

[3] See Lib., Ep. 1457.

[4] Zosimus, ii., 27.

[5] Sozomen tells us of a peremptory and offensive letter written by Julian to Arsaces, contrasting his own rule and character with those of his predecessor, and a letter (furnished from these indications ?) in all probability spurious, has found its way into the collection of Julian's letters.   He can hardly have been so impolitic as to write in a fashion certain to repel a useful ally.

[6] *Cf.* Am., xxiii., 3, and xxv., 6, and Jul., Ep., 27.

[7] iii., 12, 13.   65,000 at Carrhæ—18,000 already sent off to the Tigris under Sebastian and Procopius.

[8] Theodoret, iii., 22.   The anecdotes about Julian told by Church historians are not generally very worthy of credit, but this one seems not uncharacteristic or improbable.

[9] According to Zosimus, he turned aside to visit Edessa, but Sozomen (vi., i.) denies this, and it is inconsistent with the account of Ammianus.

[10] A relative on the mother's side (?).   Shortly before this, Julian is said (as Ammianus reports) to have given Procopius a purple robe and named him his successor.   But as the ceremony is said to have been without witnesses, we cannot regard it as a proved or even probable event.

[11] Or joined.   It is not clear whether he had met the fleet before.

[12] Not by Ammianus nor by Zosimus, but by Malalas.

[13] Mücke understands that all the eighty guards with Nabdates were burned to death, but the words of Ammianus do not seem to bear out this hideous suggestion.

[14] Bunbury (*Ancient Geography*, chap. xxx.) has some remarks on the topographical difficulties connected with our narrative.   There is still a trench bearing a name of similar import, but it does not occupy the line one would expect.   The water-system of the lower Euphrates and Tigris has probably changed in the lapse of centuries.

[15] The account of Zosimus is here strangely different from that of

Ammianus, since he represents Julian as crossing two days after the battle. We can only suppose (α) that Julian was not present at the battle, though Ammianus, apparently an eye-witness here, says he was most active in it ; (β) that he returned and crossed again next day ; or (γ) that the crossing, in the account of Zosimus, is not of the Tigris at all, but of the canal, which, according to Ammianus, had been crossed already.

[16] On this point see the pamphlet of Reinhardt referred to above.

[17] Of Libanius and Socrates. Ammianus and Zosimus do not mention another special embassy at this juncture.

[18] By the brothers Maurus and Machamaeus (Am., xxv., i., and Zos., iii., 26), who had *perhaps* been left at Circesium, and rejoined the army.

[19] Zosimus says it was a dagger. But Ammianus is to be preferred here.

[20] We cannot, of course, suppose that he delivered the harangue which Ammianus puts into his mouth, but it probably represents the main drift of his last sayings.

[21] See Mücke, Reinhardt, etc. The Γαλιλαῖε νενίκηκας appears first in Theodoret.

22

Coin of Valentinian the Elder.
Reverse, RESTITVTOR REIPVBLICAE. Emperor holding Standard and Victory.

CHAPTER XV.

OUTCOME OF JULIAN'S ENTERPRISES. HIS POSITION IN HISTORY.

> And not by eastern windows only
>   When daylight comes comes in the light.
> In front, the sun climbs slow, how slowly,
>   But westward, look, the land is bright.
>   A. H. CLOUGH.

F this had been the biography of a great hero of progress, an initiator of a successful movement, or a founder of permanent institutions, our task, after narrating his death, would have been to trace the lines along which his work was carried on by those who succeeded to his ideas and authority. But Julian, as we have seen, was not a successful initiator; rather he was one who endeavoured to hold back the chief movement of his day and to prevent the disappearance of what was old and vanishing; he founded no new institutions, though

338

he tried bravely to infuse new energy into those
that remained ; and he had, properly speaking, no
successor. Yet it seems necessary, in order to complete even a slight sketch of the man and his
thoughts and efforts in relation to the life of his
times, to consider briefly the continuation or the
abandonment of some of the tasks to which his
short life was devoted, whether as soldier, as politician, or as would-be religious reformer.

We naturally begin with the military enterprises
in the East, in the execution of which he had been
suddenly struck down. Of course the immediate
necessity laid upon the army that had lost its leader
was to choose a successor. It was not merely a general for themselves, but a head of the Roman world
that they had to appoint, for, in the absence of anything like either a constitutional rule or any definite
principle of succession, there was little likelihood
that the choice of the army, if fairly unanimous,
would be disputed by any civic authorities. But the
army was not united. The party that had formerly
been attached to Constantius, led by the dashing
Victor and the handsome, attractive Arinthæus,
wished for one of their own number. The semi-
barbarians who had been devoted to the person and
fortunes of Julian, prominent among whom were
Dagalaif and Nevitta, desired one of themselves. A
compromise, however, might have been made by
the appointment of the brave and highly respected
Sallust, the Præfect now with the army. But he
declined the honour, and suggested that the throne
should remain vacant till they arrived in Mesopo-

tamia,—a suggestion which points towards Procopius, whom they hoped to meet in that province. The general feeling however was for an immediate choice, and, as commonly happens under such circumstances, the result was the unexpected and tumultuous election of a man without remarkable qualifications of any kind, Jovian, a Chief of the Guards (*domesticorum ordinis primus*). The new Emperor was the son of an illustrious soldier, Varronian, and was a man tall of stature, dignified in demeanour, a pleasant companion, of no great capacity in the field, and too fond of a good dinner. To complete the contrast between him and his predecessor, he was favourably inclined to Christianity, though the stories which would represent him as a persecuted confessor are to be taken with caution, and he certainly allowed an inspection of sacrificial victims to decide on his next course, and also showed more obedience to their indications than Julian had sometimes done. The march was resumed. Sapor—overjoyed at the news of the Emperor's death and at the description he received of the character of his successor, continued to harass the army, and, according to some accounts, actually defeated it in battle. The soldiers who, for a brief moment, had been led by the similarity of the names *Jovian* and *Julian* to believe that the report of their beloved leader's death was false after all, were soon undeceived. The sufferings of famine and other privations became worse than ever. The soldiers begged to be allowed to recross the Tigris. Some bands were allowed to make the attempt, but they were not successful, and the army continued to march along the left bank. The Persian king took this opportunity of offering peace on terms favourable to himself, and Jovian was not ashamed to consent to conditions that could never have been suggested to his predecessor. Sallust and Arinthæus tried vainly to come to a more satisfactory arrangement. But Jovian was anxious to have something settled before they met with Procopius. Accordingly a truce was made for thirty years, on condition that the Romans gave up five provinces on or just beyond the Tigris (Arzanena, Moxoene, Zabdicena, Rehimema, and Corduene), with the strong towns of Nisibis and Singara, and many other places. The Romans further promised not to help Arsaces of Armenia against Persia. Nor did Jovian stipulate any immediate relief for the suffering army. Rather, as it ceased now to follow the course of the river, the pangs of thirst were added to those of hunger. At Thilsaphata, they joined forces with Sebastian and Procopius, who showed as yet no sign of disloyalty. It was with feelings of great relief that the soldiers approached the city of Nisibis, which was ready to receive the Emperor with all hospitality. He had not, however, the face to show himself to those whom he had betrayed. Very soon, a Persian officer arrived to insist on the execution of the treaty, and the evacuation of the city by its Roman inhabitants. Now ensued heartrending scenes. The Persian flag was hoisted. The people, of high and of low rank, begged in vain for permission to defend themselves unaided rather than to leave their native place. They reproached the Emperor with abandoning the

key to the province; they contrasted his conduct
with that of Constantius (did they not know or care
for Julian?); when an orator presented him with the
customary crown, he ironically expressed the wish
"May you be thus crowned, Emperor, by the cities
that remain!" The citizens were obliged to depart,
with such goods as they could convey with them,
casting regretful looks on their old homes and the
tombs of their fathers. It is some consolation to
know that many of them found a new home in the
still Roman city of Amida. Leaving an officer behind to accomplish the execution of his ignominious
treaty, Jovian hurried on, eager to secure the chief
seats of the empire, towards Constantinople. He
gave his men but a scanty rest at Antioch, and
thence moved on to Tarsus, whither Procopius had
preceded him with the bones of Julian. We hear
from Gregory of Nazianzen of undignified games,
and of buffoonery in which the habits and demeanour
of the late Emperor were caricatured by those who
saw the procession pass. The Antiochenes were certainly not incapable of such conduct, but Julian's body
did not rest among them, and probably did not pass
through their city. Possibly Gregory is himself
caricaturing the Pagan ritual and games which Procopius would probably celebrate on the way. Thus
for a time the body of the last Hellenic Emperor
rested in the birthplace of the Apostle to the Gentiles. A tomb was erected with an epitaph in hexameters, simply stating: "Here lies Julian, who fell
by the strong-flowing Tigris. He was both a good king
and a mighty warrior." Subsequently we hear that

GATEWAY AT TARSUS.

the corpse was removed to Constantinople, and laid by the side of the Empress Helen. To Ammianus it seemed that Rome would have been for Julian a fitter resting-place, among the temples of the national Gods and the monuments of ancient heroes.

Jovian never attained his desired goal. He was at Ancyra for the first day of the new year (364 A.D.), and showed yet again his want of regard for the dignity of the Empire by associating his baby son with himself in the consulship. When he reached Dadastana, on the confines of Bithynia and Galatia, he was one night found dead in his bed. Some attributed his end to a fit of indigestion; others to the fumes of a coal fire, such as had once almost suffocated Julian in Paris; others seem to have suspected foul play. In any case, little was said, and the army proceeded to the choice of a new Emperor. Sallust again received the offer of the purple and again declined it. The choice then fell upon Valentinian, a soldier of approved merit, who speedily requested and obtained permission to associate his brother Valens with him in the Imperial dignity. A return was now made to the arrangement of Diocletian, and though the unity of the Empire was still unimpaired, we have again two Emperors, to whom the care of the East and of the West were respectively assigned. Valens fixed his residence at Antioch, and it was thenceforth his care to meet the difficulties that arose on the side of Persia. Though the Romans had abandoned the alliance of Arsaces of Armenia, yet when Sapor invaded that country and loaded the king with chains, it was not unnatural that the Armenians should appeal to the Romans. At the same time the Persians had interfered in the affairs of Iberia, still a vassal state of Rome. Valens received hospitably the son of the king of Armenia (Arsaces had died in captivity), and an army was sent to place Roman candidates on the Iberian and Armenian thrones. But difficulties arose which induced the Romans to consent to a partition of Iberia, to which Sapor, however, would not consent till after another rather futile campaign. Meantime he and Valens were rivals for the adherence of the somewhat shifty Para, son of Arsaces, who finally met a treacherous death at the hands of a Roman emissary. If the Persian kingdom had been stronger, or if Sapor had had successors of his own calibre, the Persians might have taken further advantage of Roman preoccupation in the West. The final solution, however, was a separation between Roman and Persian Armenia, which subsisted for long, and left permanent traces in the ecclesiastical divisions of the East.

If Julian had lived, and if he had persevered in the enterprises he had undertaken in the East, it is difficult to say whether the relation of Rome and Persia might have been finally settled on a footing more satisfactory to the dignity of Rome. It would have cost Julian much treasure and probably many legions, to establish a vassal prince on the Persian throne, and even in that case, we cannot feel certain that Hormisdas and his dynasty would always have been faithful to their patrons. But we may feel sure that strong efforts would have been made to preserve Roman supremacy in Mesopotamia, and Roman ascendancy in Armenia as well as in Iberia. Yet the neglect of Julian to maintain his communications and to provide against the great difficulties of eastern campaigns prevent us from regarding him as potentially what he ever desired to become, a later Alexander, spreading in eastern lands the religion, culture, and the civic life of the Helleno-Roman world.

In the West, meantime, events were proving that Julian's campaigns and administrative reforms had not been thrown away. True, the Allemanni took advantage of the occasion offered by Julian's death to take up arms again, and if Jovian had had his will, the changes he projected in the military officers would have caused great danger to the Roman dominion in Western Europe. He sent from Asia to order that the post of Master of the Cavalry and of the Infantry should be given to his father-in-law Lucillian, and he instructed this new general to move the command in Gaul from the brave and capable Jovinus. But the only result of this mission was that the army mutinied, Lucillian was killed, and Jovinus was retained in his office, to the great advantage of the provincials. Valentinian, in his military and provincial arrangements and conduct, proved a worthy successor to Julian. He fixed his residence for a time at Paris, and laboured as Julian had done for the relief of the burdens and difficulties of the Gauls. His great achievement was to strengthen the frontier by means of strong fortifications at important points on the border rivers. He

undertook also some active operations into the enemies' country, and made Roman arms respected on
the Mosel and the Neckar. But the task of Imperial
defence was becoming harder, as in the course of the
great migrations other barbarian hosts forced their
way on to the scene, especially when the Burgun-
dians began to appear on the Upper Rhine, and the
Goths on the Danube. The plan was tried of setting one tribe against another, but this policy could
not permanently lead to the maintenance of peace.
When, just after the death of Valentinian, his less
warlike brother arranged for the settlement of a large
body of Goths within the territory of the Empire,
they gained a foothold of which even the successful
campaigns of Theodosius could not deprive them.
Meantime, the great increase of the barbarian element in the Roman army, which Julian had felt it
necessary to retain throughout his wars, continued
to influence for evil and for good the fortunes of the
Roman world. Perhaps the wisest of rulers and the
best-governed of states could not for long have prevented the irruption of the barbarians into the land
of the South. Yet, in estimating the worth of what
was accomplished by Julian and by those that followed in his steps, we must remember that here
every delay was a clear gain. For the longer the
barbarians were kept at bay on the borders of the
Empire, while their ablest men, in military employ-
ment in the Roman armies or in private intercourse
with the officials of the Imperial Court, were learning
something of organised enterprise and civilised life,
the more likely were they to respect and to spare

RELIEF FROM SARCOPHAGUS (JOVINUS?). MUCH RESTORED.

some relics of the ancient civilisation when the power over it all should fall to their share.

In the civil Government and the arrangements of the Court no violent reaction followed the death of Julian. It would seem indeed that the brother-emperors, who, by the embellishment of his tomb, showed some respect for his memory, desired in many respects to follow his policy. Both were accustomed to plain living and averse to the orientalising tendencies which had been conspicuous in the palace since the days of Diocletian. Of course there were sowers of discord eager to incriminate and supplant many of the persons who had stood highest in Julian's favour, and Valens at least was not deaf to suggestions of treachery. The dissatisfaction felt by those whose day was over found its champion in Procopius, who, after performing the last offices to Julian's body at Tarsus, had been obliged to lead an obscure and afterwards a wandering life to avoid the hostile efforts of the eastern Emperor. After a time, he appeared at Constantinople, during the absence of Valens in Asia, and by bribery or persuasion obtained from a portion of the soldiery recognition as his cousin's successor on the Imperial throne. Yet he seems to have had no large following. The best of the military officers, including Sallust, were loyal to Valens. The action of Procopius, in attracting to his cause the Goths and other barbarians, seems hardly worthy of one on whom Julian had cast his mantle; and the support of the widow of Constantius, whose little daughter was made a figure-head in the wild enterprise, cannot have lent much strength to his cause. It is even uncertain how far we may take Procopius to represent the old Hellenic principles in religious matters. He achieved some successes, but was finally captured in Phrygia and put to death with great cruelty. He was a silent man, whose intentions were not widely divulged, but we cannot suppose that he ever had much chance of showing himself the heir of Julian's ideas. Little Constantia was married to Valentinian's son Gratian, and thus some semblance of relationship between the late and the present dynasty was maintained.

But apart from personal changes, the general objects of Julian's Government were still kept in view, and the legislation of his successors shows the same desire to keep the *Curiales* to their duty and to check the abuses of officials, especially in regard to the post-system. But it also exposes the difficulty of achieving any sound and lasting reforms. Certainly within fifty years of the death of Constantine, under the weak sons of Theodosius, the complaints made of Court extravagance and official greed and oppression furnish a proof of the insufficiency of legislation alone to check a corruption which has eaten its way into the heart of the administration and of society generally. At the same time the impulse which Julian had given towards the encouragement of the arts and sciences did not cease to act, but showed itself in the liberal provisions for higher teaching in the University of Constantinople, and in the privileges which were continued to the medical profession.

Even in religious affairs there was not at once a total change of policy, certainly no return to the lines followed by Constantius. Jovian, Valentinian, and their successors were known to be Christians, though we have no ground for ranking them among the sufferers from the Pagan reaction. The fact that their religious belief did not materially hinder their recognition by the army and the subjects generally (except in the doubtful case of those who adopted the cause of Procopius), points to a want of power or of zeal among the worshippers of the ancient Gods. Nevertheless, prudence dictated a policy of comparative toleration. Jovian restored the Christian symbols in the army and issued a decree for protecting women who had devoted themselves to a religious profession. But he, as we have seen, did not scruple to allow sacrifices and the prophecies of the haruspices. Under Valentinian and Valens, the clergy gradually recovered their former privileges, and Christian teachers again received the right of educating the young. Sunday and Easter were again recognised as holidays, temple property was resumed—not, however, for the use of the Church but for that of the State—and sacrifices which involved bloodshed as well as nocturnal meetings were prohibited. Yet even here concessions were made to local popular feeling; thus the Eleusinian Mysteries were excepted from the prohibition, and for a time the State professed the intention of protecting the liberty and security of men of all religions. Where popular fanaticism raged high, this was of course often impossible. Many ancient buildings and statues fell a prey to iconoclastic zeal, and many devotees suffered, on the charge of sorcery, the penalty of their constancy to ancient and occult rites.   It was naturally the Neo-Platonists whom the latter kind of persecution chiefly affected, and the jealous suspicions of the Emperor Valens rendered it more active, and brought Maximus and perhaps a few others of his stamp to a martyr's grave.   But in general Hellenism was not capable of inspiring a desire of martyrdom.   Old superstitions might linger long among the *pagani* of outlying districts, and old associations might, in the great cities, retard the disuse of ceremonies which had been followed from time immemorial.   Yet, when Gratian and after him Theodosius, took a more decided line, shutting the temples and forbidding heathen rites, no very serious opposition seems to have been encountered, nor any large dissatisfied minority left with a grievance.   In all probability, the stringency of the acts was often eluded, unless, as in Egypt, excited monks and a superstitious rabble joined in the hue-and-cry.   A stage was marked when, under Gratian, the Altar of Victory was a second time removed from the Senate House of Rome, a proceeding which led to a controversy in which were heard, perhaps for the first time, and originally on the side of Catholic orthodoxy, arguments for the complete separation of secular politics and religious observance.

Meantime, Julian's policy of non-intervention in the conflict of parties within the Church, was for the most part adhered to, till the civil arm inter-

vened to give the final determination to what had
been already practically decided by other means
than those of mere terrorism. Jovian, while fav-
ouring Athanasius, who returned to Alexandria and
died there in peace, was unwilling to attend to the
demands of the bishops of the Nicene party, who
wished for a definite declaration in their favour.
Thus he answered their demands by general expressions of good-will towards all who sought the peace
of the Church. Valentinian likewise, though con-
fessing the Homoousian belief, preferred to leave
ecclesiastical affairs to ecclesiastical management.
" I am but one of the laity," he said, when asked to
meet a synod of bishops for deliberation on doctrinal matters; " let the bishops, to whom such matters appertain, assemble where they please." He was
not, however, always consistent in maintaining an
indifferent attitude, and his brother is sometimes
represented as an active persecutor. But though
Valens was baptised by an Arian bishop, and pursued a policy which incurred great unpopularity
among Nicenes and semi-Nicenes alike, it is uncertain
how far we are to regard his measures as aimed
against any religious party as such, and how far as dictated by a desire to check the growth of such an ascetic
withdrawal from the world, and consequent loss to
the State of the services of its citizens, as was closely
associated with opinions of the leading Homoousians.
Meantime, those who could accept in some form the
creed of Nicæa drew together. The schism at Antioch
was healed. Of factions we still hear much, but
except among the barbarian Goths, Arianism seems

not to have had much vitality, and leaders in Church and State could reasonably hope for the achievement of ecclesiastical unity. The efforts of some leading minds among churchmen, notably of Ambrose of Milan, whose influence with Gratian and Theodosius was very considerable, tended in the same direction. Finally, after his victories over the Goths, Theodosius, with a soldier's love of order and regularity, issued edicts ordering all men to accept the Nicene faith and forbidding heretical assemblies in the towns. Julian's policy of toleration was over, but possibly, while it lasted, it had given scope to the principle of the survival of the fittest.

It is not, however, by what he accomplished, but by what he tried to do and by what he was, that Julian raised himself to a position among those who must ever rivet the eyes of mankind. As, in this sketch of his life and doings, our chief object had been to portray his character and the relation in which he stood to the movements of his time, a further examination of his mind and principles would be superfluous. The reader has, it is hoped, material for forming a final judgment, such as to men of an earlier generation was well-nigh impossible. Julian has been hated by those whose religious enthusiasm was near akin to his own. He has been admired by those whose scepticism would have aroused in him the deepest abhorrence. He has been represented as an unpractical " Romantiker," and as a first-class general and statesman. If we look at him impartially and yet with the sympathetic understanding that we can only obtain after trying in imagination

to realise his point of view, we see in him, not a
genius of the first rank in statesmanship, strategy,
literature, or religious philosophy, not a character
unequalled in virtue and strength, but a man who
did something, because of his earnest devotion to
his ideals, and who would have done more if he had
been gifted with a surer insight and had moved at
a less feverish pace. He was a good king and a strong
warrior, as his epitaph said. Yet his conduct at
Antioch showed him unable to meet all the requirements of a disordered state, and his neglect of precautions, especially in the Persian War, prevents us
from ranking him among the great generals of the
world. He wrote in what, for his age, may be regarded as a pure style, but he wrote too rapidly to
produce any great work. He was a thinker, and
often throws a ray of clear light on matters obscured
by convention and prejudice, but his mind was not
calm and collected enough for us to rank him among
great philosophers. His personal character is most
attractive. He had warm affections, a strong desire
to do justice, an abiding sense of moral responsibility. He was, moreover, of a singularly trans-
parent nature, living (when the evil days of forced
dissimulation were over) always above-board, hating
secrets, proclaiming in season and out of season the
aspirations of his heart and the principles of his life.
Yet, with all his love of truth and goodness, there
were some potent types which he was quite incapable of recognising. With all his desire for equity
he could not always be fair to those whom he could
not understand. In spite of his realisation of the

littleness of human effort in the universal system of nature and man, he could not see how powerless were his own endeavours to oppose a barrier to the incoming tide.

Yet Julian is one to whom much may be forgiven because he loved much. If, turning aside from the events of his short and chequered career, we look to the main principle by which he was throughout guided, we see that it was an entire devotion to the Greek idea of thought and life, a settled determination to prevent, so far as in him lay, the destruction, by what he regarded as barbarous and degrading forces, of that fair fabric of ancient civilisation under which men had learned to venerate beauty and order, to aim at a reasonable, self-contained life, and to live in orderly society under intelligible laws and humane institutions. And who shall say that this principle is an unworthy one, or that a life lived in obedience to its dictates could fail to achieve some good results besides those that may appear on the surface?

And after all, that cause has ultimately triumphed, not by the suppression of Christian institutions, as Julian vainly hoped, still less by the extinction of the Christian spirit as a motive power in the world, but by the permeation of society, speculation, and practical life with the most permanent elements of Greek culture. If Julian was mistaken in thinking that the religious ideas lately come from Palestine would soon pale before the revived glories of Greece, no less short-sighted were those who thought that Hellenism was buried in the Emperor's grave. Sometimes for better, sometimes for worse, the two streams have blended, till it is now hard to conceive what either might have been apart from the other. We cannot feel that the triumphal cry of Julian's enemies, which has seemed ever to echo round his death-bed, has been fully justified at the bar of history. It is the Christ, not the Galilæan, that has conquered.

FINIS.

Coin of Valens.
Reverse, Spes R.P. Valens and Valentinian seated: between them a shield, inscribed Vot. V. Mvl. X. which rests on the head of a smaller figure.

INDEX.